THE WARRIOR'S WAY TO SELF IMPROVEMENT

BY ALAN BAKER

The knowledge in this book is derived from decades of instructing every branch of the U.S. military, as well as the Department of Defense, police agencies, SWAT teams, and elite-level bodyguards. The information and wisdom is also gleaned from over forty years spent in the martial arts and gaining over fifteen black belts in various arts. During that time, I have run numerous academies and been able to work as private protection for numerous VIPs, including the stars of film and TV shows such as *The Walking Dead*, *Arrow*, and others.

The lessons I've learned have shown me that, despite the many obstacles that make life feel impossible at times, there is a way forward for anyone dreaming of becoming an elite-level performer, athlete, businessman, or anyone simply seeking a happier, fuller life. I have been low and discovered what it took to get back up. I have had people from all across the spectrum come to me for guidance, and I have shown them the steps that I took, and that other masters before me took.

We are all down at some point. It is inevitable in this life. But there is a process to recovery, steps that one can take to redeem one's body, mind, and spirit. This book is a collection of those steps, a set of guidelines I have found to be universally beneficial to those that have decided to opt out of the quitter's mentality and finally seek a higher awareness and greater happiness. A sigma personality.

I have taught soldiers, and soldiers have taught me. I have been in the company of killers and monks, and found that there are a surprising number of foundational habits that they all have in common, habits allowing them to reach a higher state and keep themselves sane, aware, healthy and clearheaded.

In this book, you will learn techniques on breathing and exercising more intelligently, but you will also see highlighted the many ways you can alter your thinking to reach greater physical and mental goals.

This book is not just about how you should think differently about your body, but also how you should rethink your thinking, and begin a journey of self-discovery that, if you're lucky, will last until your dying day. There is a way forward, a path one can take to rejuvenate themselves and ascend past the normal limitations set not just by others, but by oneself.

It is not hopeless. You are not hopeless. There is a path forward. Let me show you.

Published By; Warrior's Path Publishing
Edited By Chad Huskins & Iris Rousseau

Alan Baker
2400 Olivia Run
Woodstock GA, 30188
www.sifualanbaker.com
www.atlantamartialartscenter.com

Warriors
Path
Publishing

DISCLAIMER

The author and publisher of this material are not responsible in any manner whatsoever for injury which may occur through reading or following the instructions in this manual. The activities, physical and otherwise described in this manual may be too strenuous or dangerous for some people, and readers should consult a physician before engaging in any of them.

for speaking inquiries, coaching or seminars e-mail sifualanbaker@gmail.com

This book is dedicated to to the following instructors and individuals that were willing to mentor and guide me which I am grateful.

Sifu/Guro Dan Inosanto
Sifu Francis Fong
Ajarn Surachai Sirisute
Sensei Erik Paulson
Master Pedro Sauer
Professor Greg Nelson
Professor James Cravens
Sijo Dana Miller
Dr. Richard Kobetz
Sijo David Collins
Saya John Taylor
Sifu Paul Olivas
Sifu Mark Bayne
Master Bob Byrd
Master Chunyi Lin
Tuhon Tim Waid
Saya Mike Jolley
Saya Doug boring
Saya David Croft
Coach Bill Henderson
Sifu Steve Grantham
Guro Don Garron
Sifu LaVonne Martin
Sifu Paul Vunak
Coach Justo Dieguez
Scooter Sellers

ACKNOWLEDGEMENTS

I would Like to thank those who helped in the preparation and development of this book.

Steve Grantham
Chad Huskins
Jennifer Wood
Iris Rousseau

TABLE OF CONTENTS

PROLOGUE

Imagine that you are in a jungle with dense foliage of all kinds, vines hanging in your face, pesky gnats constantly nagging you, the soil damp and easy to sink your foot into and twist your ankle. The trees are so tightly packed together you can't see ahead. In fact, the jungle canopy above you is so cluttered you can't even see the sky. Mosquitoes constantly zip into your mouth, nose, and ears. They bite your neck, your arms, your legs, and you have to swat at them constantly. It is difficult to get through this jungle, with so many things clouding your vision, ensnaring your feet, and interfering with your journey through it.

This jungle is life.

Now imagine that you find a path, one that someone has paved before you. You may not know who exactly made this road, but it has been laid here to make the journey through life easier. Someone else came before you, hacking all the briars and brambles out of the way, clearing the path not just for them, but for those who would follow. This path was created by the masters who came before, the wisest of their day, and it has been left for you.

It takes discipline to stay on this path, which I call the Warrior's Path. Many who walk it become bored, and easily lose focus by glancing off into the jungle, wondering what's out there. There's all sorts of other sounds in that jungle, so many distractions. It is so easy to wander off the path and never return. Some people remain in the jungle their whole lives and never even come upon the path.

Those that do find the path may find it difficult to stay on it, but, in the end, they will find their lives a great deal easier. Minus all the gnats buzzing in your ear, the vines snatching at you, the occasional wild animal attack, and all other distractions, you are free to walk the path and reach your goals in a reasonable amount of time, without becoming lost along the way.

Now, this isn't to say that an occasional visit into the jungle can't have its rewards—in case you haven't guessed, the "gnats" and other distractions in this analogy represent TV, internet, video games, chasing women or men, all that —but spending too much time in the jungle has never gotten anyone anywhere. If you want to achieve great things, you must find the path and keep focused on it, there is no other option for success, bet on it.

Of course, this level of discipline is to be commended, but it isn't exactly the highest form of life one can achieve. Yes, it does take great tenacity to keep on this Warrior's Path without falling for the allure of the jungle, or the cries from those within saying, "Forget the Path! Come on in here with us! You should see all this stuff!" But there is something even greater beyond the path. Or, I should say, above it.

Imagine that same scenario. You're in a jungle, and you come upon the path. You decide to stick with it, and after walking the path a while you determine that this is indeed easier. It is easier to follow the road laid by the smartest of your predecessors—after all, they worked out all the kinks for you, and the ones that came after them worked out even more kinks, down through the ages—but soon you may come to realize that, well, a lot of people are following the same road. Others around you (not many, but there will be others) are also following the Warrior's Path, traveling the exact same road as you.

Upon realizing this, you may begin to wonder, "Perhaps...perhaps there's another way we might go. Another path we might take? One of our own design? After all, why not?" In a moment of whimsy, you might even perform a thought experiment, and look upwards. You see an eagle, and you wonder what the world would look like from its perspective. From where it is, there are no roads, no defined paths that it must follow. There is the sweeping jungle below, and the untouched mountains in the distance.

After being on the path for so long, you may often cast your eyes up to the eagle. Just like Einstein who uncovered secrets of the universe by conducting a thought experiment —imagining himself racing along at the speed of light, and what effects that would have on him—you look up at the eagle, a totem of inspiration, because it possesses the vision you so desperately want, the higher perspective you want to have, and you imagine yourself as being that thing.

Incidentally, in this analogy, the "Eagle" is that rare person who soars above all, who has evolved to a state where they don't need the path, who has sprouted their proverbial wings and now knows no limits, no borders, and no boundaries.

When I talk to people about training, when I am working out a curriculum, when I am looking at a new student and seeing their potential (everybody has it), this analogy is paramount in my mind. My ultimate goal is to create leaders, eagles, but in order to do that I have to not only follow the path, what I've termed Warrior's Path, but I have to teach them to *see* it. I have to guide them to the road laid by other grandmasters—your Bruce Lees, your Dan Inosantos—and take them out of the jungle. In the jungle, they'll never get anything done.

However, it is important that we find the path first. Remember, it was only because we got on the path that we can even see the sky, and thus see the eagle. If we were lost in the jungle, so choked by trees, briars, and brambles, you would never have even seen the birds flying free in an open sky. You have to get beyond the distractions.

This is what Warrior's Path means to me. It takes a warrior's focus to ignore those who scamper in the jungle foolishly and become lost. The most I can do for them is try to beckon them to join me on the path, but I cannot make them. It has to be a choice. From the path, we can see a clearer sky, and truly recognize and respect the eagle, and aim to become it.

Next is the path to "Eagle's Flight." I chose the eagle as the symbol, rather than any other bird, because of its tendency to fly alone. It doesn't fly in a flock, it maintains itself, and it looks over all with its famously piercing vision, flying wherever it wants. You may have heard the expression, "It's lonely at the top." This is true. If you shoot for the Warrior's Path, your focus on training and discipline will indeed lose you friends—you won't even mean to do it, and it won't even be your choice, it'll just be the choice of others not to follow you on the path.

However, if one aspires to be the eagle, you will certainly find yourself shedding even more friends. Again, this won't be intentional, it just sort of happens. For instance, if you're going on a strict diet, working out an hour every day, jogging, and attending martial arts classes regularly, then that friend of yours who likes sitting on the couch all day eating Cheetos and watching reruns on TV isn't going to have much in common with you anymore. He chose the jungle. You chose the path. You're both going to have to deal with it eventually and go your separate ways.

Or, don't. Stay in the jungle if you wish. I cannot tell you that that's wrong, and I certainly can't tell anybody what to do with their life. However, I can tell you that if you want to achieve your goals in life—if you want to be a martial artist, a painter, a writer, a musician, a small business owner—then you must find the Warrior's Path and adhere to it strictly. You must walk it for a while, learning from the masters that came before. This means attending classes, lectures, and reading books written by masters, some of which may have been written a thousand years ago. Then, only after many years of focus and discipline on the path can you hope to see the open sky, the eagle, and your truest potential.

That is the goal of the Warrior's Path: the actualization of potential. If you're reading this, you're probably either lost in the jungle (where most people are) or you are peeking your head out of the jungle and becoming curious about the path. I would like to encourage your curiosity and invite you to walk the path a while with me.

In my opinion, the individuals who choose the path of the eagle are our warriors. Even though the concept of the warrior has roots in the yard of war, you do not necessarily have to train in combat or fighting to strive for, or obtain the warrior mindset. Like the warrior, you just have to decide that you're going to set yourself on the path of improvement, the path of growth. You are willing to invest time, effort and energy into growth and development. You are willing to hold yourself to a higher standard and push for greater levels of achievement. This book is about assisting you in that growth, pointing you to the path. I hope to do this by sharing my knowledge and experience that I have gained over 40 years of continuous training in the martial arts, under some of the best instructors and mentors in the world. I do not claim to have all of the answers, but I do claim to pursue answers with unyielding tenacity.

Sometimes martial arts can be intimidating to some people who have never been involved with it before. People may associate martial arts with the UFC and envision training, including getting punched in the face and kicked by some huge sweaty guy. Others may roll their eyes at martial arts, imagining a room full of people in white, chopping the air, and yelling, "Hi-yah!" Some people have tried martial arts but went to a school full of ego, that sees new members as fresh meat instead of welcoming and caring for new members. Because of these preconceived biases, opinions, and negative experiences, lots of individuals will choose not to engage in the martial arts community. It is unfortunate because under the surface, it possesses some of the most effective and advanced character building and self-improvement methodology that is available anywhere.

Martial arts will teach you things about your mind, your body, and your spirit that you never knew existed. It has allowed me to learn how to use my mind more efficiently; it has taught me mindful focus and has given me tools of developing personal drive and motivation. It has taught me how to breathe more intelligently, to be able to control stress, anxiety and tension levels in my body regardless of the situation I'm dealing with. It has taught me intelligent ways of strengthening the body and improving overall health and longevity. This ancient wisdom has taught me how to improve my daily amounts of vital energy. It has given me a highly detailed owners manual to one of the greatest machines that has ever been created: the human-machine.

It is unfortunate that a lot of this information is hidden and is not taught openly, even inside its own culture. And it is not unusual for it to take years in training before getting to the point to have access to the information.

My goal with this book and the Warriors Path Community is to give you access to this incredible information. Not only do I want to make it available to you, but I also want to try to do it in terms that are easier to understand, make it attainable, so that you may apply it to your life, regardless of whether you train in the martial arts or not. This information is universal, and it can be applied in any area of life. I have taught this information to high-performing business people, executives, special forces operatives, and high-level executive protection agents (bodyguards). I have seen this information personally improve performance in every industry that I have shared it.

We are going to start with *The Three Basic Disciplines* that I start with my students at the Academy. These are Physical Discipline, Mental Discipline, and Emotional Discipline. Physical discipline is the ability to take control of and gain a higher command of your physical body. Mental discipline is your ability to tame your internal landscape and focus your consciousness in order experience and achieve more. Emotional discipline is your ability to calm the emotional fires of your body and eventually use them to increase your overall energy and passion that is available to you daily.

All of these things will be connected to your breath. The art of breathing has been brought to the surface more and more in the last few years. Learning to control the breath is an extremely powerful thing and we are going to discuss it in depth. But the important thing to remember is it is just the beginning. Breath is only a tool to start the journey, it is not the destination.

I see it taught as the beginning and the end in a lot of places. It's important to remember where you're going when you begin your study of this tool. I do believe that you will not reach the destination without it though, it is something that must be studied and mastered.

Your ultimate goal is control of yourself in the human-machine. Control of the mind and your consciousness. Control of the emotional centers and reactions of the body. Control of the physical body itself on a greater level. All of this can be reached through the study of the breath.

We are going to look at a lot of these areas individually, but you will notice as you go through the book there will be a common thread that brings you back to the breath because it is the bridge of control.

FORWARD

I first met Alan Baker in the early 90s when I was teaching at the Francis Fong Martial Arts Academy in Atlanta and by that time had been training in the Martial Arts for about 10 years. He and I got to know each while I was teaching Wing Chun and Kali at the Academy and when I opened up my own school in the late 90's I was lucky enough to have Alan come and train with me. I was as impressed with how much time he put into his training outside class as I was with how consistent he was in showing up to class. Many students are constantly looking for the next technique, always focusing on accumulating new information before they even master the last one. Alan was different though. When he learned something new he would drill it mercilessly until he had internalized it before he would ask for more information. When I met him, he was already a tough and very accomplished fighter, so we focused more on the concepts of Martial Arts as taught by Francis Fong, Dan Inosanto, and Pedro Sauer, which at the time I had more exposure to than he had.

I believe a good teacher strives to help his students grow as much as they are capable of learning, and if possible, to assist them in surpassing the teacher. It quickly became apparent that Alan would surpass me, and I am happy that we have been training partners for so many years now.

Alan transitioned from being my student to being my teacher and training partner faster than anyone I had ever met. To highlight this, a story I often tell is our journey training in Gracie Jiu-Jitsu together under Professor Pedro Sauer. In 2000 we started our training together, and while I received my blue belt shortly before Alan achieved his, we both received our purple belts at the same time. And he quickly progressed earning his brown belt about 6 months before me, and finally his black belt a full 2 years ahead of me.

The single most impressive thing about Alan is his incredible work ethic. In my entire 35+ years in the Martial Arts, I have never met anyone who worked harder or more intelligently on his self-development. He constantly seeks out new challenges and when he finds one that he is not able to immediately accomplish, he relishes the opportunity to step back and design drills and training methods until he can conquer it. It is this single-minded focus on growth that has allowed him to achieve high level ranks in multiple martial arts under world famous martial artists, as well as develop his credentials in the personal protection industry and beyond. Alan's pursuit of growth was not limited to training Martial Arts. Often when we met over the years, he would share with me what he had been researching and working on since we last saw each other, finding ways to improve himself as a teacher, improve his business, and his organizational skills. He was always looking for mentors and teachers to help him in areas where he felt he was lacking in some skill.

Since we met, he has evolved in so many areas that it is almost impossible to reconcile with the young man I met so many years ago with the person he is today. And yet, he has continued to be humble and respectful to others and is often a mentor in the many organizations to which he belongs. He has become a role model to many martial artists that I know, and I continue to learn from him to this day.

In this book, Alan has laid out in a very organized format about how his training has helped shape him into the person he is today, and he gives others the tools to begin their own journey. He does not prescribe a one size fits all approach, and in the true spirit of his instructors, notes how every individual is different and is starting from a different place. The only prerequisite for reading this guide is to have an open mind and a strong desire to develop your full potential. No matter where you are in your own personal journey today, if you read this book with an open mind and consider and practice the material, I am confident that you can also evolve towards becoming the person you strive to be. Whether your goal is for improving physical defense, gaining emotional stability, changing your habits, or just becoming healthier, I believe you will find the guidance and suggestions in this book to be the path you need to take in order to achieve your goal.

When I read this book, in the midst of the 2020 pandemic, I was amazed at how it helped me organize my thoughts about my current training and refocus my goals to maximize the time and energy I am gaining through this quarantine. If you are looking to make a change to your current circumstances, I believe reading this book, and converting this information into action is the smartest thing that you can do for yourself.

Steve Grantham, **Wing Chun/Gracie Jiu-Jitsu/Kali/JKD/ Muay Thai Instructor**

1.
DISCIPLINE

Discipline is a popular word that is thrown around quite a bit in today's society. Discipline is often referred to when someone desires to make a change in life, create a new habit, or reach a new goal. I have been involved in martial arts for 40 years. In that time, I have been immersed in the culture of discipline.

I got to approach it and study it from multiple different angles under many different instructors. Instructors in Karate, Judo, Jiu-Jitsu, Kung-Fu, Filipino martial arts, and Indonesian martial arts, just to name a few. I remember having a conversation with my Burmese Bando instructor, Saya Mike Jolley, when I was sixteen, and explaining to him what my life plan was in the martial arts, and his response to me was, "Well, you are going to need about three lifetimes to achieve all of that, or you are going to have to greatly discipline the one you have now." He was right, many times in my life I have had to discipline myself to put in the time and effort needed to build that life plan.

I have also watched others who were making the same plans give in to human nature and not achieve what they were pursuing. The Martial Arts were not the only place that I would see the lack of discipline affect someone.

When I worked as a bodyguard for high-profile entertainment professionals, sometimes I would work details for clients that would be active for days and still have to work as the clients sleep. I have seen many protection specialists lose their employment because they lack the discipline to stay in the game until the job is done.

Because of this, the word "discipline" came to hold many different meanings in many other areas. It is my goal to share that experience and knowledge with you through this book.

Discipline has been a point of discussion between myself and my students quite often over the years. The first place I start is finding out what their definition of discipline is, and then challenging it. Some of the most common examples I get back are having the ability to wake up early each day, and the ability to do something which I do not want to do.

I have recently had the opportunity to teach an eight-year-old, Adam, the importance of making his bed on a daily basis. Needless to say, this is not something he really wants to do or has any interest in. Elements of the educational process were conversations about disciplining yourself. When we discussed discipline, part of the definition I used to educate him was learning the ability to do that which you don't want to do. It was a challenge to say the least; Adam spent quite a bit of time being irritated and unhappy with me. My attempts to have him be more disciplined in his environment was definitely outside his comfort zone and something he could do without. At that time I was also responsible for his schooling during our days together, so I came to an agreement with him that if he would give me focused periods of discipline throughout the day, I would arrange for Adam to have time set aside to play as well. Of course, I clearly defined what I was looking for as far as those periods of discipline. And when the time came to play, I tried to put in just as much effort as he did during playtime. After some time, Adam was waking up on his own and making his bed before starting the day.

Therefore, by the definition I would receive from my students, Adam had obtained discipline.

Yet, the question that will arise for me is this: is there nothing more to it, no further room to grow, when developing the ability to make yourself do something you do not wish to do? Fortunately, I had teachers that taught me otherwise. In my opinion, from my experience teaching students, there are different types of disciplines, as well as levels to each, that you can develop.

The word discipline is synonymous with the warrior. Whether it is in the Armed Forces, law-enforcement, the security world, or the martial arts world. Discipline means different things to different people, based on their training or life experience. One of the goals for this book is to convey my mindset, training, and experience with discipline, based on my training and life experience. I believe there are multiple levels to discipline, and the deeper you study and pursue it, the greater levels of improvement you can obtain for yourself and your life.

It is a warrior's responsibility to inspire, to lead by example. It is his or her responsibility to demonstrate hope in his actions. He doesn't just speak it; he lives it, demonstrates it, and does it out in the open in front of everyone.

I believe that everyone has a gift, and a warrior's gift is a fighting spirit that never gives up. He may not always be the best trained or the best fighter but he is the guy in the room that will not stop in the face of chaos or challenge. In fact, a warrior does not have to be a fighter at all, it could be someone driven by passion to make a positive change in their world. It may be a change that will seem impossible, but that is why it becomes the warrior's task. I have seen society change over the years and become a population that shuns the warrior; they look down on warriorship. Because of this, a lot of the training, philosophy, and mindset is not openly available to everyone. One of my goals for this book is to change this and try to make the information more available to those that may not have access to an academy, teacher, or the time to commit to obtaining the information.

I learned and developed the mindset of continuous growth and self-improvement from my mentors and teachers. My path was not the path that is commonly taken. I did not get exposed to self-help programs or books to obtain the information. This knowledge was given to me by the multiple teachers I was fortunate enough to be involved in the martial arts. Most of these principles and thought patterns I have no names for, so when it got to the point when I was beginning to pass them on, I found myself looking for labels to put on the information to classify it and organize it.

This was when I started to do more research outside of the academy; I started to get introduced to the self-improvement industry. What I found was that I had been taught much more than I had realized. I also found that my path to that information was unique. Most of the lessons were introduced on the academy floor and were taught through the physical, mental, and emotional challenges that were created in the environment of that ecosystem. I was actually living it. I did not just read the information in a book or get introduced to it through a video or seminar, then have the challenge to find out how to implement it in my life. Sifu (teacher) would create live opportunities to experience and implement the knowledge.

The challenges were created for me by my peers and my instructors. Sometimes those challenges were far greater than any I have run into in life. I was also held accountable by my teacher and my peers for continuous improvement. When I was starting to show a sign of being comfortable in the middle of the chaos created, the people around me would step up the game and increase the pressure or resistance. All to push me to the next level. Most of this was done through physical training; these are the things you commonly see in the ecosystem of the martial arts.

But these environments were not just about learning to fight. They created the opportunity to develop a strong spirit and determination, unyielding willpower to push forward regardless of your conditions and regardless of whether or not you thought you could win. Most of the time, winning did not seem to be an option. It seems like almost every day on the mat, the little voice in your head would tell you, "You cannot win this, you are starving for air, physically exhausted, and mentally shot; why are you continuing to move forward?"

These moments are when you center yourself, and learn to apply the thought patterns and physiological changes that are available to you, to not only survive but to win. This is another reason I wanted to put this book together; I wanted to have a broader method to share this different approach to self-improvement. I understand that not everyone will be able to place themselves in this type of environment. Regardless, I have found on my journey through life that you do not necessarily have to go to these extremes to create these learning environments. You just have to know what you want to develop and be creative.

One thing that I had in the academy was a community of like-minded individuals. On the surface, we were all there to learn self-defense, the ideologies and methods to protect ourselves and our families. This was probably the bulk of the individuals that would be on the academy floor night after night. They would primarily focus on the physical techniques and attributes that were needed to survive a physical encounter against one or several other opponents.

Out of this, a small group of us started to realize that there was a deeper level of information that was not necessarily written on the curriculum, it was not necessarily required to pass a test. This information was introduced to us in the social settings outside of class. They were introduced when we would have a challenge that would put us in check.

Sometimes you would run into a problem you could not handle on the mat, and you had to get up and walk off to take some time. This is when Sifu would come over to you and share information that had nothing to do with the physical technique, but instead, it would have to do with how you handled yourself mentally, how you handled your internal landscape.

Some would pay attention to this, and others would ignore it and re-focus on the techniques. The small group of students that started to see the value in this information eventually would come together into its own sub-community in the academy. I was fortunate enough to be a part of this group. We realized that we could use the things we were learning and the environments that we were creating as tools to hone our own metal internally. We could use the environment to create opportunities to not only bring ourselves face-to-face with the emotional, mental, and physical challenges that would force personal growth and development. But additionally, we could do it repeatedly in a safe manner, in order to ingrain those internal skills into our being.

Most of the time, as you go through life, you are not aware of the event that may be just around the corner that will anger you. It will sneak up on you, make you angry, and before you know what you were, react in a way that you may regret later. That anger will take you over sometimes and consume you at that moment. Imagine having a group of individuals, inmates that could come together and help create an environment that would produce this challenge for you and give you the opportunity to not only face it but to work on how you face it and improve your internal thought patterns and reactions to it at that moment.

You wouldn't have to wait for life to throw one of these opportunities in your lap. You could create it on your own with your team. Not only could you create it, but you could control the level of intensity of the exercise as you improved with your performance. This type of training environment could be created around any of the self-improvement topics or methods that were given to us by our teacher. Having this group of individuals training in this manner was one of the most potent periods of personal improvement of my life. I learned to clear and control my mind, which in turn gave me the ability to control my body.

I learned to calm heightened emotional reactions to the things that were going on around me and gain the ability to remain calm in chaotic events. I was able to gain the ability to sharpen my willpower, spirit, and determination.

All of these things carried over to the rest of my life outside of the academy and gave me the abilities to pursue and achieve successes in life that I would have never thought possible. The experience and knowledge I gained allowed me to maintain an advanced level of physical fitness and youthful daily energy levels even into the later years of my life.

It is the goal of this book and Warrior's Path to create a community of growth and development-minded individuals interested in pursuing opportunities to develop themselves following the same warrior philosophies and methods.

Over the years, the types or subsections of discipline that I have taught in the academy have grown in length, but when I start teaching these concepts, I will generally narrow them down to a list of three fundamental basics. These three basics are where most of my students and the people that I coach start their journey into the study of the discipline. Next, we will take a look at those basic areas of study to gain a little insight into each one and what they have to offer each of us on our journey to become high-level achievers.

A story of discipline:

In the middle to late 80s I was a teenager, and I was training with a Grand Master and Sijo (meaning grandfather or founder), a man that had created his own system of Kung Fu. Sijo was over six feet tall, lean with an athletic build, and had a beard. He was involved with a special forces unit in the Vietnam War, and he had a stern hardness about him. His presence was not only impactful because of his appearance, but also because he gave off this energy or glow.

When Sijo entered into a room, everyone would look to him; their eyes and attention drew to him. He would command attention without needing to say a word. One of the things I admired about him was that Sijo was always sharp and clear. He never had a fog blurring his attention or vision like many other people I would come into contact with. Sijo had a sharpness and directness about him that also felt open and engaging. He never lacked anima, and he was never one of the people I now call the walking dead (the average person mulling about through life without passion and drive).

A friend and I would drive four hours one way to eastern Tennessee every week, sometimes for a day, sometimes to stay for weeks at a time to train with Sijo. In addition to running a martial arts school, Sijo also ran an expedition company in these mountains. He taught rappelling, mountaineering, rock climbing, and scuba diving. Sijo knew the mountains like the back of his hand

and had built training sites throughout them for his students.

During one visit, we went to a training site in the mountains where there was a balance beam. The balance beam was about three feet above the ground and only a couple of feet away from the edge of a cliff. The day was cold, about 38 degrees. Sijo began by having us do different basic exercises on the beam. We would warm up with these exercises, doing various movements and drills while trying to maintain our balance.

This wasn't our first experience training on a beam. At the school, we had a balance beam we regularly practiced on. That beam was about 4 inches off the ground and the floor was padded all around. When we trained on the beam at the school, we would do drills and spar. During our training, we would fall off the beam many times. We never really had a "successful" day of training without falling off many times.

This beam on the side of a mountain was a much different animal than the one at the school. It was in a dangerous spot where falling off and over the side of the cliff was a very likely possibility. Not only was it in a perilous location, but there were also many environmental factors to deal with.

While we trained, our minds would shift focus between training on the beam at the school and how much we fell off, and how dangerous this beam would be if we fell because of its location. We knew that if we fell off of this beam on the mountain, we would very likely get injured or die.

After completing the basic exercise, Sijo instructed us to begin sparring. It wasn't long before Sijo pointed out to us how much tension in our bodies we were carrying. He explained that the first factor he noticed was the cold. A second factor would be our fear of falling off the beam. Sijo questioned us as to why we allowed this tension to be in our bodies. He explained that we were allowing our minds to control us and not the other way around.

We realized we were unable to focus on dealing with each other as training partners because we allowed our minds to be distracted. "You have to be in the here and now," he would tell us. The thoughts we allowed to race through our minds and build emotion were affecting our bodies physically. I could feel my fear lifting my energy from my root, limiting my ability to push it down to stay grounded on the beam. He said, "It does not matter what is in front of you or around you. You have to control your mind. Don't allow it to wander down the cliff or to what may happen if you fall. Don't allow it to focus on the cold and create tension in the body. Your mind has to do what you tell it."

As we continued our training, our legs grew tired and began hurting. We allowed the pain to creep into our bodies. Sijo would ask what was wrong, and we explained our legs were hurting. He would ask, "How do you know? Why did you take the time to listen to it? Why would you let that stop you?"

So we continued sparring. We were tired, cold, scared, and in pain. Sijo sat about eight feet away from us on a tree. The tree had a massive trunk that split into two main sections. One side was cut off while the other continued growing and forming branches. Sijo was sitting on the side that was cut off. At the base of that tree was what seemed like an endless supply of pebbles. He observed our training. We were sparring on the beam and finally getting comfortable with the training.

Then came the pebbles.

The first time Sijo hit me with one, it struck me on my head. I was distracted from sparring and looked over at Sijo with surprise. That was the moment when my partner punched me in the head, and I began to fall off the beam. My only thought was to try to avoid falling off the cliff, so I reacted by grabbing the beam as I fell. I landed right on my ribcage and I remember thinking I had broken my ribs. As I righted myself on the beam and stood up, I asked Sijo why he hit me with a pebble. He replied, "What pebble?"

At that point, I knew exactly what he meant. He continued his questions, "Why does the pebble make a difference? Did you fall off because of the pebble?" I said no. Sijo asked if I fell off because my partner hit me. I again said no. Sijo began to explain that I fell because I allowed my mind to be distracted, which in turn disrupted my control of my body and emotions. I got back up on the beam and gathered myself. I reigned in my mind, body, and emotions, then continued sparring with my partner. More pebbles came, more shots to the head, more kicks to the body, but after a while, it didn't matter. I remember wondering if Sijo would sneak up on that mountain with buckets of pebbles just to keep them on hand.

I learned it's not so much the storm on the outside, but instead what's going on internally and how I dealt with those things that made the difference. Through experiences

31

like this, I learned how to regulate my emotions and my body's physical response to what was going on around me. I spent many hours on that beam and, in turn, learned numerous lessons about myself that I would carry for the rest of my life.

You may not have access to a Grand Master or may not have the time to spend on a balance beam on the side of a mountain. Yet, this does not mean you don't have the ability to learn and apply the same knowledge and wisdom into your life. It is my goal to impart these lessons to you through this book. I have heard it said many times that knowledge is power. So I believe it is extremely important to take a subject, especially when it can have such a tremendous influence on your life, and study it in depth.

One of the key principles for my personal study and growth is the fact that you don't know what you don't know. This is something Sijo and other teachers would point out to me many times when I thought I had learned something. It applies when I have learned a skill or a set of skills to the point where I think I understand something or I think I know a certain subject.

The fact that "I think" I know actually will hinder me in my continual growth in that area. So for me personally, remembering that I do not know what I do not know, keeps me continually searching for depth of knowledge in a given subject. There is always more knowledge, wisdom and understanding that can be found with aggressive research and study. You just have to remember to keep yourself honest and look deeper.

For me, this is a core trait of a warrior. The warrior will have a code of standards they will follow that will keep them in check and make sure they are continuing on the path of personal growth.

This warrior mindset was introduced and taught to me in my journey in martial arts by my teachers and mentors. There is a difference between a martial artist and a warrior. You can attend a class two times a week at your local martial arts school and call yourself a martial artist, but you are probably not a warrior. You may have been training for years and are a teacher at a school, maybe a professional martial artist, yet you may still not be a warrior. Because of this guiding set of principles and checks and balances that these Warriors will follow, they will operate at a higher level of proficiency and achievement in the pursuit of knowledge.

How can this benefit you? The more you grow and improve yourself, the greater change you can create in yourself. The closer you will get to achieving your goals, and the better you will be from the journey. Having and abiding by a set of principles will guide you in your journey and help keep you on your path. You will be less likely to make unnecessary detours and will reach your goals faster. You will become more proficient and accomplish more in a shorter amount of time. Keep this in mind when we take a look at the topic of discipline; we want to search for the deeper wisdom and knowledge that may be unknown to us currently.

With that said, let's introduce the basic three areas of study that we use when teaching discipline.

The Basic 3 Discipline Studies

Physical Discipline (Body changing)
Mental Discipline (Internal landscape)
Emotional Discipline (Taming the fire)

PHYSICAL DISCIPLINE

The first area we're going to take a look at is the study of physical discipline. In Kung Fu, we refer to this as body changing. I have studied multiple forms of Kung Fu: Shaolin Kung Fu, Chuan Fa, Tai Chi, and Wing Chun Kung Fu, just to name a few. One thing they all taught was body changing. They believe that there is more to learning than just putting knowledge in your head. I was told that a system, if properly trained, would change your body. After training for a time, you would change physically in some way through achieving the ability to discipline your body.

One example of this is the strength-building methods that are taught in some of the systems. Unlike Western methods of building strength, these exercises literally rewire the body's muscular system to the point where it can activate a higher number of muscle fibers than what is normal. In several systems, this training is referred to as stone warrior training. In my experience, it is probably the best method I have ever seen for strength development in the students that I have taught over the years and in myself.

There are many different forms of body changing that are taught in Martial Arts. Here, we are primarily going to focus on the ones that are in relation to discipline and the body. The mind-body connection is a common discipline to begin with.

Building connection between mind and body

In a martial arts class, it is common for the class to begin with the students lining up in order to pay respects to start the class. Generally, when they line up, the students try to do so with a certain level of discipline and control of the body based on the expectations of the instructor. Sometimes the instructor will take a moment to look at the line to make sure everyone is uniform.

A very common occurrence that I have run into is seeing a student standing in line, and their toes will not be touching, so their feet are not together. I will approach the student and ask them to correct this. Upon making the request, I will often get a confused look from them because in their mind, they have told their body to go into the proper position and think it has listened and done so. They have told their feet that they should be together with the toes touching. When they look down to see that their body has not responded as requested, they will be surprised, fix their feet, and go back to attention.

This is important because at the moment of the lineup, the student told themselves mentally, "I am going to put my body in this physical position." Prior to looking down, they believed their body was in the proper position. Yet, the reality was the body did not respond to the mental command. In other words, it responded in an undisciplined manner.

Another example I have seen with many people, in general, is that they hold residual tension in their bodies. I see this a lot in the shoulders because it is a place where tension is stored. It appears the shoulders are being held up towards their ears and sometimes rolled forward. This tells me that they have not developed a strong mind-body connection. When working with a client or student, I will ask them to relax their body. Many times their response is, "I am relaxed," or they will sigh but not change their body.

The first step is helping them focus attention and noticing their body more to build awareness of the tension they are carrying. Once they have become aware, they are able to gain the ability to command their body. They will begin to relax, and the shoulders will drop down by a few inches. In this situation, the tension came from stress and a lack of awareness of the buildup. Without awareness, the body is undisciplined.

My partner, Jennifer, has helped clients who have experienced another kind of mind-body disconnect due to trauma. Sometimes when a person undergoes trauma, the mind will learn to protect itself by disconnecting from the body. The person is unable to escape the abuse, so the mind will try to leave the here and now and be somewhere else. This can lead to a break in the mind-body connection. One example is someone who has experienced repeated sexual abuse. As a survival method, the mind would go to another place during the abuse. Some people have described having an "out of body" experience during abuse where they watched themselves or were in another place altogether.

Through repeated experiences, the mind builds new neuropathways that strengthen the response. Over time, the result can be chronic pain, unexplained illness, digestion issues, and a lack of awareness of the body. One example

Jennifer experienced was while utilizing trauma-sensitive yoga.

Jennifer was helping a client work on interoception, becoming aware of the inner feelings and sensations in the body. Using yoga forms, the client would move through each motion and pause in it while reflecting on sensations they are feeling, or a lack thereof. Jennifer was inviting a client, who had their leg extended behind them and out of view, to move their straight leg in circles or up and down. The client had a bent leg and was struggling to move it in the way they wanted. Jennifer inquired about what the client was experiencing and found out that the client could not tell if their leg was straight or bent.

They had a weakened mind-body connection as to where they could not tell what position their leg was in without looking at it. To help rebuild the connection, Jennifer offered for the client to look at their leg to see if it is bent or straight, then practice noticing differences in the way they felt in each position. In time, the client gained a level of physical discipline. Their body would respond to commands, and they had an awareness of the body's actions.

For me, this is one of the first areas of discipline. It is the training of the body to do what it is told. I use the lineup as an example because it has been one of the most common things I have run into in my career.

Another example of this in the martial arts industry is the use of forms. When the student is in the lineup, they really are not moving; they are trying to stay in one place and discipline their body to maintain a position. When a student does a form, you're starting to add movement into the equation. This sounds like it's easy, but once you start trying to rein the body in with movement and have it do as you wish, you quickly will find out that it does not always listen to what you're thinking.

For those of you that don't know what I mean by the word "form," in Martial Arts, a form is a series of movements that are related to fighting or to some kind of combat. A student will learn the series of positions, memorize them, and then practice the movements until they are second nature. The goal is to get to the point where they do not have to look down at the body to make sure it is in the proper position.

Most of the time, this is looked at as a way to learn different martial arts techniques. Of course, that's true, but that is only scratching the surface of a form's true purpose and beauty. For me, it is a tool used to develop the body. It can be used in many different ways, and one of those ways is physical discipline, teaching the body to respond correctly to commands of the mind. This is a skill that can be applied to more than just your physical body. We will find that out shortly as we discuss additional topics in this area.

Now is this the only way? Of course not. There are many different ways to train this concept. You do not have to study Martial Arts necessarily to develop this level of discipline. I have met people who have reached a high level of the mind-body connection through the study of yoga. I have seen it done with high-level strength athletes, as well as bodybuilders in the fitness industry.

Though I personally learned this initially in the arts, I later carried it over to my own training in the gym. I found out quickly that the more physically disciplined I became, and the more control I gained over my own body, the more positive change I was able to develop through training in the gym.

Control of muscular flexion

Your body has three different types of muscles: the cardiac muscle, smooth muscle, and skeletal muscle. The muscular system is the engine of the body. Skeletal muscle is connected to the bone structure of the body, and generally, they will come in pairs due to the fact that they can only contract. So in this pair, one muscle will pull a bone in one direction, and the other muscle will pull it in another direction. Muscle fibers can only contract or pull; they do not have the ability to push.

The percentage of contraction or flexion that you can create in any given muscle is directly related to your level of strength. Additionally, the size of the muscle will have an effect on the amount of output it can produce. With this in mind, I will generally have two options when I want to increase strength in a muscle group. We are going to take a look at the first option. The question is, how does someone train their body to flex at a higher percentage? Fortunately for us, martial arts holds the answer.

I was initially introduced to high tension training from a study in kung fu called stone warrior training. At the time that I learned this part of the art, I was not doing much training inside the gym as far as weightlifting. All I did on a daily basis was practice the stone warrior exercises I was taught. One thing I noticed from this training was a huge increase in my own personal strength. I did not put on much muscular size during this time, and at the time, I thought that muscular size was the only way to increase strength, so this seemed odd to me. I noticed that muscle I already had became denser as the form taught me greater control of it. Because of this training, when I was younger, I never had a problem with lacking in strength. I would commonly train with partners that were larger than me at that time, and I would always at the very least be evenly matched, if not stronger. I would often get the comment that I was a lot stronger than I looked.

It wasn't until later in life that I decided to combine the principles I learned from this martial art study with the basic movements I was learning in weight training. Combining the two methods not only brought me more strength in the gym and on the mat, but I noticed that it did it at extended ranges of motion. For example, if you are fully extended in a given range of motion, generally, you will be weaker at the end of that range. The stone warrior training seemed to build strength all the way through the range of motion.

I have been doing this now for over 25 years, and the additional benefit is that I have been maintaining higher levels of strength as I've gotten older. Even at 50, I have been able to maintain a decent percentage of my strength from years prior. I definitely feel that it has allowed me to maintain a higher level of overall physical strength and be able to do it later in life than if I had not put the two sciences together.

Regardless, I do believe that martial arts training is one of the best tools available to do the study and practice of disciplining the body.

High Flexion Training in the gym

The first strength exercise I learned in the stone warrior training was a movement set called snake turns over, or "snake turns." Snake turns is a movement done while standing in a low stance. Most of the movements in the exercise are done with the arms and the muscles of the upper torso.

Just to give you an idea of what this exercise would look like: if you're standing in the low stance that I mentioned above, you will have your hands pulled back next to the sides of your rib cage. Both hands will be in a fist with the palms up. From here, you will punch out in front of you, and when the arms are fully extended, you will curl the arm so that the hand comes back to your shoulder. From here, the hand rotates to face forward (like the head of a snake), and then it will open, and you will press the open palm forward in front of you.

At this point, the hand will turn back over and roll into a fist, and you will pull that arm back to its position next to your rib cage. Once you do this on both sides of the body, that is considered one repetition. I don't explain the exercise in order to teach it but just to give you an idea of what it looks like. We are going to take the principles and apply them to a more commonly known physical exercise in just a minute.

As you are moving through these motions, you are attempting to do them at a higher level of tension or muscle flexion.

This is not necessarily a form but more of a drill. Each time when completing the exercise, I would stand in one position and repeat the upper body movements for a certain number of repetitions. Every day I would add on an additional repetition to the movement with the goal of eventually getting to 100 repetitions in each session. When I first began, it sounded easier than it actually was in practice. Then as I progressed and the numbers grew each day, it became more difficult. Many may say, "Well there's no weights, so how could this be that difficult?" The answer is it is only as difficult as you make it.

My focus was to put forth as much effort and stress on the muscles as possible. As I moved through these movements, the goal was to do them with as much muscular flexion in the muscles of the upper body as possible. This flexion does not turn on and off with each movement. I would maintain a high level of tension in my muscles for the entire exercise. So if you end up doing the exercise for an hour, you are literally going to maintain a high level of flexion for the entire hour. If you are doing this correctly, it will be extremely difficult. You have to have a high level of physical discipline to be able to maintain the flexion that long while combating fatigue.

This is something that I had to build up, hence the addition of the repetitions each day. I remember doing this exercise in one spot in the academy for an hour and a half. When I finished with the exercise, I looked down at the floor to see a large puddle of sweat.

After about 100 days is when I started to notice a distinctive change in my strength. Those I trained with in the academy took notice as well. I soon surpassed the strength of students who were larger in size than me. Things that took effort three months ago, I was doing easily. As I said earlier, I did not put on much size during this time, yet I could tell that the muscle structure of my body had become much denser. I went to my teacher to inquire about the exercise to learn more about what was happening through the practice.

He explained that I was training my body to have the ability to flex at a higher percentage of what I had been able to previously. The average person has the ability to flex a muscle around 15% out of 100% of their total capacity. In other words, if they have 100 muscle fibers, they are only able to switch on 15 of them.

The goal of the exercise was to help increase that percentage to 25 or 30%. So I was literally trying to rewire my muscles to allow me to flex a higher percentage of muscle fibers through the training, in other words gaining more physical discipline and control of my body.

This training intrigued me at the time, and I wanted to know more, so I began searching for additional information to dive deeper into this study. What I found is that the body has a sensory organ called the Golgi tendon. In simple terms, this organ controls the amount of tension you can generate in a muscle. If you had complete control of full flexion of a muscle, you would have the potential to tear joints and connective tissue with the amount of power that it would create.

The Golgi tendon reflex keeps you from flexing at those high levels and damaging yourself in the process. Imagine doing a set of curls in the gym. You put the weight on the bar and start curling. You may get 15 reps into the set, and suddenly your muscle just gives out. This is the Golgi tendon reflex turning off your muscle to keep you from doing damage to yourself.

I believe from doing the high flexion training over time, you are not only strengthening the muscle fibers but also rewiring this response to allow you access to a greater percentage of muscular flexion.

This is the knowledge that I took into the weight training gym and applied to what I was doing in that arena. For my own training, I would still do about 20 minutes of the stone warrior training prior to going onto the gym floor. The practice gave me a greater connection with my muscles, and it also seemed to warm up the nervous system prior to doing any type of lifting. Then once on the gym floor, I would pick an exercise, and regardless of the weight, I would try to go through the movement with the same level of muscle flexion that I had learned in the stone warrior training. With this new knowledge and way of training, it felt like I was starting all over again in the gym.

It took a little time to get used to going through these movements while under flexion. Once I started to get comfortable with the exercise, that's when I would start adding gradual increases to the weight I was using. It wasn't long before I noticed a huge increase in strength in the basic exercises that I was working with. I also noticed a considerable change on the academy floor when I was training with my partners in resistance exercises.

An example of this would be pummeling or grappling. You are literally putting your strength and skill against another opponent while you try to move into superior positions so that you were able to submit them. The changes I noticed immediately was the moves that my training partner would normally get me with were not working anymore. Additionally, I noticed that the things I was attempting were starting to get easier and smoother. My endurance during that time seemed to almost double; it was taking twice as long to feel the same muscular fatigue that I would normally feel while training.

By taking what I learned through martial arts and applying it to my work in the gym, I noticed some other side effects of the training. For one thing, I was as hungry as a bear every day. I would do this training in the gym. I started eating more but still seemed to be leaning out with the additional intake. So I did have to increase the amount of calories I was taking in on a daily basis.

The second thing I noticed is I started gaining in muscular size. Even though I was not putting a tremendous amount of weight on the bar, I started to see the physical change in my body. By gaining more flexion control of the muscle, I was able to make a noticeable change without using a lot of weight.

I was increasing in size and strength without putting unhealthy wear and tear on my body using the heavier weights. I had used the heavier loads in the past, and it would put more strain on my connective tissues extending my amount of recovery time and potential for injury.

I recovered faster and had more energy for martial arts training later in the day. Over the years, I have noticed how dense the connective tissues in my body have become. This has directly affected my ability to withstand injuries on the academy floor while training.

I first started doing these experiments when I was in my mid-30s. I am currently entering my 50s, and I am still implementing these exercises and this training method into my daily routine. The only thing that has changed for me over that time is learning to implement recovery time in my overall training strategy intelligently. I have also had a tremendous return from implementing periodization routines and progressive resistance. In my experience, the older you get, the more you have to lean on a greater understanding of the science of training in order to maintain growth. You have to be a perpetual student in your own physical education.

It is my hope that his knowledge can be taken by you and used in some form to acquire the same benefits I have seen in my life.

Now, how do we get you there? Let's use a common exercise to start with to practice these concepts.

Once you've got the concept down and are ready for more, check out my website at: www.sifualanbaker.com. For now, we will use the pushup. I am going to assume you have worked your way up to being able to do one push-up. If you are unable to do a standard push-up, then you can start out on your knees and work your way up. You can also do these exercises standing and leaning against the wall and doing your push-ups there. As your strength increases, you will be able to gradually work your way up to a regular push-up.

I would like for you to have some push up handles to use so you have something to grip as you do your push up. I'll go into why in just a second.

Stone Warrior Push Up

First, I want you to stand up and flex your entire upper body. If you have never done anything like this before, start with the muscles in the chest by crossing your arms in front of you to activate them.

Next, you can flex the muscles in the back by pulling your hands back, next to your side, about waist level like you are rowing a boat. Pull your shoulder blades back and down.

Next, try to activate the back muscles at the same time. Once you have done this, try it once more, and try to flex the muscles in the arms and see if you can get them to activate at the same time as your chest and back. Try to feel flexion in the arms, the chest, and the back. Next, tighten up your abdomen like you're going to receive a punch to the gut. Try to turn on all of your muscles in the upper body, then relax.

Now we are going to do the same thing, but this time make a fist with both hands and imagine squeezing a ball in your fist as hard as you can. You should notice that you can flex your entire upper body much harder when you grip your fist. Hold the flexion for a few seconds, then relax. Now we're going to do it a third time, but this time, I want you to add contracting your rectal sphincter as if you are trying to stop yourself from going to the bathroom.

This additional move will assist you in creating greater intra-abdominal pressure that will increase your strength. Flexing the muscles of the pelvic floor will not only increase your strength, but it will help avoid hemorrhoids if you are performing exercises while using intra-abdominal pressure.

Intra-abdominal pressure or the Valsalva maneuver is a buildup of pressure in your abdomen. This is a common thing you will do when you are attempting to have a bowel movement.

This pressure buildup stabilizes the torso as well as increasing strength. We are going to learn more about this later when we learn the power breath.

Now, we are going to do a pushup on the pushup handles using the method you just learned. The reason for utilizing the handles is to give you the ability to grip and squeeze your hands. As we mentioned, the tension in your grip will additionally increase strength for this exercise. Start in the top/up position of the push-up. Before you begin lowering yourself, grip the handles hard and flex all the muscle groups as we did earlier.

Once the tension is on, slowly drop to the bottom of the pushup. Try to time the drop so that it is about 4 seconds. 1.... 2.... 3.... 4.... Now maintain the flexion and go back up to the top of the position. 1.... 2.... 3.... 4. Then relax. Congratulations, you just did your first stone warrior pushup. You are on your way to rewiring your muscle and gaining greater control of your body.

Though this is one example, this principle can be used in most other forms of exercise. I personally have done it with bodyweight exercises, Russian kettlebell training, club bell training, weightlifting, strength training, and obviously, in the martial arts forms. If you currently do not do a lot of physical exercises, I would suggest starting with bodyweight exercises for a little while prior to moving into weighted exercises.

Releasing tension or turning off muscle

Now we're going to take a look at the other end of the spectrum. Your ability to turn off the tension in your muscles. Most of the people I introduce this to look at me strangely and say, "Well I just let go and let it release, right?" The thing is, even though you think you're turning off your muscle, most of the time you're still holding on to a certain level of residual tension that you can't release. There are several things that will cause this. One main cause of residual tension is stress.

The level of social stress you are under on a day-to-day basis can have a direct effect on the levels of tension in your body if you are unable to process the stress and release the tension. If a stressful environment is something you are exposed to for an extended amount of time, the effects of it will just keep getting worse. Even if you are able to manage it at first, it will tend to overwhelm you. It may be that the tension shows up in new areas. You may focus on working tension out of your body but then find you've started grinding your teeth at night.

Another result can be a dysregulated digestive system. That stressful tension will end up being stored in your body to the point where you are not in control of it. Today it is common knowledge that this type of stress and tension is the forbearer of different types of disease for the body.

A toxic diet will have a direct effect on the levels of tension in your body. Not eating healthy can continually put toxins in the body that it is unable to process and eliminate in a timely manner. If the body does not have the ability to eliminate these toxins and get them out of the system, they will end up being stored in the fatty tissues and the muscular system. This build-up over time can begin to create tension in the muscular system.

Excessive physical training of the body will also build tension in the muscular system over time. You can see this in some people who have spent a lot of time in the gym. There's a gradual loss of range of motion in the joints. Most of this is due to building up residual tension inside of the muscles. It's one of the reasons why it is important to stretch and loosen the body as part of your weight training routine in the gym.

With this in mind, it is equally important to learn how to relax the muscles of the body as it is to learn to flex them. When I'm teaching this concept in the academy, I will have the student imagine a scale of 1 to 10. Ten represents being fully flexed and one being completely turned off and relaxed. Most people will land on a scale between 4 and 7. Our goal is to learn to train your body to be able to increase its range in both directions. Our focus is trying to turn that 4 into a 2.

Shaking the body loose.

This exercise is one of the first basic exercises I learned to drop tension out of the body. It is very simple, and it will literally "bounce" the body and force the release of tension in the body.

We will begin standing with your feet shoulder-width apart. You will want to find a position where you feel a solid connection with the earth through the bottoms of your feet and your weight distributed through the pad of each foot. With your knees slightly bent, you start bouncing up and down. This isn't a huge move, maybe just one or 2 inches. Movement is primarily created in the knees with your feet flat and in continuous contact with the floor. Arms are going to be hanging loose, trying to mentally release all the tension in them that you possibly can.

Each time you bounce, release a small exhale. As you are doing this, you're going to mentally scan the body from the top of the head all the way to the feet. As you mentally address each part of the body, try to let any tension go and think about softening that body part even more. You can imagine shaking and bouncing the tension out of each area. You may find that you spend longer in some areas than others as your body may naturally be trying to resist the bouncing.

As you progress, releasing tension and finding a more fluid movement in your body, the bounces will gradually get smaller and smaller. You can do this practice anywhere from 2 to 5 minutes. At the end of the drill, you will simply stop bouncing in a standing position. Usually, when I stop the movement, I am still mentally passing through the body from head to toes, telling the body to release and let go. You can imagine tension running down through the body and out the feet like a light or a liquid. You may notice at the end of this exercise a warm feeling in the body, and areas of the body may tingle. This is normal and part of the exercise.

A few things to remember when doing this exercise: you have to find the right pace of bouncing. Sometimes if you go too fast and too hard, it will just create more tension in parts of the body. You should feel looser and more relaxed at the end of the exercise. Additionally, as you are mentally passing through the body, you can focus your attention on three areas as you go down. The first area is the skin, muscle structure, and external flesh of your body. Secondly, you can think of the organs of the body as you scan. Thirdly, you can focus on the bone in the skeletal system of the body.

You can do these one at a time during the drill. Another option when doing this drill is to just focus on the different levels of the body. For instance, just do the head, then the neck, down to the shoulders, and so on and so forth. If at first you don't feel the deeper tissues in the body, that is okay; it will come with time and practice. Each time you do the scan you're going to imagine releasing stress from whatever part you're focusing on and let it flow down the body, through the feet, and into the floor.

The nice thing about this exercise as it can be done pretty much anywhere. At home, in the office, in the field, when traveling, anywhere at all. All you need is enough room to stand in one spot for a few minutes to yourself. There are many benefits to this relaxation training— specifically the development of the ability to be physically relaxed while operating in a high-stress environment. Stress will obviously increase tension in the body, and this tension will act like an involuntary brake system slowing you down and sometimes causing you to freeze.

Depending on the situation, this could be the difference between losing the deal, game, fight, or the difference between life or death. Maintaining a relaxed physical state increases your athletic ability, your agility, and your all-around performance.

This drill can be done in five to ten minutes each day. With practice, it will gradually increase your ability to relax. The individuals I have taught this method to operate on very tight schedules or are placed in the field where they do not have the equipment or a lot of time to spend on daily maintenance of strength development.

Tension to counter and release tension.

In Kung Fu, we learn to use tension in order to release different areas of the body that we are having problems getting to relax and release. I learned different exercises in which we would flex and create tension in different parts of the body in a progressive manner, in order to coax the muscles to release to a greater extent than when we started the drill. I also noticed this as a byproduct of training the stone warrior forms and exercises. Sometimes these exercises of hard tension would be done for up to an hour at a time.

After spending this much time working on half flexion in the body and taking the opportunity to rest, I noticed that I was in a much greater state of relaxation than when I started doing the training. Naturally, as my strength increased with this training, I also noticed that my ability to relax had increased, as well as my range of motion in my major joints. Later I discovered that this method of stretching was called proprioceptive neuromuscular facilitation, or PNF.

Dr. Herman Kabat developed PNF stretching in the 1940s as a means to treat neuromuscular conditions, including polio and multiple sclerosis. PNF is based on the physiology of the stretch reflex. This reflex is caused by the activation of the Golgi tendon response that is located in the muscle spindles of any given muscle group. The Golgi will send a signal to the brain that will lead to a contraction in the muscles.

Using variations of tension and release drills, we can attempt to re-educate this process, thus leading to greater relaxation in the muscles of the body or the area we are focusing on. PNF is commonly used in different stretching routines to increase the range of motion for other body areas. We have used this form of stretching in the academy for years.

As I stated earlier, I was first introduced to this idea in Kung Fu and Chi Gong to remove tension from the body gradually. This, like the bouncing exercise we spoke about, is a very effective way of coaxing residual tension out of the body and giving you access to the greater range of release that we talked about on our 1 to 10 scale.

This exercise can be done by laying, sitting, or standing. When first introducing these methods to students, I will generally have them attempt them in a lying-down position. The only reason for this is to put the student in a relaxed position that they are familiar with. If you do this in a seated or standing position, you will need to learn to align the skeletal system in a balanced manner and hold the muscular system and the organs on its structure. This allows the soft tissues the ability to relax entirely and just hang onto the skeletal system. Sometimes this takes a little time to learn, which is another reason to introduce the training method in a lying-down position.

So from your lying-down position, begin with the feet. Try to flex all the muscles in the feet, hold this for a few seconds and then release. When you release the tension, exhale and mentally focus on relaxing the muscles as much as possible. You can do this flex release cycle several times if needed.

Next, you can move up to the lower leg, flex, and hold the muscles in the lower leg. When you release the tension, you're going to do the same thing that we stated previously. You can follow this process and go from the feet all the way up through the body, out the arms, and to the top of the head. The more you do the exercise, the better you will get at activating the muscle structure equally, releasing it on the other end of the flexion.

We have gone through a couple of different methods of coaxing tension out of the body. You don't have to do all of them; you could pick one and focus on it for a little while and then switch to another one once you have some time in. You may like one method better than another one, and that is okay; the main thing is that you find a method that works for you and will allow you to release residual tension in your body.

Breathing, The Power Breath.

Another aspect that I teach in physical discipline, after a student has obtained a certain level of control over their body, is to start looking for a level of control over their internal operating system—specifically focusing on the pulmonary system. So they will start learning to control their breath as they are doing whatever exercise they've chosen to focus on for their growth.

Basically, for myself, there are two fundamental forms of breathing. Right now, we just want to realize that the breath is also connected to the body and that it is one of the things that you have the ability to control. Because of this, it is one of the fundamental areas of study in physical discipline. Later in this book, we're going to go into greater detail on the art of breath overall. For now, let's look at a power breath to add to your pushup to increase your power.

Take a breath and exhale. Now take another one, but as you exhale, pinch your lips together so you can restrict the airflow. Don't let air pass out of your nose, only your mouth as you do this; flex and tighten your abdomen. Your goal is to feel air pressure in your stomach. This is The Valsalva maneuver or sometimes called intra-abdominal pressure. You are not holding your breath, just releasing it against pressure to build pressure in the torso.

Once you have tried this, you can apply it to your pushup. Inhale at the top. When you start the exhale, you will start the pushup. Try to time the exhale so that you have air pressure during the entire pushup. At the top of the pushup, take a full breath before performing another rep. You will notice that you will be stronger and more stable in your core when you add this breathing method to your exercise.

Weightlifters and kettlebellers will perform the Valsalva maneuver when they are lifting heavy weights. They do this to provide stabilization to the trunk. Intra-abdominal pressure will have a tremendous effect on your strength. I have witnessed it personally and used it myself many times in the arts. The most common are Karate's systems, but it does exist in almost every system or method that I have personally trained in or studied. If you watch a Karate practitioner demonstrating a form, you will hear them cry out during certain parts of the form.

What they are doing is producing an explosive Intra-abdominal pressure to give power to the move. The interesting thing is that the noise they make will additionally amplify their levels of strength. After learning this, I realized I could apply it to the different strength training exercises myself, just by using a low groan. So when you perform the stone warrior pushup, you inhale and then activate the flexion in all of the parts of the body we discussed.

This will create that internal pressure. Personally, I will release it slowly through the back of my throat with a low groan or growl. Depending on the capacity of your lungs, you could do the entire repetition with one breath. If it's too difficult, you can just pause at the bottom of the rep, take another breath, activate flexion, and then finish the rep.

MENTAL DISCIPLINE

Mental discipline is a student's ability to discipline or control their internal landscape, their ability to concentrate or focus their consciousness, or that little voice in your head. Every idea, every action starts with your thoughts and your internal dialogue. In other words, the conversations you have with yourself have a tremendous effect on your life.

Consciousness

Additionally, most of the time, we perceive what is around us on a daily basis unconsciously. It's like we're cruising through life on autopilot, not 100% paying attention to what's going on around us. You are not asleep, but you're not really awake either. You were not entirely in the moment, in the here and now.

Our consciousness is concerned with our personal history, fears, worries, regret, pride, desire, and ego. It also processes our daily anxieties that we hang onto from both the past and the present. The consciousness also processes thoughts of potential future outcomes or perceived challenges. Additional mental space will be consumed by daydreaming, fantasy, and our wants and desires.

All of these things consume space in our conscious minds. They are there whether we choose to recognize them or not. I believe most of us when we do turn our eye internally, realize that it's there. This leaves us the minimal mental capacity to direct into the present, the here and now, to be able to focus on what we wish or need to consciously. If we considered that all the things mentioned above consumed 90% of our mental capacity, that would leave us with only 10% to use in the here and now, only 10% left to focus where we need it. In my experience, 10% would be a gift. I believe most people are cruising around with about 5% available to them on a daily basis.

Subconscious

Our mind's subconscious aspect is like a massive computer hard drive in your mind that collects and stores all of your knowledge, memories, and experience from life. It stores information that you don't need to carry around in your conscious mind all the time—for instance, riding a bike, driving a stick shift, or swimming. If we consciously had to store all of the information that is in the subconscious library, it would overwhelm us mentally. It not only stores this information, but it will process what you need and deliver it into the conscious mind on demand.

That is, of course, if your mind is operating optimally and is not clouded or distracted. Freud compared the subconscious to the submerged half of an iceberg, "the bulk of it lying below the surface, exerting a dynamic and determining influence upon the part which is amenable to direct inspection, the conscious mind." It has also been credited as a source of creative and transformative thought. We are going to come back to this a little bit later. But first, let's focus on consciousness.

How do we activate consciousness? How do we pay attention? How do we move those mental obstacles and gain the ability to FOCUS intent on what we want and where we want to go? In the study of meditation, spending time in that 90% is referred to as the lower levels of consciousness. This is further amplified by our pursuit of the accumulation of possessions.

If you stand back and take a look at the input that is put into your mental landscape on a daily basis (television, advertising, movies, social media ads, road signs), all of it is about accumulation and materialism. The Google gods are even tracking everything you do online in order to have more influence (control) over your thoughts, over your conscious and unconscious mind.

All of this will have an effect on the available mental capacity we discussed above. If you are at 90% available consciousness, and then we add in all of the noise that comes in from media, marketing, and other areas, how much more will that consume? Let's say it takes another 5%, and that will leave you with that small 4 to 5% to use in the here and now.

The more we clear the inner landscape and gain the ability to be in the "now state" or the conscious mind, the more ability we have to live at a higher level, a higher intelligence. In the now state, mind does not split between the subconscious and the conscious; you are fully aware of the here and now and able to experience the present moment.

I found that the more time I spend in this now state of mind, the more things that do not truly benefit me in my life (actions or things that equate to an unnecessary waste of time and energy) get discarded. In addition, I experience true gratitude for those beneficial people and things that are in my life. This reminds me of watching an infant who is experiencing his surroundings for the first time. He is uncluttered and fully in the present moment. The infant mind has the ability to learn and process new things at an incredible rate. They seem to be in a constant state of growth and development, completely unclouded by the drama, complications, or life issues. This is the state we strive to regain with our practice.

The times in life when I have been able to silence the mind and truly be in the here and now are where I experience some of my greatest moments of clarity, change, and growth. You will know when you are in this mental state, and sounds will be clearer, colors will seem brighter, your hearing will be sharper. If you have experienced this in the past, it usually is one of the most elaborate memories that you have.

Moments are usually connected to a near-traumatic or traumatic life events. Sometimes an intense physical activity will cause this. Something that immediately forces you 100% into the current moment pushes the mental cloud to the side for a time. I have heard students use the term being in "the zone," there's a feeling of being completely alive and the experience of evolving and expanding.

Although we list this as an area of discipline, mental discipline alone could be the topic of an entire book. I have written entire curriculums around this topic for both my students and the high performers I've coached over the years. And even now, I continue to revise and change those curriculums as my students and I continue to grow in the topic. It is our goal with this chapter to give you some fundamental tools to begin to take back control of your mind and your consciousness. The most powerful tool you possess.

The Creative Subconscious

Earlier, we talked about the subconscious being a source of creative and transformative thought. If you have ever experienced waking up in the middle of the night and realizing that you suddenly have a creative idea or the answer to a problem you've been pondering for a while, then you are familiar with this feeling. Maybe you just woke up in the morning and lying there getting ready to get out of bed, you are struck with a creative stroke of genius, a new business idea, or a side hustle endeavor.

Many people are able to do their most creative work immediately after awakening. Those moments of relaxed, clear thought allow you to connect to your creative subconscious. These moments between being asleep and awake are referred to as a hypnopompic state or your "threshold consciousness." Many past artists, writers, scientists, and inventors have credited hypnagogia and related states with enhancing their creativity. Including Beethoven, Richard Wagner, Walter Scott, Salvador Dalí, Thomas Edison, Nikola Tesla, Benjamin Franklin, and Isaac Newton.

There are times when you will be so fully immersed in a task that your conscious mind seems to take a back seat, and you slip into that creative, focused zone. Again, connecting with the transformative subconscious mind.

Meditative mind work can clear the connection between your conscious and subconscious, giving you more access to the mind's creative engine. As you progress, this connection becomes more readily available to you during your everyday consciousness. The great thing about it is that the exercise needed to both make available more of your conscious awareness, as well as connect you to the creative subconscious, is the same.

The Focus Lesson

As a kid, I was an uncontrollable ball of energy. So much so that my school had a conversation with my mother regarding having me placed on medication to dull my senses and slow me down enough for the teacher to control me in class. They told my parents that I did not have the ability to focus on anything in my current state.

Thank God my mother told them to go to hell, and instead of drugging me, she told them they should learn how to do their job better instead of relying on drugs. I am extremely grateful for this. I had since had the opportunity to work with individuals who were unfortunately placed on these drugs when they were kids. I have seen the effect it has on them both when they are on it and the effects it has had on them once they were removed from the medications. No thanks!

For most of my life, I was told that I needed to learn how to focus and control myself. I would get that comment from multiple people growing up. School teachers, employers, and even my friends would notice it.

One day, I was working with one of my kung fu instructors, and as usual, my attention would stray, and he would have to bring me back to the topic at hand. He looked at me, and he said, "Son, you really need to learn how to focus." After hearing this over and over, I just lowered my head and simply said in a defeated tone, "Yes sir, I know I do."

And then something happened that had never happened before. He asked me if anyone had ever taught me how to focus. Of course, my answer was no. No one ever got past the point of just telling me I needed to learn how to focus. It's not really something they teach you in school. And at that moment, he said, "Then I am going to teach you how to do it and harness this power you have." This was a huge turning point for me.

Turn Off the Noise

One of the first things he had me do was to turn off what he called external noise. He told me to shut the TV off at home. He told me to turn the radio off when I was in the car. He told me to cut back on certain kinds of music; he gave me a list of acceptable music (none of which was my taste at that point in my life, but I did it anyway). He told me that I was going to need to turn off any gossip that I'm exposed to.

For a teenager, this was quite a request. But I did it. I pretty much put down television completely. When I was in my car driving, I got to the point where I would not even turn on the radio. When I was with friends, and unnecessary drama or gossip would start, I simply would walk away from it. I learned to remove myself from it. I was fortunate that I had a good friend at this time who understood what I was doing and jumped in there and did it with me.

He was also a regular training partner for me in the martial arts, and like myself, he was endlessly curious and willing to work for additional knowledge in the arts. We became "accountability partners" in training and in the life changes that we were going through at that time.

My teacher told me that it would take time but if I could maintain what I have started, then eventually I would start to have quietness in my mind, silence to the unnecessary noise. And he was absolutely correct. It did take some time, but after a while, I started to realize that all of these things he had told me to put down were putting unnecessary noise into my mind. It seemed that even if I wasn't listening to the radio or watching TV that those things would still be echoing in my internal landscape. It was almost like they left a residual noise in the background.

Later in life, I realized that all of those things were just unnecessary input. At first, I thought that because I was not listening to the news or watching it on TV, this would make me uninformed. But quite the opposite happened. I did not add in sources of information for years. Honestly, I think I was in my 40s before I even started looking for a method to get the daily news and other information in a quick, concise manner.

Now I only receive information that I feel is needed every two or three days, and I still limit it tremendously. I have not owned a TV since the early 90s, and I've got to say it has been wonderful for me. They were unnecessary information, unnecessary noise that was just being put into my mind. Once I started to see its effect on me, I realized that I had to intelligently choose what I allowed to be put into my internal landscape. We are going to be talking about this more a little later on.

Do you ever feel like you can't turn off your mind? Like the noise in there can't be shut off sometimes? Do you have moments at work when you seem to dull out or zone out for a few minutes, like your mind is forcing you to take a break from the overstimulation?

Maybe it's time to start taking a look at what you are putting into your internal landscape. Find those things that really are just noise, just garbage input that you don't really need. Tibetan Monks will isolate themselves in search of the quietness of mind. There is great power when you can calm the seas of the mind and focus it properly.

I think this is most important in the early part of the day. Your conscious mind and subconscious are open and are the most susceptible to new information and knowledge in the mornings. It still has a state of relaxed quiet from the night's sleep. This is one of the reasons I like to choose exactly what goes into my internal landscape in the mornings for my morning routine.

If you do this, too, you will find it will help you set the tone for the rest of your day. Not only is it important to choose what you expose yourself to at this time of day, but additionally, you should pick the things that you do want to feed the mind. Choose what your daily influence will be.

Take the time to see what your unnecessary inputs are and start to remove them. You don't have to do it all at once, you can do it a source at a time, or you can go cold turkey as I did under my teacher's guidance. After I had eliminated some of the external inputs, I had an opportunity to have another lesson on focus. Sifu sat me down and had me explain to him everything I had done since the last lesson.

I talked about all the different mental input I had eliminated. He told me it was good, and he said he wanted to discuss consciousness with me. This was a very unusual topic for me. I immediately thought to myself, *But I am conscious already.* He told me that most people only have control of a small portion of their consciousness. He went on to explain that the conscious and the subconscious mind will exert energy on different things, and sometimes it will do it without me even realizing it.

He explained that people with untrained or unfocused consciousness would allow parts of their internal landscape to be consumed with past life history, fears, and worries of the unknown, regret, or disappointment from negative events in life, past and present. It will be taken up by ego and pride, desires, or our daily anxieties. He told me that these things could accumulate with age as well.

Though I was young at the time, he told me that I would experience these things as I grew older and if it was left unchecked, it would only get worse. My lesson was to become aware of these things that were consuming my focus, my consciousness, and as I became aware of them, attempt to disconnect from them as best as possible.

This, for me at the time, was even harder than what he had given me to do previously. As I practiced, I was able to become more aware of these different things. But becoming unconnected to them is a continuing challenge.

Regardless, for myself, with practice came change and achievement. And the more I practiced, the more I was able to obtain more control of what he called consciousness. The ability to be in the here and now, to live in the moment. And the more ability I gained, the more I could direct the energy into the more important things in life.

Your breath is the bridge of control for your mind and body.

Emptiness.

About 6 to 8 months later, I went back to my teacher and told him of my progress. It was at this point that he gave me my first real mental exercise to work on. He wanted me to create a new daily habit. As part of this habit, I would spend 10 minutes doing breathing exercises and attempting to empty my mind even more.

He told me my goal was to get to the point where I could have 10 minutes of emptiness or quietness in my mind. In other words, 10 minutes of no thought. This was one of the hardest things I ever had to do. Just imagine how difficult it is to sit down and just clear your mind for 10 minutes and try not to think of anything. At that time, it seemed almost impossible to me.

This drill took a few years to get even remotely good at. During this time, he taught me two fundamental breaths. And I mentioned this earlier when I discussed physical discipline. As you read through this book, you're going to hear it a lot more. Your breath is the bridge of control for your mind and body. You will find that it is the beginning, the launching point of control of yourself.

So in this exercise, my teacher would have me start a basic full-cycle breath. The full breath is a very natural breathing method. I first learned this method in a lying-down position. If you ever watch an infant breathe, you will notice that it does not breathe from the chest. They will breathe from the stomach using the diaphragm. Chest breathing is a learned habit, sometimes learned unconsciously. It is also a response to having residual tension in the body, something we tend to pick up more as we grow older.

The full breath will start with the expansion of the abdomen wall outward. As the stomach fills up with air and extends outward, it reaches the point where it has no more room, and it will force the chest to rise. So the rise in the chest is the last part of the movement, not the first. On the exhale, it is the first area to drop.

At the end of the movement, I like to pull in the abdomen wall, which will raise the diaphragm and completely empty my lungs of air. This is a basic explanation of the full breath. There are different rhythms that are tight with this breath as well to gain different effects in the body.

There are so many incredible benefits to this exercise that will affect multiple areas of the body. We are going to discuss this more later in the book when we study the breath in detail. But this will give you a basic idea of what you're looking for in this exercise, just to get you started on the emptiness exercise.

You're looking for a long, slow inhale, then a long, slow exhalation. You want to find someplace that you can lay comfortably with the arms and legs straight. As you're breathing, you will notice your ability to hear the breath inside your body. By opening or hollowing out the back of the throat, you will be able to amplify this breathing sound.

You will focus on this breath as the air goes in and out of the lungs & torso. Your goal is to attempt not to focus on anything and empty the mind. For a long time, what helped me in the exercise was listening to the breath and focusing on that as I tried to empty everything else out of the mind.

Once you have the breath, the next thing you want to work on is relaxation. The more tension you hold in the body, the more it will draw your focus and concentration away from your exercise. You will notice in the beginning that it may be difficult sometimes to just lay still for an extended amount of time.

Most of the time, this is related to the amount of tension you're holding in your body. Sometimes it's a residual tension that you are completely unaware of. So it is not uncommon to spend some time recognizing this tension and just gaining the ability to let it go during your practice.

Doing the exercise first thing in the morning is usually one of the best times because of your relaxed state. This is just to allow your body to obtain the greatest level of relaxation as possible. As you progress in the exercise, you will begin to work on different seated postures, and eventually onto some standing postures, so that you will become aware of the different tensions in the body.

A simple way to do it is breathing, mentally running from the head down to the toes. As you come to each area, focus on that area and release it, tell it to let go and try to relax. You will notice that each area of the body that you address may hold residual tensions that you were unaware of. After doing a single sweep of the body, you can move on to working on the mental landscape.

So now you have set your breathing pattern, and you have achieved a certain level of physical relaxation. As you do this exercise, you are going to have thoughts that will jump into your mind. It's important not to try to push them away or force them out. When you have a thought enter your mind, simply address it. Think about it, consider it, and give it some time until you are able to release it and let it go.

Some thoughts will come back again and again. This is normal; treat them the same. Sometimes these things are areas of life that might need to be addressed. They may be related to a problem or difficulty that you are currently having. Several times I have come out of this exercise with answers to questions or situations I had to deal with in my life.

Those days, the training may not have been a successful exercise of emptiness, but it gave me an empty slate and a higher level of focus to concentrate on whatever it was and come up with an answer or a solution to it. I have found once I deal with those questions and I get an answer, they generally do not come back. I ended up dealing with several situations in life that were creating mental noise that I had to deal with.

Sometimes as you lay in meditation, you may experience pain in your leg. Just like the thoughts mentioned above, do not become attached to it. Once you pay attention to it, you are giving it energy, you become attached to it. Again, mentally address it and then ignore it. Don't give it the mental energy it's trying to demand. Most of these things are just illusions in the mind. You are not those thoughts or experiences that will stray into your consciousness and internal landscape.

In the beginning, many things will demand your attention while you're trying to do this exercise. They will come to take your attention, you will take it back. They will come and take it again, and you will take it back again. Thousands of times, they will attempt to regain control of your mind, your consciousness, and your focus. Remember, this is normal, and everyone that goes through this exercise experiences the same thing.

Over time, I have experienced less and less of this interference, and my ability to find a state of nothingness increased. My ability to silence the mind increased. This exercise was done daily, and like anything you do consistently over time, it becomes a habit. And I believe if you create intelligent habits, those habits will help you build your desired future. This one became a part of my morning routine. It is something I do every day.

For me, this is the ground floor of mental discipline, the beginning. This is the fundamental basic that I will have my students and anyone I coach to start with. Gaining the ability to clear your mind will give you a canvas that will be available to you to focus on and create. It gives you the ability to clear your mental landscape so that you can insert the things you need to work on or the things you need to hear.

"If you create intelligent habits, those habits will help you build your desired future." - Alan Baker

Bringing Mindful Focus Into The Daylight

Okay, let's say we've had a student who has been practicing the focus exercise for a while. He has gained the ability to spend most of the ten-minute drill controlling where his consciousness is focused. Let's say he finishes his morning exercise and gets ready to go through his day. During his day, he runs his own business.

Let's say this business is having some financial difficulties. And this is creating a bit of anxiety for him, and he continuously thinks to himself throughout the day, "I don't know what I'm going to do if I don't fix this problem." The thought stays in his mind throughout the day consuming his mental energy.

Every time it comes up, he spends mental energy focused on the problem. This is a common thing. For the practitioner who has reached an intermediate level in his mental work, he wants to attempt to bring the skills he's developed in the morning exercise into application during the day.

The skills he's developed of taking a look at a thought that comes into mind, processing it, and then letting it go. He wants to be able to carry this skill outside of his morning exercise and into the rest of the day. This takes some additional willpower over your focus, over your consciousness.

Most of the time, those thoughts will just jump into your mind, and they control you. We are not really mindful that we are able to address those thoughts as well as choosing to ignore them and not give them mental energy. Now, does this fix the problem? Of course it doesn't, but neither does wasting worrisome energy on it. This is an example of what a student will attempt to do after they have reached a certain level of success in the morning ten-minute focus drill.

My teacher had me doing the same thing after reaching a certain level of success, and it was just like starting all over again from the beginning. Mindfulness and being in the moment, fully awake in the here and now, can be a challenge. It takes a bit of self-aspiration that has to remain consistent throughout your day. But it is absolutely possible with practice and consistency. Achieving this can give you greater control over your attention and focus.

The Power Of Your Focus Ability

One of the most important conscious decisions you can make every day is what you are going to focus your consciousness on. If we let the past consume all or a large portion of our focus, we will have none available to live and enjoy our life in the present moment. You will miss out on that sunset because your head is slightly down as you think about a problem that is in the past and you have absolutely no control over whatsoever.

Don't let that garbage consume your present moment because once it is gone, you will never get it back. Time is a precious commodity, live it, and don't miss out on the life and time you have left. This is a daily battle because one minute, you could decide that you were going to be in the moment and mindful, and then in the next minute, you can let your mental guard down, and your mind will take off in an unhealthy direction. This is especially the case if you have developed the mental habits of focusing on the obstacles and complications of life that you have no control over.

Just like the bad physical habits that we all try to correct, we have to recognize and correct the bad mental habits that we acquire over time as well. Some habits you don't even consciously choose; they just develop over time because of small shortfalls in discipline, or a lack of knowing what you truly want in life.

The more you practice and increase your focus ability, the more mental energy you have available to become aware of these things and correct them. I remember finally becoming aware of these mental habits and asking myself, "Where the hell did that come from?" I could not remember when the mental tendency was even created. I had these cerebral programs running in my mind, and I was never even aware of them until I took the time to look.

Additionally, we spend so much time focused on the accumulation of what we do not have in life. I am not saying we should not have goals or make life plans. It is important to have a plan for your life so that you can focus your attention and energy on things that will carry you into the future you want.

What I am saying is, do not let it overly consume space in your mind and take you away from the here and now. Or take you away from the family who are all right next to you. There is a time and a place for it, and outside of that designated time, don't let it devour your consciousness in the now.

The Gratitude Drill

One of the most powerful things you can do once you have gained control of your focus is to exercise gratitude. The word gratitude comes from the Latin word *gratus*, meaning pleasing and thankful. The gratitude drill not only brings your attention to the current moment but also helps you focus on the truly essential things that you have. Also, the gratitude drill will create powerful emotional energy around these people and things.

Emotional energies have the ability to make your mental landscape a dark and consuming place, or they have the ability to bring power to the image that you were focusing on. One will pull you farther inside, and the other will amplify what are you are focusing on externally, bringing you more into the moment. When I first discovered the gratitude drill, it was something that I would do maybe once a day. But after learning its power and how it affects your conscious focus in the moment, it is something that I started to apply throughout my day, every single day.

The therapeutic benefits of gratitude are abounding. For myself, the gratitude drill has become such a powerful influencer when exercised that it will prompt a change of state. The "gratitude state" will have powerful effects on your attitude, passion, and physiological capacity. Gratitude will lead to long-term happiness, self-esteem, optimism, and feelings of well-being. It has powerful positive effects on anxiety, depression, and daily stress. Expressed outwardly, it will improve relationships that you have with family and friends.

It is extremely simple to do, and I will usually start by focusing on my immediate environment. I can easily look around myself at any given moment and recognize the blessings that have been placed in my life. Of course, there can always be things present that may not fit in this category, but you must remember that you are in charge of your focus and what you place it on.

You can choose to look at the good, or you can choose to look at the bad. In other words, the perspective of good, your ability to recognize those good things and immediately have gratitude for them, can change more than just your state. As I mentioned above, it can assist in bringing you into the here and now. This is one of the reasons that I choose to focus on my immediate environment first.

This has the ability to bring you into a state of mindfulness, the state of now. When I do this, I have a small saying I will add here to myself as I am reviewing my environment. It goes like this: "people, places, things." The first things I will direct my focus on are the people that are around me.

Most of the time, they are the ones that are in my inner circle. The ones that are your do-or-die team, these people are a tremendous blessing to me. Secondly, I will move on to places and things, all the while keeping the perspective of good.

Once I have reviewed my immediate environment, I will mentally move out to things that may be outside my current sphere of reality. Regularly practicing gratitude will bring benefits to you that are endless. It is a common habit to only express gratitude in certain moments of life that may be around some type of achievement. Make it your goal to create a daily habit, the daily gratitude practice, or a drill, as I like to call it.

Doing this will start to affect your behavior outwardly. Everyone that I have taught this to in my school will start to display what I call the attitude of gratitude. This is when you start to express what you are building internally outwardly to those around you, especially the ones that are most important.

These are the people who we mentioned earlier that most of the time might be in your inner circle. This regular expression of gratitude outwardly will start to change your daily environment, whether that is your goal or not.

There have been several studies done on the effects of gratitude on your physical health, such as improving sleep, boosting the immune system, and helping counter the effects of stress. It has been shown to have an effect on your mental health by reducing toxic thoughts and emotions.

The benefits of the gratitude drill will eventually go far beyond using it as a trigger to increase your daily mindfulness. It is a mental multi-tool, a tool that can be applied in many ways and can achieve many benefits for the user.

Internal dialogue.

After my teacher taught me how to create a blank canvas and to empty and clear a space for thought, he then taught me how to put in positive, designed information. At that time, a lot of my goals were based on achieving things in the martial arts, different abilities, and skills that I wanted to obtain.

He asked me to choose one of them that I wanted to focus on. And based on my choice, we picked out some verbal reinforcement that I could use internally that would motivate me to stay focused on obtaining that goal. It pretty much came down to having a mantra that I could say to myself internally. A mantra is a commonly repeated word or phrase used to help you focus on for motivation.

The first ones that I came up with on my own were very broad and, therefore, not very specific to my goal. He taught me how to break down my goal into individual steps. I would have to decide what the first major accomplishment would be on my journey to achieving whatever goal I had set for myself. So the first mantra that we created was based on this initial goal. And once I had achieved that goal and knew what the next step would be, he and I would get back together and create an additional internal dialogue that would keep me focused on that next step.

The use of your mantra is not limited to your morning meditation. I have used them many times when training to find the motivation to keep driving forward. I remember a particular phrase I would use when grappling with some of the "monsters" on the mat. "Not dead, keep going" was a common one. I have used them in moments of high stress in order to control the mind and body throughout my life.

Creating a mantra depends on your personal beliefs, interests, and your goals. When you create a mantra, use something that motivates you. Make it something that will keep you calm and focused. Something you can easily chant to yourself, when alone or with others, like when in training.

In one of my mantras, I started with the sound "Om." From what I understand, it is considered the first sound, and it is the creator of all other sounds. The "Om" sound is a Delta wave and vibrates at the pitch of 432 Hertz. This universal sound can be used by itself to help with focus, and to clear and purify the mind. Because of this, I usually use "Om" regularly in my emptiness exercise, or sometimes I will connect it to other mantras I have put together.

Science has begun to recognize what the ancient mystics have told us for centuries. Everything around us is in a constant state of vibration, and this vibration or resonance can have a powerful effect on the mind and body. 432 Hz resonates with the frequency of 8 Hz in the standard musical scale. You can actually use these sounds played eternally to have the same effect as what the "Om" mantra would. I have been told that Tibetan monks tune their singing bowls to 432 Hz, and Mozart based his music on the vibration of A-432.

Conscious Intensity - Focus

Gaining command of more of your consciousness can increase your ability to focus. It can give you more mental energy to process your current environment. Your intensity with the available consciousness is equally important. Your intensity will determine how well you are able to focus on an individual task without being distracted by the little annoyances that will pop up while you're training or working.

Additionally, the intensity will be the level of energy that you are able to put into a task. There's a difference between just standing up and lackadaisically throwing a punch. Or throwing it with strong mental and physical intensity, putting everything you've got into it even though you may just be training. The ability to explode into an intense state when necessary is very valuable. You never know when you are going to be placed in a situation where you have to defend yourself or someone you love.

The ability to go from 0 to 60 in terms of intensity is very important in the situation. Someone who is slow to rise to the occasion may just show up late. I have trained students in the academy to be able to tap into this and use it in training. I have had students in the past who have been thrust into real-life situations and had the same level of intensity, and it changes the outcome of the situation.

This intensity can be both a mental, emotional, and physical state, but everything starts in the mind. Demand is the ultimate driver of the body. I have seen this level of intensity applied in the gym. I will see guys walk around in circles, getting pumped up prior to doing a bench press. They may have never been trained to do this, but they know if they can enter into that intense state that they will be stronger and more focused on what they are about to do. Individuals have this gift naturally. Some have to seek it out and be trained on how to do it.

I have had many of these individuals come through the academy doors. We generally start, just as you have, by clearing the mind and just cleaning up the mental landscape to the point where we have some available mental material to work with. Then we start working on this level of concentration in their practice on the mat. At first, some of them feel strange doing it because you are pretty much acting out the level of intensity at first.

I will see this demonstrated in martial arts forms. After students get the movements down, they start to work on the level of mental intensity and focus that they can add to the movements. It's just another method to train the idea. They are posturing, attempting to create a state that they can recall at any given moment in case it is needed.

There is a big difference between "intense" individuals and individuals who are just going through the motions, aimlessly repeating what they believe are good repetitions in practice or daily routines. The thing is, it doesn't take long for them to notice that their other classmates have surpassed them. This is the same thing in life; only we don't see the guy out there who is busting his ass with high intensity and passing us until it is too late.

We are usually seeing that guy at the finish line and witness what he has achieved. Sometimes you have to double-check yourself while you're training and make sure that you are not falling into that mindless routine.

One of the best things you can do to stay focused on proper levels of intensity is to know your goal and keep them simple and obtainable. Secondly, have someone keep you accountable for your level of intensity when training or working routines towards goals. It doesn't hurt if that accountability partner also has the skill of motivation. I have had accountability partners in the past that would just check my progress, and I've had ones that were highly motivated.

The motivational ones were well worth the extra time it takes to seek them out. You will know these personalities, and generally, they are the ones you like having in your inner circle anyway. Take the time to find those individuals that make the difference and take that extra mile. And remember, you may be doing it for someone yourself soon.

Power Presence

I have also seen this type of training increase an individual's personal power, that personal presence that seems to follow some individuals into the room and makes heads turn. Personal presence can affect almost every area of life. It will have an effect on your level of persuasiveness, whether you're using it to make a sale or negotiate a deal.

People with strong personal power look more confident and comfortable and are generally strong communicators. In my experience, one of the first steps into developing this type of presence is developing your conscious intensity. Just doing the basic exercises of focus and gaining clarity to be more at the moment and mindful will affect the power of your presence.

I have spoken to people who seem to be preoccupied and in another place or "zoned out." They seem to be lost somewhere in their mind. Then there are those individuals who are right there with you, listening and engaging with their conscious mindfully present in the moment. You can tell the difference between these two types of interactions immediately. The meditative exercises I've written about here are very powerful in assisting with this development of personal power. There are other things you can take into consideration.

A huge part of communication is understanding other people's body language. I'll look at the body as an antenna; if the antenna is bent, it will not transmit or receive clear information. Pay attention to how you use and express your body, straighten your antenna and allow the energy that you are creating with your training to come out. Take into consideration your speech rate, the gestures you make, the amount of eye contact you make when communicating, the timing of the things you say. All of which will be enhanced by your mind-body connection, your level of physical discipline.

Tested By Life

Probably one of the most difficult life events for me to deal with mentally was going through a divorce. I didn't have too many experiences in my life that had as much of a mental effect on me as this event. It was a mental and physical kick in the balls. Up until this point, I generally had control of my internal landscape because of my training in martial arts. It's not that I would not experience a moment where it would get away from me, and I would have to regain focus and control; everyone has to do that.

But this was different; this rocked me on my heels and literally put me in a mental state of shock for a month or two. I had absolutely no control of anything in my internal landscape, and it was chaos in there. I remember just reacting to everything that would come in front of me emotionally. It was during this period that I met several other people who had gone through the same experience or were currently going through the same thing.

While speaking to several of them that had gone through a divorce in the past, I found that they were still dealing with it. They were still chewing on it mentally, they really had not given it up, and it was still a controlling entity in their mind. After seeing this, I remember thinking to myself, "That is not where I want to be or where I want to go in the future." I remember asking myself, "What am I going to have to do to avoid it and go in a better direction?"

At that moment, I realized that ever since I got the paperwork for the divorce, I had stopped my morning practice. But this time, I realized that I had not done any type of mental training for two or three months. I had just dropped the training altogether. I had let the jungle in my mind overgrow and take charge.

That next morning, I woke up early and restarted my morning routine. Let me tell you something, finding 10-20 minutes of mental silence, of emptiness after this period of time, was one of the most difficult things I've ever done. I believe it was even harder than the first time I learned the exercise over 30 years ago.

Although divorce is not something I would wish on anyone, I now realize that going through it took me to another level of mental control in my practice. It was not easy at all, and there are still things that I am processing, but the journey has strengthened my mind, focus, attitude, and mental control.

Because of this, I have achieved more professionally and monetarily in life in the two years since the divorce than many years prior to it. It all came down to an exercise I learned in a small martial arts school in Tennessee and the words "the breath is the bridge."

Morning routine

As my teacher introduced internal dialogue to me, it was also at this time that I was also introduced to doing a morning routine. My teacher already had me doing the different training routines, Chi Gong, and breathing exercises in the morning. The next thing he had me add was the mantra that I had put together around the steps to my goal.

He asked me to start my day by reviewing these every day. Since I had already been working on spending 10 minutes breathing and emptying my mind, he asked me to start using this blank slate in the mind to focus my intent and energy on obtaining my goals. I would do this with the last 1-2 minutes of the exercise.

This morning routine is something that I have done the majority of my life. And like anything that you spend time on doing repetitiously, over time, I have seen improvement in it. It has had a tremendous effect on my life as far as keeping me focused on my goals and achievements as well as multiple other areas of personal growth.

At the time, I didn't realize that I was getting introduced to a method of intelligently designing habits. It wasn't until later in life, when I started looking back on what I was taught and what it had brought me in life, that I realized the tremendous worth that was taught to me. Waking up early and doing a morning routine is a high-performer success habit.

A morning routine can include many things to help you get your day started on a good note. It can put your mind into high gear and set your attitude for the entire day. The mind is fresh and relaxed in the mornings, and it is easier to study and learn new things. You won't have the anxiety and stress that you build up during the day. You are more open to input in the morning.

This is an example of my morning routine:

Breathing & Focus Exercises

Visualization exercise

Music & Motivational audio intake

Gratitude Drill

Drink Water / Supplements

Brain Coffee / Power Juice / Protein Drink

Make Bed / Brush your teeth

Writing, Scripting & Research

Physical Exercise & Stretching

I have experienced such good success with the morning routine that I put one together to do first thing when I get into my office every. I use this just to get organized so that I can spend my "open" time more appropriately during the day. That looks a little bit like this:

Review overall goals and baby steps.

Review to-do list for the day.

Make one new business connection for the day.

Review your finances, expenses & check budget.

10 Min news and finance podcast

The Mind's Eye - Internal vision

Webster's definition of mind's eye: the mental faculty of conceiving imaginary or recollected scenes. This is sometimes referred to as visualization. Visualization is the process of creating a mental picture of a goal that we would like to manifest in our reality. Elite athletes use it, the super-rich uses it, and high-level performers in all fields now use it.

Using the mind's eye can activate and program the consciousness. it can build your motivation and keep you focused on your chosen goal. Visualization can also have an effect on the subconscious.

I like to think of the subconscious mind as your computer's hard drive. You can use visualization to download new programs into the drive. It is believed that the subconscious cannot tell the difference between what is real and what is imagined. So to it, your visual imagery seems like reality.

Earlier, we discussed attempting to tame the subconscious in order to gain more consciousness. Visualization can guide and direct the subconscious in a direction that will be more conducive to the goals of our life. Of course, the conscious mind is in control of the subconscious, but there are times when the subconscious can take over and operate commonly made habits for you: this is your autopilot.

Imagine you were doing something at work that you do five days a week. You've done this so many times that when you begin the task, you don't even have to think about it. It's almost like your body just starts doing the work for you. Subconscious autopilot at your service. The cool thing is, with visualization, we can start to implement new routines or change and improve old autopilot routines.

Just as we learn to create internal dialogue, we must also learn how to tune in the mind's eye. When I started doing this, I would imagine a television set in my mind. At first, I had no control over what this subconscious television was playing. And when I think back on the things that were on it when I first learned the exercise, they were not necessarily a good influence or positive information.

The mind was running wild; no one was at the wheel. Just as I did with the internal dialogue, I learned to intelligently create what I wanted to visually see in the mind. I could see myself achieving each step on the way to my goal as well as achieving the ultimate goal. Often your internal vision is referred to as visualization.

With practice, you can gain the ability to generate images using all five senses and doing it with clarity. It is important to be absolutely clear and specific when you are creating your visual images.

As I mentioned above, you are creating a new program for the subconscious, and you are in complete control over it. You will see what you see in your vision, feel what you're feeling, hear what you're hearing, and you can even get to the point where you involve taste and smell as you work toward the goal of overall total experience in your visualization. The more of the senses you can involve, the more powerful this tool will become.

You can use visualization to modify a bad experience or vision that is coming into the mind or use it to amplify a positive event or vision that enters the landscape or one that you have created yourself.

Let's say you have a reoccurring negative image. This could be connected to something that has happened in your past, like a bad experience. When there's a negative image or vision coming into the mind, remember you have the ability to make adjustments to this vision. You can adjust the color, make the colors dimmer, softer. You could distort your internal vision of the image entirely. You could put it out of focus, make it fuzzy and unclear. You could move the image farther away from you or move yourself farther away from it so that it seems distant and far off. If there's a sound that is related to this image, you can do the same thing to it. You could make it full of static and indistinguishable. You are in complete control of the imagery in your mind.

Obviously, this image could show up again and again. It will just depend on how dramatic the event was, but the thing is, every time it comes into your internal landscape, you have the ability to do the same thing. Over time, this can change the effect the image (or the event it was connected to) on you.

Now the opposite can be done for a positive event. You can add color, bring yourself closer to the image, turn up the sound and give it more power and energy in your mind. So now, imagine this is an image that you have intelligently created for yourself. It could be designed around a goal that you have in life or anything else you wish to achieve. It could be an image that brings you joy and gratitude in the moment. Whatever it is, you have the ability to give it more power by making these little adjustments.

My teacher and I would discuss how it felt when I would see myself achieving this goal. It eventually became part of the emotional discipline of the overall exercise as well. Once the emotional element was added to the exercise, it made it very powerful and very motivating.

Using my imagination, I could visually put my goals in front of me. Anytime I lacked the motivation to get myself going for training or working on an exercise, I could tap into this vision internally and draw energy from visually achieving that goal. Remember, you are in charge of your internal environment. You can direct your imagination. You have the ability to mold and guide that environment in a way that can help you achieve more.

Visual Event Chaining

It's not uncommon when you get introduced to using the mind's eye to visually create the goal that you go straight to the end result. This is OK because seeing that end result, that big goal at the end can supply a lot of motivation, and it can be a passion source to develop drive and energy. But it is important to take time to look at the chain of events needed in order to step your way up to that final goal.

Don't just create one vision of the final destination, and it is important to have a visual path that is required to walk to that point. For example, let's say you are putting together a new business model. The final goal is a successful business. But think about what the required steps would be between where you are now and your end result:

Obtaining and finishing the training you will need.

Saving money and fundraising.

Meetings with potential business partners.

Securing a location.

Building it out all the way up to opening day.

For me, I will even do these visual steps in phases. I will lay out the process, and it's entirely in my notebook. I will separate it into phases and possible timelines. And then, I will only focus on the steps that will be in Phase 1, with the ending of Phase 1 being a major event or personal accomplishment on the overall journey. It is important to remember to keep the different steps realistic and attainable.

Different links in your visual chain could be in relation to the personal development that you need to obtain on the way to your goal. Sometimes at the beginning of a goal journey, you may not yet be the person you need to be to attain certain levels of your goal. Think about what you might need to change personally, who do you need to be to obtain that goal.

Think about the different qualities that will guide and assist you in achieving your goal. Better listening and communication, sales skills, dealing with criticism, or maybe improved confidence. All of these things can be turned into individual steps between you and your end goal. Each step can, in turn, become a powerful visual motivator.

Create a visual path to your goal

This is something that I have done inside the academy for my students for many years. It is important to have visual representations of what you want to achieve in front of you every day. Just as we did with internal vision, it is important for these goals you place in front of you (visually) to be broken down into steps as well.

Don't just have one photo of your end goal. Have a photo of the first event on your chain of events that will get you to your goal. This puts it right in front of you every day. For me, I will get a photograph that represents the first link in my goal chain. I set it on my desk, so I will see it every day. Sometimes I will have it hanging on the mirror in the bathroom.

Once I reach that initial goal, I will change the photo to a representation of the next goal I need to achieve. So this is something that you can change as you go through your process. Some people will create a vision board. If you create something like this, remember the principle we just introduced. Create a line of photos on your vision board. Each photo will represent a point of achievement along the way to your end goal.

It is good if you can have more than one visual representation connected to each link. In other words, additional photos that help you hone in on the little details of each event. Just like when you create an internal visualization, the more details you can have, the more real it is to the mind.

I usually exercise visualization as part of my morning routine. I will start with breathing exercises, go through the focus drill to clear the mind. Then I will do a visualization exercise. Here are just a few points that you can take into consideration when you are designing your own visualization routine:

1. Find a few minutes where are you can be alone and relaxed. This is one of the reasons I like to do it in the morning, and your mind is sharper and clearer in the mornings.

2. Be comfortable. This exercise can be done lying in bed in the morning, or you can sit in a chair. It depends on your body state, but you want to be relaxed and comfortable so that your mind is not drawn into the body. For instance, if your back is tense because your posture is incorrect, your mind will go to the tension.

3. Reference the visual representation for your goal. Earlier I mentioned photographs that are in relation to your goal. This could be as easy as taking a look at those photographs. Remember, you are looking for details in relation to all of your senses.

4. Be a first-person player: when you create your vision in your subconscious, don't see yourself doing

something, be yourself doing something. Place yourself in the experience and visualize it in the first person. Mentally connect all the details that you referenced earlier.

5. If your vision becomes blurry or seems to leave your mind, just take a break, then come back to the visual stage and re-create your subconscious image.

6. As your ability to visualize improves, your goal is to gain more clarity and add more detail and power to your vision. Make the colors more vivid, make the sounds clearer, become more aware of what you're feeling physically as you go through the exercise. Be aware of what you smell and what you hear. Eventually, add in the emotional content of the moment.

7. This exercise can last anywhere from 5 minutes to 10 minutes. If you have more time available, I suggest adding a different session later in the day.

EMOTIONAL DISCIPLINE

For me, the study of emotional discipline can be broken down into two parts in the beginning. The first study is learning the ability to take control of the different emotional energies inside the body. The second is to use the emotional energy to drive and motivate you or add drive energy to a state or internal vision. This is an example of that idea; imagine driving in traffic, and as you're going along, someone goes to great effort to get in front of you and cut you off sharply. I choose this example because I'm sure a lot of you have had this experience or something similar.

When the offense happens, sometimes there will be an emotional jump in energy in the body. A reaction to the experience. Emotional discipline is the ability to take back control of that emotional surge you experience. Because if you do not have control of your emotions, those emotions will control you. And an out-of-control emotional state will cause you to make decisions that are completely illogical. Most of those snap decisions that I have made out of high emotional events I have regretted.

I was taught this not in an automobile but on the academy floor. In training, we would do multiple types of sparring environments such as kickboxing, pummeling, and grappling. Quite often, while we were in these environments, we would choose to set a certain pace. We would set the intensity, and we would usually try to base it on a percentage. We would explain this percentage to our training partner in hopes that he would make as much effort to maintain an equal level of training force. Doing this would allow us to train safely and for a longer amount of time.

It was inevitable in the training that you would run into that one partner that would, in an effort to showboat or "be supreme," up the tempo and the level of force. And like the driving experience we mentioned above; sometimes you would have an emotional reaction to that. As a warrior, when these moments arise, it is an opportunity. If you can keep your wits about you, it is an opportunity to train emotional discipline.

Any time your emotions get away from you, they have the ability to take control of you. So as warriors, we want to control these emotional energies as best we can, especially when we are in a combat situation.

Not everyone will start learning this while sparring. I was first introduced to it in drills that I would do with my instructor. He would give me a task or a drill and help me do it. Even if I'm doing it by myself, there were many times that I would become aggravated with my performance. Sometimes it even seemed that my teacher was picking obstacles for me to overcome that I did not have the ability to overcome. And while doing the exercise or drill, he would generally be right next to me, giving me commentary on my performance.

As you can imagine, this irritated me even more. But now that I look back, I realize that he was doing exactly what he needed to do. He was getting inside my mind and igniting the emotional centers of my body. He did it intentionally, first for me to experience it, and secondly for me to eventually learn how to deal with it and control it.

Taking these drills and exercises into consideration, we are not even in front of another human being, and we are not in any form of combat or physical exchange. So you can see how sparring can create even greater opportunities to deal with this or not deal with it intelligently. Part of the emotional discipline is getting control of these runaway emotions to avoid them taking control of the mind and the body.

The Emotion Centers Of The Body

I was taught that the different centers of the body were related to different energies that it was able to produce produce. The chest or heart area is one of the strongest emotional centers of the body. Second to the heart was the solar plexus. Each energy center can loosely be related to different emotional energies that are experienced in the body.

Untrained chest breathing will amplify the emotional center of the body. If you take note when you are in an emotional situation similar to the one we spoke about in traffic, you will see that your body automatically starts breathing higher in the torso. If this is left unchecked, it will only amplify whatever emotional state you are experiencing, potentially making it worse.

Learning to lower the breath in the body and centering yourself in the lower torso will help you control those emotional energies. Syncing the emotions back down to the center of the body. This is an additional reason for learning the full cycle breath because it will bring your breathing pattern low and will not amplify unwanted emotion.

Different methodologies will connect different emotions to different centers of the body. Generally, in my experience, I stick to three basic areas. I find that more than that in actual application just ends up being an over-complication for most people. Suppose it is trying to be applied in a high-stress environment. In that case, it's important to remember to keep it simple: the more complicated any method is, the less likely you are to continually apply it consistently over time.

Become Comfortable Being Uncomfortable.

Another environment that had a huge influence on me as far as controlling emotional energies was grappling. I was fortunate enough to be introduced to grappling in the late 80s from the system of Burmese Bando. This Burmese martial art had a subsystem of grappling it taught. I would train it off and on but did not become fully immersed in grappling until 1995, when I was introduced to Combat Submission Wrestling and Brazilian Jiu-Jitsu.

I immediately fell in love with the systems that taught this and dove into them wholeheartedly. Grappling will create multiple opportunities for you to train emotional intelligence and emotional control. Many times I have been sparring with a larger, stronger opponent, and I was placed into a bad position, and there were times when I thought I would never get out of that position. The opponent was stronger, better trained, and sometimes fresh in the fight whereas I had been training for the last hour. Believe me, being in this position will challenge your ability to control your emotions.

It is commonly said in Jiu-Jitsu that you become comfortable being uncomfortable. I can remember many times when I have been stuck under a larger opponent with no escape in sight. I had to learn to breathe and calm myself in order to just survive. Prior to learning this skill, I had to tap or give up to the opponent, and I remember it not being so much from their pressure but more of the fact that I lost control of myself under their pressure. It's a lot of input from a lot of different senses all at one time.

Just like in life, sometimes you get caught up in the moment before you realize that the moment is controlling you. It would be nice to always have the ability to recognize when you are starting to enter the state of no control. The truth is that that is not always what happens. We are human, and sometimes we react instead of think, react instead of consciously choosing to control ourselves.

Iris Rousseau was a student of mine who eventually became a business partner. Iris came to the academy initially to study the art of Brazilian Jiu-Jitsu. The Jiu-Jitsu class was not a comfortable environment.

She was a small girl in a class with several large men. If anyone ever had to learn to deal with pressure, she did. Just as I did, I got to watch her learn to control her body, her mind, and her emotions while learning and developing in the art. There were many times over the years I would watch the guys in the class be ready to give up, and they would see her still going, not quitting, and it would give them the motivation to stay with it.

The knowledge is available to anyone willing to seek it. Iris went on the achieve the rank of Black Belt in Gracie Jiu-Jitsu under Master Pedro Sauer. This is an accomplishment that has only been achieved by a handful of women.

I wanted to include this as a training option because these systems have become readily available today because of their popularity. However, these systems do not teach the finer details of emotional control because it is just not part of the curriculum that they offer. Regardless, they are a great environment to experience and train these ideas.

Due to the nature of the training, just being involved in the classes will teach you to be aware of these things and address them. If you do choose to seek out a school, seek out one with a genuine learning environment. They should have an organized written curriculum that they can show you. Safety and intelligent growth should be ingrained in their class culture. You should not be getting injured if you are in this type of culture.

Now, this is not the only way to train these ideas. The art of Kung Fu has tightened these concepts and methods in their systems for hundreds of years. They would do this by placing the student into physical positions (stances or postures) or training methods (drills, forms, sets) that will create stress and discomfort in the body. Additionally, they will place a certain level of mental stress on the student. Stressors can be increased by having the student perform under a set time, alternating environments (hot or cold), by challenging strength or balance (balance beam).

Just like the Brazilian Jiu-Jitsu class mentioned above, it creates an opportunity for the student to control the body and emotions in the mind. A lot of these training methods have been lost behind the popularity of the grappling arts in the last 20 years. People commonly look at them and believe that these exercises and drills have no combative value.

I am not arguing whether they do or don't, but they do possess the ability to train someone to reach greater levels of control of themselves. As well, a lot of this type of training can be done alone. So if you are a high performer who does not have a lot of time to go find a school and devote to three days a week to training, these ideas and methods can work for you as well. They could easily be added into a daily routine or be done one or two days a week and still give you the ability to progress on the areas we are speaking of.

The principle of making the uncomfortable comfortable applies in everyday life just as it does on the mat. It is not uncommon that we fall into our everyday routines and these routines become comfortable for us. One of the best ways to force growth in life is to try something new.

The thing is, "new stuff" can be unfamiliar, which can create discomfort. And it is human nature to avoid challenging and/or uncomfortable situations. It is also common to overthink yourself into an "analysis paralysis" when considering stepping outside of your comfort zone. It can be a vicious cycle that would trap you into the day-to-day mundane repeating routine.

I believe it is part of the warrior's mentality to put himself on the line and take the risk to get out there, just like you do on the mat. When you "put yourself out there," you come away from that event with new experiences, know-how, knowledge, and memories. It is the same thing in life. Though putting yourself out there may not be the easiest path, and it definitely is a rewarding one.

This mindset can also prepare you for anything that life will throw at you later on. Discomfort, frustration, fear: they are all part of any journey to success and achievement.

For me, the Jiu-Jitsu mat or the Thai boxing ring are the best places to achieve this, but not everyone can walk out on the mat. So what can you do to get better at dealing with being uncomfortable? Here are a few ideas:

1. Breath and mind work. If you have been doing the exercises in this book up to this point, you are already on your way to dealing with discomfort effectively.

2. Use your mantra; we discussed this earlier as well. A favorite of mine has been "this too will pass." Just like any major storm, there is a beginning, and there is an end.

3. Reframe or reprogram the discomfort you're experiencing into a source of growth. Recognize that stepping into the unknown will create great change and improvement.

4. Focus on what you can control. Part of your situation may be out of your control, but part of it may be within

your reach. Determine what those things are and focus on them.

The Breath Is The Bridge

Here we are again, hearing that same quote, "the breath is the bridge," just as I heard it many times from my teacher. The reason for this is simple. On your journey to reach higher levels of discipline and a deeper understanding of what discipline truly is, the beginning point is going to be your breath.

Your body's autonomic nervous system controls your respiration rate, your breathing, as it does many other functions in your body, such as heart rate, your digestion, your "fight-or-flight" response, and your pupillary response. If you were to try to hold your breath for an extended amount of time, your body will override your action and force you to let out that breath and start breathing again.

The wonderful thing is you can also control a part of this system. Yes, it will control your respiratory rate, but you have the ability to command this as well. Once trained, it will eventually give you the ability to reach out and control the other things that are involved with this system.

You can also retrain this system to operate in different ways to improve performance or help control emotions. Different patterns of breath will allow you to control or regulate the body according to what you need. This, combined with being consciously aware of your physical state, can allow you to gain greater control of the human-machine, your body.

I always give this example, imagine you had a long day at work, and you finally make it home and sit down on the couch. For me, a home is a place of solitude, and it is one of the few places I can go to release and relax. So after that long day at work, when I finally get to sit down, one of the first things I will do is a deep, long exhale. I'm sure many of you have experienced this. One of the reasons for this exhale is that when you do it, you can feel tension released from the body.

Well, just as the tension is released from the body, emotions can also be released. And the better you get at doing the breath, the more experienced you become at intelligent breathing, the more tension you can release and the more emotional energy you can release.

Remember the aggressive driver we spoke about earlier that put us in an emotional spike due to the situation. Another example of this would be training with an aggressive partner at the academy. Both of these examples could create an opportunity for us to train emotional control. The trick is recognizing that you are on the front end of an emotional spike and being able to deal with it before it gets out of hand. The ability to recognize that moment is connected to your state of awareness.

One of the first breaths I teach in our breath programs is the full cycle breath. Whenever you feel that emotional jump, the first thing you want to do to take control of it is a deep full-cycle breath.

As we mentioned earlier in the book, fill the bottom of the glass first. What I mean by that is fill the belly first (we focus on this area because we want to avoid raising the chest first). As you inhale, imagine filling the stomach with air or breath. Your belly will push out, and eventually, it will feel like it has reached its max capacity and the only way to pull more air into the body is to raise the chest.

The chest will rise at this time. It almost seems like filling a glass with water from the bottom to the top, right? As you inhale, do so through the nose in a slow, controlled manner. As you exhale, slowly blow the air out through the mouth. On this exhale, the chest will fall first, and then the stomach will fall after that. At the end of the exhalation, pull the stomach inward. I like to imagine that I want to touch my abdomen to my spine. As I am doing this, I'm trying to empty all of the air out of the lungs.

When you do this exercise in one of the stressful environments mentioned above, you may not always be able to get a full breath, which is okay. As with anything, when you start training, it is good to do the exercise in the full range of motion. It is the same thing with learning to breathe. A lot of times, I will do this exercise while sitting in a chair in the morning. This allows me the opportunity to train the breath in its fullest capacity.

This may not always be an option when it is done in reality, especially if there's stress involved. Stress will tend to shorten the arc, so to speak. But after many years of training this exercise, I have found that that becomes less the case. Even under stress and in those difficult environments, I have found that the more I practice, the better I get at having that full range of motion or the full range of breath. This has made a huge difference for me if I am using this knowledge in a real-life situation.

Charging The Body

If training the breath is part of your daily routine, you will find that you are generally better equipped prior to a stress-inducing event. Regular breath training charges the body with higher levels of oxygen. This means there's more available to you if you are suddenly forced into a situation where you need it. You can use proper breathing to charge and wake up the body prior to an expected event.

Additionally, as the mind considers the impending event's possibilities, it will start to prepare itself by releasing hormones into the body in preparation. Your adrenal glands will release cortisol, norepinephrine, and adrenaline.

This is commonly referred to as the "fight-or-flight" response. This chemical soup is responsible for the immediate physical reactions you feel when you are threatened with a stressful event. They generally will make you more aware, responsive, and focused.

They will bring blood flow away from the extremities and into the organs, all of which is in preparation to take action. The problem is if your mind triggers this response prior to having to take action, and then you have to hurry up and wait. In other words, you don't get to jump right into the fight, but instead, you have to put yourself on hold. Dealing with these chemicals during that hold time is the trick, and this can be done with the proper breath.

I will have students use this on the academy floor regularly by having them do a breathing cycle prior to training. They often enter into a training environment with more energy, and they perform more optimally than if they would have entered the exercise in a breath-starved state.

I have also done this with several of my scuba diving students in the pool. Part of their requirements to obtain their basic open water certification is to do an underwater breath-hold dive. I have had individuals come through the class who have struggled with this qualification quite a bit.

Up until that point, their daily routine never really required them to hold her breath longer than maybe 20 seconds. I have spent some time with these individuals and taught them how to breathe properly and charge their bodies with oxygen prior to attempting the underwater swim. I have had a lot of success with this, not only with them achieving their goal but also becoming much more relaxed after doing the breathwork.

I have also taught this to individuals who are going into extremely stressful environments with success. Personal protection agents, law enforcement officers, security drivers, and special forces operatives. The same knowledge can be applied in your life as a high performer. Not only will discharging breath prepare you for the event, but it will also help you get a jump on the body's response to extreme stress.

Additional benefits of breath
The additional benefits that come to you from training your breath are numerous. It seems that the psychology and medical field is continually discovering new benefits to breath. With that in mind, we're going to take a look at

some of the primary benefits my students and I have received from doing this training over the course of 40 years.

Full Pulmonary Activation

It has been my experience that most people only use a small percentage of their lung capacity. They will go their entire lives and never tap into those additional areas that are untouched. Your lung capacity is the total amount of air that your lungs can hold. Typically, someone who is untrained will see their lung capacity decrease slowly as they age. It usually starts around the mid-twenties, perhaps the early thirties.

As you experience this decrease in lung function over time, it can lead to shortness of breath or difficulty in breathing later in life. Other conditions such as asthma or chronic obstructive pulmonary disease (COPD) can worsen this process.

One of the first things the full cycle breath will teach you is to use the thoracic diaphragm to its full capacity. The diaphragm is a musculomembranous partition separating the thoracic and abdominal cavities. It controls the pressures between the thorax and the abdomen. On its sides, it attaches to the six lower ribs, at its front to the sternum, and at its back to the spine.

The body has three diaphragms: the cervical, thoracic, and the pelvic. I have studied some systems that teach that there are more in the body. I generally only focus on the big three with my students in order to keep things simple and obtainable. Stale air can buildup in the lungs if you are not properly using the diaphragm.

Training the full cycle breath will teach your pulmonary system to operate close to or at its full capacity. You will be able to tap into areas of your lungs that are normally dormant and more than likely have been for a long time. I have taught these exercises to students and have received comments back from them about literally being able to feel the upper lobes of the lungs stretching after they have done the exercise for an extended amount of time.

When I first learned the exercise from my teacher, I believed I was using my full-on capacity. After using it for a time, I believe that just learning the exercise gave me access to more of it. But I didn't realize the truth until much later after repetitive work. I could literally start feeling my ability to tap into greater areas of my pulmonary system.

I had not obtained the skill to do it without the effort and intent that I would use in the drill. In other words, it was not just coming naturally to me yet. As I practiced, this became less and less the case.

Another area that had a huge effect on this was that, with practice, the connective tissues and muscles that are in the upper torso/rib cage began to loosen and open up to more range of motion.

In Qi Gong, we would learn different movements with the body that we timed with full-cycle breaths. These movements were designed to help the body loosen up and relax the different areas that are related to pulmonary action. The exercises would increase the articulation of the rib cage as well as the shoulders.

The area's ability to expand and open up increased over time. So not only were we learning how to rewire our pulmonary system to operate at a higher level, but we were also changing the physical structure of the system as well.

This was driven home even more for me when I visited a close friend of mine who is a chiropractor. He was going to do a little work on me for an injury I had acquired while training at the academy.

Before he wanted to make the adjustments, he asked me if it was okay to take a couple of x-rays of the torso and chest area. I said, of course, and we proceeded to go through the process. Once the images were finished and he had taken a look at them, he walked into the room and wanted to show me something that he thought was curious.

He had looked at a lot of these images over the years, and he has been in this business for almost thirty years. What he had noticed was that the bone structure and the connective tissue in the rib cage were much denser and thicker than what he would commonly see in this imagery. When he brought it to my attention, I immediately knew what it was. My teacher had always told me that this would be a benefit of the process. I guess I just never had it register until I had those images put in front of me by the chiropractor.

Improved Performance Under Stressor

One of the other areas of improvement that I experienced from my training was my ability to operate in my full pulmonary capacity while dealing with outside stress. In other words, I could access this full capacity whether I was dealing with a stressor that was from someone cutting me off in traffic or the stress you deal with when you're on the mat in the academy, dealing with a stronger opponent.

As I practiced, over time, I noticed that it became easier and easier in those moments of stress, whether it be mental or physical, for me to take a full breath. It almost seemed that I had increased my range of motion through my practice to the point that even if I was experiencing a stressor that limited me to a smaller amount of that range, I still had a greater capacity than I ever did prior to starting the training.

In the fitness field, whenever you want to increase your endurance, your trainer will usually direct you into cardio training. One of the things I've discovered is that the training introduces another option, and that is your ability to train your pulmonary system to actually operate more intelligently.

You're not just training it in the gym or on the treadmill, you're actually teaching it how to use a greater capacity of what is available to it. Not only that, but you're teaching it to operate at a different pace, a different time that is separate from the timing of the body. In addition, it is my experience that doing the training over time actually increases the available capacity. This is something I've seen in many of my Kung Fu teachers in my career.

Here is an example that I usually teach my students after they have gone through the basic exercises. I will have them start doing the same training as they are slowly jogging. This is just a way to introduce another level of stress to the exercise. I will start with a slow jog in the beginning. You can always adjust how fast you're running to increase the stress on the exercise.

The thing to remember is I'm not doing the running in order to tax the system in a way to improve cardio. You will start with a slow run that will force you to speed up on its own. Sometimes I have noticed that your breathing pattern will match the pace that is set in your jogging or running.

Once you feel that starts to happen, it is your goal to take control of your breathing pattern. You want to slow down the breath as well as increase the capacity that you're using. Your pattern should be slow, long, all the while taking deep breaths, regardless of the pace that your physical body is taking up.

As I mentioned earlier, you may have to slow down your running in the beginning. Once you gain control of your breathing pattern and you're able to separate it from the pace the body is setting, then you can start running a little faster and see if you can maintain that level of control.

Our goal is to train the system to operate intelligently and in its own timing and pattern. I do not want the pulmonary system to chase the body. I want to train the system to operate more intelligently while under stress. If you are someone who finds a slow jog to be excessively challenging, just start out with a fast walk.

Again, it is not about developing cardiovascular endurance as you do in the gym on the treadmill. It's more about showing the pulmonary system a different way to operate. Cardiovascular endurance can definitely be trained as well, and it does have a huge impact on performance.

What we're saying is to recognize the other options and add them into the routine. For myself, I will work on training the system first for about 20 minutes, and then I will pick up the pace just to test the system in order to stress cardiovascular development.

The Amygdala hijack

Amygdala hijack is a term coined by Daniel Goleman in his 1996 book Emotional Intelligence:

"The amygdala is the emotional part of the brain, which regulates the fight or flight response. When threatened, it can respond irrationally. A rush of stress hormones floods the body before the prefrontal lobes (regulating executive function) can mediate this reaction." I'm sure all of us have felt this dump of hormones when we are startled or taken by surprise.

The term amygdala was first introduced by Karl Friedrich Burdach in 1822. The amygdala is a group of nuclei located in the temporal lobes of the brain and is considered part of the limbic system. It is involved in the processing of motivation, long-term memory, decision-making, and emotional responses. It also determines the body temperature and blood sugar level and enables the process of respiration. The hijack refers to the amygdala's ability to quickly take over control of the brain in order to trigger the response needed to deal with a potentially dangerous situation.

It is this emotional response and its connection to respiration that we want to focus on here. When the amygdala senses danger, it sends a signal to the main control center of the brain, which is the hypothalamus. The hypothalamus is a small region of the brain. It's located at the base of the brain, near the pituitary gland. Then this signal will travel through the sympathetic nervous, and the adrenal glands are activated.

The adrenals respond by dumping a chemical cocktail into the bloodstream to prepare the body for either fight or flight. This causes a number of physiological changes in the body. The heart will start beating faster, and you will begin to breathe more rapidly; more nutrients are dumped into the bloodstream to supply you with more available energy. You literally stepped on the gas of the human-machine to prepare you to take action.

Deep breathing is extremely helpful for managing this stress reaction, which we are going to discuss more later. Being placed in a stressful situation will trigger your fight or flight response. This response was ingrained into early humans as a preparation to deal with physical threats or harm.

The stress response chemical dump into the bloodstream will consist of: Adrenaline, Dopamine, Endorphins, Norepinephrine, and Cortisol. Each member of this chemical cocktail is going to affect you in different ways.

Adrenaline

Adrenaline is also called epinephrine. It is released by your adrenal glands, which sit on top of the kidneys, and it is the boss of the fight or flight response. It will cause the airways of the lungs to open up more in order to provide your muscular system with more oxygen. It can give you temporary increases in your strength.

It will cause your blood vessels to constrict in order to push more blood to the center of the body for the organs in the major muscle groups. The temperature of the body will increase. You may even begin to sweat.

Adrenaline will decrease your sensitivity to pain as well as give you increases in strength in order to improve performance. This is commonly referred to as your adrenaline rush, and the effects from this rush can last up to an hour.

Adrenaline can sharpen your mental focus, increasing your ability to think quickly and react quickly. All of this can take place within seconds, and it will sometimes feel like a rush that comes over you quickly, which is why it is sometimes nicknamed the adrenaline rush. It can vary per individual.

Dopamine

Dopamine is the chemical messenger of the body, a neurotransmitter that transmits signals to the cells. The brain makes an amino acid called Tyrosine, which then is processed into dopamine. Dopamine is considered a regulator of your mood and behavior, and they are the natural "uppers" or reward system of your body. It plays a large role in how you feel pleasure. It is produced in the brain in two places, the substantia nigra and the ventral tegmental area.

Cocaine stimulates the production of dopamine in the body that gives the effect of a euphoric natural high. It also affects the vascular system, helping to widen blood vessels to increase blood flow. It will also help maintain a level of alertness under stress.

Endorphins

Endorphins are also released from the pituitary gland, they act as the body's natural painkillers. They do this by blocking the pain messages that are traveling from the body to the brain. They are also neurotransmitters, chemicals that pass along signals from one neuron to the next.

They will enhance the immune system as well as produce a state of euphoria. They are natural "feel-good" chemicals for the body as well.

As stated, they are the body's painkillers, which is beneficial in a dangerous high-stress situation. An example of this is sustaining an injury during a car crash and not feeling the injury until after you start to calm down 30 minutes later.

Cortisol

Cortisol will shut down the nonessential systems in the body when under stress. For example, they may shut down the digestive system or the reproductive system.

Cortisol will help control blood sugar levels in the body, it will regulate metabolism, and it can even help reduce inflammation. Cortisol is one of the primary anti-stress hormones. It is what keeps you from going into shock if you are exposed to trauma.

Norepinephrine

Norepinephrine, also called noradrenaline, is one of my favorite additions to the cocktail: it is the driver of your fight or flight response. Noradrenaline acts to increase the amount of flexion or contraction of muscle fibers in the body. It will also affect the rate of the contractions. Just preparing you to either react or retreat. This includes the heart muscle, which will increase the heart rate and its output, as well as the blood pressure in the body.

Serotonin

Your blood platelets release serotonin to help heal wounds. Serotonin will cause tiny arteries to narrow, helping form blood clots in injuries.

One of the most common responses is the short and shallow breath cycle that will center in the chest. Being in the moment and in control of your breathing cycle will allow you to control this response.

Now the stress response is not always a bad thing in the body. Say you're having to deal with something that is an emergency, and you need that extra boost. In this situation, it might help you out, but sometimes life will create stressors that will place you in the fight or flight mode when you are not able to act. So since you're not able to do something physical, your body does not burn off this additional adrenaline, dopamine and cortisol that is dumped into your system.

Audio and visual exclusion

To add to your troubles, this chemical hijack will also cause tunnel vision. The brain hyper focuses on whatever the immediate problem or threat is, and we lose peripheral vision and the ability to be fully aware of what's going on around us.

It will also affect your hearing, and you may lose the ability to hear surrounding noise. This has been shown in police officers who are placed under a tremendous amount of stress in a gunfight. They would commonly report that they thought their gun was not firing because they could not hear the shots.

They basically had tunnel hearing. Additionally, this can cause you to have problems recalling events of the stressful occurrence, or it will cause you to feel like you're having an out-of-body experience. In other words, it's like you were above yourself and watching what is going on.

Your perception of time can be affected as well. Victims of car wrecks have reported feeling like everything went into slow motion as soon as the wreck started to happen.

Another possibility on the fight or flight spectrum is that you could freeze and take no action at all. In the law enforcement and military security world, I have heard this referred to as condition black. This is probably the worst possible condition you could slide into if you are in a stressful situation that requires action.

The full cycle breath is your lifeline when you are thrust into stressful environments that can cause the amygdala hijack to occur. It allows you to rein in the body and its responses to the situation. It will empower you to pull your consciousness out of the limbic system and into the rational brain.

Damage from the stress response

There are times when your fight or flight response is a good thing, and there are times when it is not necessarily working in your favor. There are times when this response is tricked into action. You may have a sudden scare that will trip the switch. You might experience an insulting interaction with another person that will bring on the same response.

PTSD is an example of being in a perpetual state of fight or flight. A similar condition could be developed for someone who has experience domestic violence. All of these things can create a state of chronic stress in the body because it constantly has to deal with the same chemicals, the same physical response that it would have in a moment of danger.

The difference is it doesn't take physical action in order to burn up the chemical dump. This can eventually lead to a host of physical problems and disease if it is not dealt with.

Many people use breathwork to counter these stressors from their day-to-day life in order to keep them from building up. The amazing thing about it is you can do it anywhere. You can take it with you to work, you can do it in traffic. The main thing is that you learn it and apply it.

Tonification

Anything you exercise or place under a growing amount of stress over time will get stronger, or it will become more tone. In Traditional Chinese Medicine, tonification can include several areas. Some of them are acupuncture, moxibustion, variations in diet, herbal tonics and treatments, and massage.

For the purpose of this writing, I'm primarily going to focus on massage. If you were to hire a massage therapist, and you had that person massage only one of your biceps for a month, then after a month, you would notice that the bicep he focused on would be more tone. There are many ways to achieve this, and massage is just one example.

As you are doing the full cycle breath, part of the process is to pull in the abdomen, either back toward the spine and slightly up into the ribcage or down into the pelvic area as you exhale. The basic version is to just pull back toward the spine. As you become more familiar with the process, you can change the angle of the vacuum in order to access different diaphragms that are located in the torso.

Activating the different diaphragms will affect different organs that are in the body. This movement applies pressure to the internal organs every time you do it. Over time, this massage-like movement of the abdomen wall will start to make the organs in the body healthier and more toned.

Additionally, blood flow is increased to the organs as this breathing massage (combined with the oxygenation of the blood system) brings tremendous benefits to the body. This, as well as the release of toxins, helps to promote organ health.

The more you are able to train these breathing exercises, the more you will be able to gain control over the muscular structure of the abdomen, which will increase the exercise's effectiveness. All of these benefits can be accessed with a minimum of 10 to 15 minutes of breath work a day.

This is a simplified look at tonification in relation to breathing exercises. For those looking for more detailed information on the art and practice, Chinese medicine and many forms of Chinese kung fu have taught this information and have for hundreds of years. More information on this can be found on our website at sifualanbaker.com.

Oxygenation

To me this is one of the obvious benefits of doing the full breath. As you begin to move more air through your system, the percentage of oxygen is obviously going to increase, both in your body and your bloodstream.

If you've never done this type of breathing before, you may notice that you experience dizziness after one or two breaths. This could be caused by that increase in oxygen in your body. I personally found that I was not used to having higher percentages of oxygen in my body, and it took me a while to get used to this.

The benefits of oxygen to the body are numerous. It affects the operation of the brain. Oxygen will contribute to the cell regeneration of damaged tissue caused by inflammation, improved immune system, and increased available energy. Today, experts believe inflammation may contribute to a wide range of chronic diseases.

Examples of these are metabolic syndrome, which includes type 2 diabetes, heart disease, and obesity. It has been found that people with these diseases have higher levels of inflammation in the body. Some of the signs of short-term inflammation are pain (whether continuous pain or only when you touch a certain area that is inflamed) and redness of an area (this will happen as the body increases blood flow to an area that is inflamed).

Loss of function is also a symptom, for instance, a limited range of motion in a joint. Swelling in an area is also a common sign of inflammation. In martial arts, all of these things are common at some point or another due to the intensity of the training over time. If the inflammation continues over an extended amount of time, it can become chronic or long-term inflammation. There are several factors that can increase the risk of long-term chronic inflammation as well, like older age, obesity, a high-sugar diet, smoking, and obviously stress.

Probably the most common answer for dealing with inflammation in the body is to take drugs of some type. In my opinion, this can only add to the problem of toxification of the body. This is one of the beautiful things about learning the ability to control the level of inflammation in the body with your breathing exercises.

I have personally benefited from this for many years, and the older I get, the more I see the benefit. If I regularly train in the school and miss a few days to a week of my breathing exercises, I can feel it in my joints almost immediately.

Increased oxygen levels in the blood cells will help provide their maximum potential of oxygen to the body's cells. With that, toxins are more efficiently removed from the cells, which allows them to perform more optimally. Many viruses and bacteria will not survive in oxygenated conditions because they are not anaerobic.

Increased levels of oxygen will boost the immune system and help build resistance to infections. The state of hypoxia, which is a deficiency of oxygen in the body, can develop serious health problems, especially if it is below adequate levels for prolonged periods of time.

Increased Daily Energy & Mental Clarity

One of the major changes I noticed after starting to do these breathing exercises was the amount of energy I had on a daily basis. For me personally, it seemed to triple. I was able to get more done every day because I seemed to have an abundant amount of energy to focus on my goals.

Even to this day, when something happens in life that prevents me from being able to do my breathing exercises in my morning routine, I will notice a drop in energy.

The full cycle breath sends a signal to the brain to release feel-good neurotransmitters such as endorphins, serotonin, and dopamine. This is on top of the oxidizing effect we spoke about earlier. These things combined have a tremendous effect on your daily amount of energy and clarity. Increased oxygen benefits the body all the way down to the cellular level. It provides fuel for each and every cell.

Cells rely on available oxygen supplies to maintain adequate levels of ATP molecules. This process is called cellular respiration, and it allows cells to convert glucose into the fuel they need to function normally. With proper breath, you are literally charging your energy system at the cellular level and helping your body to operate more optimally every day. The absence of this process causes the cells to lose the ability to maintain a healthy function. This can cause sickness and disease to develop.

The brain represents about 3% of the body and its weight, and what is interesting about this is that it uses about 20% of the oxygen that is circulated through the body. The brain uses more energy than any other human organ. The brain is a build-up of billions of neurons (or nerve cells), each of them is transmitting electric or electrochemical signals. Unlike other cells, neurons never divide, and neither do they die off to be replaced by new ones.

Electrical signals pass between these neurons continuously as the mind is in charge of all the functions of the body, both conscious and unconscious. It is the engine of the body, and its cells need oxygen to create energy. If oxygen supplies in the body are limited or cut off, the brain will actually receive more damage than the other organs of the body. Something that is influenced immediately by implementing breathing exercises into your routine. Even if you're just including a consistent 10-minute session in the mornings.

One of the first things my students have noticed after learning these methods is the effect on them becoming lethargic and cloudy midday. They will tell me that around 2:30 or 3:00 PM, they would generally go and get a big cup of coffee in order to compensate for this lag.

Once they were actively doing the breathing exercises for about a week, they started to notice that this drop in energy in the afternoon seemed to go away. They also noticed a higher level of mental clarity throughout the day in general. And this was just from a 10-minute routine. I would often tell them, "imagine if you were doing 20 minutes a day."

There are actually products that are available today that are based on this information. These products are simply canistered oxygen. They offer all of the benefits we have spoken about here. But the good thing about learning the exercise is it's free. You will never forget it at home or in your car. You don't have to carry it with you when you're running or if you happen to be dealing with a stressful event.

All it takes is building an intelligent habit of breathing properly. I believe consistency is key to greater success. Just starting the habit will create great change, but doing it consistently over time will lead to even greater changes in benefits for the body.

Alkalization of the body

When taking a broad view of the body, there are several factors that make your internal systems, your tissues in your cells, work correctly. The temperature of your body, the number of nutrients, how much water your body is holding, and the pH of the blood in the body. pH stands for "potential of hydrogen." It is a measurement of hydrogen ion bonds in a solution, the more ions that are in the solution, the more acidic the solution will be.

Our bodies are generally designed to operate in a very narrow range of pH. On the pH scale, anything higher than seven is alkalizing, and anything less than seven is acidic. The scale ranges from 0 to 14.

Higher levels of pH in the blood will increase the acidity levels in the bloodstream. Modern science has started to realize that this acidic environment inside the body can lead to various forms of the disease.

Of course, there are other aspects that can affect us as well, like high levels of daily stress, certain elements in your diet, like sugar, caffeine, and processed grains. The great thing about this is we have the ability to affect this level of acidity with the breath.

It has now been shown medically that the full range breath or rapid, hyperventilation-type breathing can increase the alkalization of your blood. It has also been shown that shallow breathing can cause an acid buildup in the bloodstream.

A failure to breathe deeply can create a carbon dioxide buildup in the bloodstream. The CO_2 levels decrease pH levels, leading to the acidification of the blood. This alkaline state has a direct effect on the amount of inflammation in the body. So proper breathing exercises can give you control of the inflammation levels in your body to an extent.

I personally have experienced this in my recovery from hard training, either in the gym or on the academy floor. If I am regularly doing my breathing exercises, I have noticed that I recover much quicker from my training. Lactic acid is produced in your muscles and builds up during intense regular exercise. It can lead to soreness in the muscles.

I noticed a quicker recovery from this soreness when I was regular with my breathing practice. When I noticed this, I started to increase the amount of time I spent doing the breathing exercises, and it had a direct impact on the amount of recovery time I was experiencing from my training in the gym. Once I experienced this personally, I started to teach this to my students, who trained equally as hard in the academy. I taught it to several individuals, and I got the same effect in them that I found in myself.

Better Sleep

I had already been doing different practices in order to improve my sleep. We've covered a few of these earlier in the book. I did not expect breathing exercises to have this type of effect on sleep as well.

I have spoken in the last section about going through a period where I wanted to do personal research on the effects of full breathing on the recovery of muscle soreness when training. During this time, I increased the amount of time I was doing daily in my breathing exercises. At one point, I was up to an hour each day. I was surprised to notice an additional benefit to this increase in breath training was better sleep.

When I started to increase the time, within two days, I noticed that I was sleeping more deeply. I also noticed that it seemed that I required less sleep time than what I was scheduled. The first day it happened, I thought it was just a fluke. Then the following days, I woke up earlier and earlier. I also felt fully rested and empowered when I woke up.

When I finished the research I was doing on the effect of the breathing exercises on muscle soreness, and I decided to start doing an additional breathing session at night prior to going to bed. So I ended up doing 10 minutes in the morning and then 10 minutes again at night before I would go down for sleep.

I noticed the same effect with this routine that I had noticed previously while doing the study. Doing the 10-minute breath work prior to going to bed also released tension and relaxed my body. It turned into a great preparation cycle for sleep.

Again, I was waking up earlier refreshed and feeling like I did not need more sleep. I want to point out that I did not get out of bed when I would wake up earlier. It is important to maintain a regular sleep schedule to improve the quality of your sleep. The schedule will be directly related to the circadian rhythm cycle, which we are going to discuss later. Whenever I wake up earlier, and it doesn't seem like I'm going to go back to sleep, I generally will just lay there and do breathing exercises.

Here are a few symptoms from having low blood oxygen during sleep;

Being Restless

Elevated pulse rate

Elevated blood pressure

Daytime drowsiness, fatigue or lack of energy

Slower Heartbeat & Reduced Blood Pressure.
A blood pressure reading has a top number, which is the systolic pressure, and a bottom number, which is the diastolic pressure. The ranges are:

Normal: Less than 120 over 80 (120/80)
Prehypertension: 120-139 over 80-89
Stage 1 high BP: 140-159 over 90-99
Stage 2 high BP: 160 and above over 100 and above

Deep controlled breathing will lower your blood pressure. One of the ways it does this is by bringing down the CO_2 levels in your bloodstream. CO_2 levels will cause blood vessels to constrict so as to eliminate it from the blood system through deep breathing, and the vessels will relax and dilate. This dilation will decrease pressure on the system and allow your blood pressure to come down. This effect is called vasodilation. Vasodilation will occur naturally when oxygen levels in the blood system are low or when there are increases in body temp.

Its purpose is to increase blood flow to the internal organs when you need it. This is also a fight or flight response reaction when the body is placed under stress or what it perceives a stress. In addition to your fight or flight response, there are several other potential triggers for vasodilation. Here are a few of them;

Exercise - generally, it occurs in exercise because of the body's attempt to deliver extra oxygen and nutrients to the muscles during exercise.

And alcohol will also trigger vasodilation, and you will feel this sometimes when your face feels flush after a few drinks.

Inflammation in the body. The body will trigger vasodilation in times to increase blood flow to inflamed or damaged areas of the body.

Stronger Immune System
Controlled breathing will have a tremendously positive effect on the Auto Immune Response of your body. It has been shown to lower cortisol levels as well as lowering blood pressure.

In the past few years, Wim Hof has become famous for using his breathing technique to boost his immune system to such a level that he can achieve some amazing feats. He has demonstrated the ability to withstand subzero temperatures without protection. The man climbed Mount Everest in his shorts.

Wim has literally learned to control his body in ways that society previously thought were not possible and does it through his breathing technique. He has had been tested by various universities and researchers from different respective organizations and has not been disproven. He has achieved some amazing things in his career and done so by taking active control of his daily breathing patterns.

I remember my Kung Fu teacher having the ability to change his body temperature and do it at will. At that time, I did not think much of it, until years later, seeing Wim demonstrate this. The first time I saw an article about Wim, I dove into the information that was available about his breathing and his program.

Come to find out, and to my surprise, it is exactly what I had learned years ago as a teenager. He has just taken it to a level that I had not seen before. It was an incredible demonstration of the power of what the breath and its proper training can provide to you.

Researchers at Radboud University Nijmegen Medical Centre injected Hof with an endotoxin bacteria that causes flu-like symptoms. The researchers found that the injected bacteria had no effect on Hof. His breathing and meditation method activated his immune system to the point where it was able to counter the endotoxin.

They actually did a second test on twelve of his students after this initial test and produced the same results. And what did he teach them? His basic breathing method. It would be easy to say Wim was just special and unique, having the ability to demonstrate a high level of control over the immune system. What testing his students has shown is that it is something anyone has the ability to obtain with the knowledge and practice.

What you take away from this is reinforcement that you absolutely can influence your immune system. This was very impressive, but imagine what you can achieve by making this a consistent daily routine. Imagine the powerful changes that are within your grasp by doing something that you already do every day, by just learning to operate it had a more advanced level.

Sitkovsky Cancer Study

In 2020, Michail Sitkovsky, an immunophysiology researcher at Northeastern University, posted a new study that shows supplemental oxygen and treatment could help in the reduction of tumors in cancer patients. The research found that breathing in 40-60 percent oxygen compared to the 21 percent that our atmosphere provides could help weaken immunosuppression and fight the development in tumors by releasing T-lymphocytes. "I was looking to solve the problem of existence of tumors and anti-tumor killer cells in the same patient," Sitkovsky told NBC News. "Since the root of all problems is the lack of oxygen in tumors, a simple solution is to give tumors more oxygen." Now this study was done on mice, not human beings, so there's not a lot of research yet in regards to how this will affect humans.

The reason I wanted to discuss this study is because they're looking at an individual who has already developed a cancerous environment inside the body. They have already experienced a certain level of damage and break down internally. At this point, they start to add elevated levels of oxygen to the body in order to counter the event.

Imagine if you are increasing levels of oxygen in your body every day as part of a normal routine. And you're doing this consistently over time. It could possibly produce an environment that would help the individual avoid reaching the disease's physical state, to begin with.

Dealing With Sadness And Depression

According to the National Institute of Mental Health, major depression is one of the most common mental disorders in the United States. For some individuals, major depression can result in severe impairments that interfere with or limit one's ability to carry out major life activities. Depression is said to be the leading cause of disability in the United States. This is a growing problem in society that we are dealing with and will continue to have to deal with moving into the future.

Even if you are not experiencing it yourself, you are highly likely to be involved with someone who is or will be in the future. I believe all too often, and these problems are dealt with medications in an attempt to cover up the symptoms instead of actually dealing with the internal struggles causing them in the first place.

We are taught in our culture not to express sadness. Unlike anger, we tend to keep it inside and try to cover it up, which is the opposite of what we need to be doing. Often it is considered a weakness to lead the show outwardly. I disagree with this. I believe it takes a lot of strength and personal power to release it and let it out.

In traditional Chinese medicine, each organ of the body has a relationship to different human emotions. For example, the liver is generally related to anger, the kidneys are related to fear, the heart is related to joy, and the lungs are related to sadness or grief. Through this, certain breathing patterns and exercising the lungs can help calm and center someone who is experiencing depression, but it can also help them release the emotions trapped in the body that could be causing a lot of the problems.

When I'm training my instructors at my academy, I will list what I believe their job descriptions are going to be while teaching at the school. The list goes like this; janitor, counselor, janitor, and then a martial arts instructor. This turns into a common in-house joke between us.

Most of the guys who are new to the program will laugh at the thought of being a janitor twice as much as they will be an instructor. But I always get that curious head tilt at the thought of having to be a counselor. I'll tell them that they will be surprised how often one of the students will take them to the side to discuss things that are going on in their life outside of the school and ask for advice.

I remember being told this myself in the early 90s when I started to teach full-time. And I thought the same thing, "I'm not going to end up being anyone's counselor. Why would someone want to talk about their life with a knuckle-dragging Martial Arts instructor?" But I quickly found out otherwise.

After getting placed in the situation multiple times, I began to suggest a lot of the breathing exercises I had learned from the arts in order to help some of the students with some of the problems they were dealing with. Some of those problems were sadness or grief over a recent life event.

When I started to share these breathing methods with the students, it was equally surprising to me how quickly, after learning the exercise and starting to do them, they would begin to weep. It seemed to me that the exercises would be helping them release emotions that they were trying to cover up. This intrigued me and motivated me to look deeper into the material that I was learning and its relationship with dealing with different emotional problems.

What I discovered was a wealth of information right in front of me. As I studied more, every time the opportunity would come to share this information with someone who needed it, I was blessed with the opportunity to see that it did help them tremendously.

Additionally, just like everyone else in life, I myself have come to moments where I had to implement the knowledge for myself. It has never failed me. Not to say, some of those moments were not difficult, but the breath training I learned and trained over the years helped me get through those moments, as well as recover from them afterward.

One of the things I found through this experience was that the breathwork was one of the easiest places, to begin with, these individuals. I see meditation being taught to two individuals who are struggling with sadness and depression before they are introduced to breathwork. In my experience, it's very difficult for someone who is dealing with a difficult life event to sit down, close the rise, and just try not to think about anything.

Of course, they're going to immediately let their mind go to the problems they are suffering. I have found that it's much easier to teach them a breathing pattern first. It is much easier to sit down and focus on your breath and allow that work to bring you into a state of relaxation and calmness first. The breathwork will put you into a physical state that will be more conducive to meditation later on if it is needed.

Now, I am not a certified counselor, nor have I ever claimed to be. I have simply had the opportunity over the years to share knowledge with other people who needed it and were asking for it. And through that opportunity, I had the blessing of seeing it benefit many people. It works, and it can work for you as well if it is needed.

The daily breathwork and mindfulness that I do in my morning routines have become daily emotional maintenance that has become a method of handling the things that show up in life daily and not allowing them to build up over time. Holding onto these emotions and the stress that is connected to them consumes a tremendous amount of energy inside the body. Processing and dealing with it and thus releasing it through your daily exercise gives you back this energy that is consumed so that you can focus on other areas of life. Not to mention the health benefits that accompany it.

Fundamental Breathing Patterns for Warriors Path

OK, guys, we have talked about it, now let's take a look at doing it. These are the first fundamental exercises I teach to introduce the art of the breath:

The Full Cycle Breath
The Cleansing Breath
The Reverse Breath

Breath 1 The Full Cycle Breath - Building The Bridge

We went into a brief explanation of this breathing pattern when we were discussing emotional control. The first time we introduced this, we did so in a laying position. For this version, we're going to do it in a sitting position.

The first thing we want to achieve is the alignment of the body. We want to get the skeletal system aligned and in a balanced position so that the soft tissues of the body will be supported and are able to relax.

Find a chair that you can sit in that will allow your thighs to be close to horizontal to the floor. I personally prefer a wooden chair just for stability. When you sit in the chair, you're not going to sit as you normally do but instead on the edge of the front of the seat. You can imagine that you're going to sit on the tailbone and not the gluteus maximus, which is the main extensor muscle of the hip.

Place your hands comfortably on your knees or your thighs. They should be in a position where they can relax and be loose. Once you are in this position, imagine you have a string attached to the top of your head. The attachment will not be dead center but about an inch back from the center. Imagine the string pulling up and lifting and straightening your spine. As you stretch the spine, tuck your chin back slightly. You may also need to pull your shoulders back slightly to adjust your posture.

As we do the exercise, we will be sitting in this posture for at least 10 minutes. During that time, you may feel certain parts of your body start to fatigue. When this happens, it means that the muscles in that area of your body have to flex in order to maintain the position.

This is what we want to avoid. If you feel this, you want to try and adjust your position to have the skeletal system support the area and not the muscle. This takes a little time to find your individual posture due to the fact that we are all built differently. In this position, it will feel like you are balanced on the tailbone with the spine straight, the head up in the bone structure supporting everything.

With your imagination, mentally scan the body from the top of the head down to the feet. As you pass through each area, relax and release each part. Our goal is to release any residual tension that we may be unaware of so that it doesn't influence our breathing pattern. After you have done this, we will start a full cycle of breath.

You will take your first inhalation through the nose. You should feel the breath start to fill the lower abdomen and torso first. The chest will not move during this part of the process, and it may feel like you are pushing the breath into the lower stomach. The abdomen will protrude outward as your thoracic diaphragm moves downward in space for the lungs.

This movement will feel like a balloon expanding in your abdomen. As it starts to get to the point where it is full of breath, you will next feel your solar plexus expand. The expansion of the abdomen, and the lungs in the chest, will cause the chest to rise. What you want to avoid is lifting the chest yourself. Let the expansion of the breath in the torso lift the chest. Once it starts to rise, you can pull the shoulders back and open up the front of the chest. Your goal is to feel the breath expand from the bottom of the torso all the way up to the clavicle area of the shoulders.

At the top of this breath, you will have a slight pause. The pause may be anywhere from a second to three seconds, and then you will start your exhalation. Let the exhalation pass out through the mouth naturally, and don't force it. The chest will drop, and you will slowly return to your original position. When all of the breath has exited the body, pull in the abdomen is slightly toward your spine. This will bring the thoracic diaphragm upwards toward the lungs.

When you do this, you will notice that you will have a little bit of air that will exit. This is not a hard flexion of the abdomen, just a slight pulling in order to completely empty the lungs. The timing of the inhalation could be anywhere from 5 to 7 seconds. The holes at the top of the inhalation will be two or three seconds. The exhalation will be another 5 to 7 seconds. The amount of time you spend on each part of the cycle should be comfortable for you.

Some of the things you may experience when doing this breath will be dizziness or tingling in the extremities. This should not be too severe and if it is, stop doing the breathing exercise. You may need to begin by just practicing three or four breaths in the beginning. Sometimes different individuals take longer to adjust to the higher levels of oxygen in the body. This is not uncommon. You may start with three inhalations on your first day and then just add an extra one every one or two days. There is no rush. Consider it a life change that you will benefit from for many years to come.

This breath will introduce the basic motions of the breathing cycle. Parts of these can be used individually. And parts of the cycle can be emphasized more than others. The timing of the breathing cycle was adjusted. All of these parameters can be changed to get in different effects depending on what you want to achieve.

Breath 2 The Cleansing Breath

This breathing pattern was introduced to me first in the art of Kung Fu. I had practiced it for years and eventually met several yoga practitioners who did a similar cycle, and they help me to improve the process of this breath. In Yoga, the breath of fire. In Kung Fu, we referred to it as the cleansing breath.

This breath can increase your physical endurance when you are extremely active or under an excessive amount of stress. There is a training method we use inside of the academy. This method will usually last about 10 minutes long, and it is done with ten different partners. You will start the timer and start grappling with the first partner. You are generally going to go at an elevated rate, trying to push yourself. When the timer goes off every minute, you get a new partner, someone who is fresh. After 10 minutes of this exercise, you are just struggling to survive and keep from getting submitted or smashed.

Once you reach the state of fatigue and your body feels like it is overloaded from the training stress. One of the things you will recognize is the sensation of air starvation, and you will feel like you can not get enough air in your body. We call this sensation hitting the air starvation wall. I have recovered from hitting the air starvation wall multiple times using the cleansing breath. I have also taught this to multiple law-enforcement and military groups to use as an in-action recovery breathing method during a moment of rest to help pulmonary recovery.

It clears the lungs and body of toxins, thus detoxifying them. It helps you replace the stagnant, toxic air with fresh air in the lungs. It's also believed to clear and cleanse the mind. By expelling all of the air in the lungs, there are no residues left in the pulmonary system. This makes room for cleaner air coming into the lungs on inhalation. It will also trigger the full use of the pulmonary system if the user has unknowingly reverted back to shallow breathing.

I use this breath regularly when I am training on the mat to reduce the amount of lactic acid that builds up during exercising, as well as built-up carbon dioxide. Lactic acid is what causes muscle soreness, fatigue and weakness.

Putting this breath into your routine will cause abdominal organs to become more toned and strengthened from the repeated movement of the thoracic diaphragm and the abdomen. This movement will additionally increase the blood flow to the organs, releasing toxins and making them healthier.

Variations of this breath can be used to raise the temperature of the body as well. It will act as a stimulant for the entire body. Have you ever hit that point in the mid-afternoon, usually around 3 PM, when your energy starts to drop? Usually, this is when everyone will pick up a cup of coffee. This breath can be used for the same boosting energy not only during your midday energy drop, anytime you need a boost or a wake-up.

Okay, so, to start a breath, you can set up in the same seated posture we spoke about with the full cycle breath. Go through the same process of aligning the skeletal system and relaxing the body. The primary difference between this breathing exercise and the first one is that this will concentrate more on exhalation than the long inhalation. If you take a full inhalation, as you exhale, you're going to flex and pull the abdomen inward.

This is done slowly in the beginning in order to learn how to properly activate the abdominal muscles. Once you have learned how to do it, the pace of this breath is a little bit quicker than the full cycle breath. The breathing pattern is controlled with the abdominal muscles and the thoracic diaphragm. You will emphasize the exhale as you sharply pull in with the stomach. This is similar to a sneeze or a cough.

On the exhalation, I have practiced both exhaling through the nose and through the mouth. Generally, if I am very physically taxed in training and I'm trying to recover with this breath, I will breathe through the mouth. In just a sitting practice, I commonly will breathe through the nose. For me, it depends on how you're going to be applying the breath after you have learned it.

You will learn this at a slower pace than you will apply it later after getting better with the breath. In application, the pace of the breath is similar to that of a panting dog. Learning to inhale and exhale in this manner takes some time to learn how to do physically. It's okay in the beginning if it is slow and methodical, just to introduce the pattern to your nervous system. Don't rush; take your time and allow your body to learn the new process at its own pace. It will not be long until you are applying this regularly in your daily routine.

Staggered Exhale

This is a variation that I have used in this breath when placed under significant amounts of stress. I will inhale in the same manner and try to get a full breath. As I start to do the exhalation, I will stagger the exhalation into multiple parts. It will sound like you were doing several small coughs in a row.

This allows me to force the exhale to its very limit, completely emptying the lungs when I reach the last cough. I will then follow with a slow but full inhalation, trying to completely change the system. This allows me to eliminate all of the stale built-up toxins in the lungs that are present from the physical training or stressful situation.

When doing this exercise, I will not only feel the abdomen pull in to its fullest extent, but I will draw up the thoracic diaphragm as far as it will go. Being able to physically feel your diaphragm inside your torso is something that you develop over time. Even in the full cycle breath, if you practice it on a daily basis, you will start to become more familiar with your pulmonary system. You will begin to fill the ability to activate your abdomen to a greater level, as well as your internal diaphragms of the torso. Usually, the first one you become familiar with is the middle diaphragm or the thoracic diaphragm. All it takes is practice.

Breath 3 The Reverse Breath

Reverse abdominal breathing is a common breathing method of Taoism. The reverse breath reverses the natural movements of the abdomen that one finds in natural breathing. The abdomen will contract inward during inhalation and relax outward during exhalation, which is where the name is coined. As you contract the abdomen inward, gently pull up on the perineum or pelvic floor from the inside.

This starts to introduce the lower diagrams of the body and the fundamental movements to condition them. The reverse breath was traditionally used by chi kung practitioners and martial artists to push energy deep into their tissues and bones and charge their bodies with energy.

When beginning with these exercises, it is important to remember not to force the movements. One of the most common mistakes is using too much force when first being introduced to the movements. Additionally, take the time to practice the first two breasts that we introduced in this book prior to advancing to the reverse breath. I will commonly have students at the academy who are training this information spend at least a year just becoming familiar with the full cycle breath before moving on to anything else.

We actually use the reverse breath often without realizing it. There's a completely normal breathing process that is usually controlled by the autonomic nervous system. It is often the breath sequence we use when we yawn. This breathing pattern is used unconsciously when we are expressing emotions, especially strong ones. Laughing or crying commonly will use these same breathing methods.

Earlier, when we were talking about adding the power breath to the stone warrior push up to increase pressure in the body and increase the amount of strength you can produce, the power breath is a form of the reverse breath. You will tighten your abdomen and pull in as you inhale to increase internal abdominal pressure.

In the power breath, we are creating resistance against the exhale in order to maintain internal pressure during whatever strenuous exercise we are doing. This can increase your strength as well as stabilize your spine and torso. Reverse breath normally does not create this resistance against the exhale but does train the abdominal area to a greater extent.

There are several benefits I have received from the reverse breath over the years. Here are a few of the main ones.

Strengthened Abdominal Muscles

Reverse abdominal breathing will help you develop a greater connection and control of the lower abdomen and its different working parts. This familiarity with the lower center of the body will allow you to ground yourself more efficiently when needed.

You also will become more familiar with the abdominal muscles, increasing your ability to activate and have greater control of these different muscle groups. Most exercises that are taught will concentrate on the rectus abdomens, which is the muscle that gives you a six-pack.

The reverse breath will additionally train the transverse abdominals. The transverse abdominals are situated like a horizontal belt around the lower belly. All of this will strengthen and increase the overall tone of the abdominals.

Strengthened pelvic floor muscles

On the inhalation cycle of the reverse breath, contact your perineum muscles, which are the muscles that are located on the pelvic floor. These are the same muscles you would use to stop the flow of urination. This is actually a common method used to locate the muscles if you are unfamiliar with them.

Next time you are urinating, all you have to do is stop the flow. The muscles you use to do this are the muscles are looking for. You will feel them pull up at the base of the pelvis. As we mentioned above, this muscle group is contracted along with the abdominal muscles on the inhalation of the exercise.

The practice of contracting this area can also be done separately from the breathing exercise. It is a common method that is tight for conditioning the area. Sometimes called Kegel exercises, or sometimes the deer exercise.

Kegel exercises are used to manage urinary incontinence, erectile dysfunction, and premature ejaculation. The exercises can also improve nocturia (awakening at night to urinate).

I was first introduced to this exercise in Kung Fu. It is a Taoist exercise. They recognized the deer as an animal with a long life in a strong sexual appetite. One of the things they observed about the animal is that it constantly exercises its anus. After seeing this, they mimicked the exercise, which led to the creation of "the deer exercise." The deer exercise was used to increase blood circulation and build the tissues of the sexual gland. Like the Kegel exercises, it also will strengthen the pelvic floor, which they believed would create longevity and increase sexual energy and performance.

These exercises are generally done in the beginning by holding the time of flexion for 10 to 20 minutes. This is a lot longer than what is done in the reverse breath, but holding the contraction will develop a greater amount of strength in the area. As your ability to hold tension in the area increases, I will have students eventually practice holding it as long as it is comfortably possible. I will usually add these exercises to the end of a breathing routine. If you have trained a reverse breath in your breathing exercises, you can connect it to the end of that exercise easily.

Increased lung capacity

The thoracic diaphragm will flex in order to create pressure in the lower abdomen. In the reverse breath, this is usually in conjunction with flexion of the abdomen and the lower pelvic muscles. All three will pull inward toward the center of the abdomen. This will cause the thoracic diaphragm to expand downward entirely; this creates a vacuum in the lung cavity, which can helpfully inflate the lungs to their capacity.

Additionally, part of the reverse breath is learning to open and expand the rib cage. This expansion of the rib cage will also create more room for the lungs to inflate. The more you are able to train the reverse breath, the more familiar you will become with the techniques of lung cavity expansion.

Over time, this can change this section of the body's structure, strengthening, loosening, and opening it. Imagine having the information to completely overhaul and rebuild your vital pulmonary system. For me, it was like getting a high-performance engine put into my car.

Resistance Training

Like many areas I have trained in, once I got the fundamental patterns down, I would add some form of resistance or pressure to the material in order to slowly strengthen the process. This type of exercise enhancement is something I would add to a student's schedule after about two years of breath training. When I first learned to add some resistance to a breathing exercise, my instructor would push against my abdomen wall while I would attempt to do the full cycle breath against the resistance. Eventually, the internal pressure would move around to different points on the lower torso. Do you further strengthen that area and learned to send intent or breath to different parts of the area.

This is something that can be done without a partner by using your hand to apply the pressure yourself, but as you progress, you are limited in how much resistance you can create. Another option is to a weighted tool and set it on your abdomen as you do the breathing cycle. I have used leather medicine balls for this in the past, and they worked great.

Sometimes, when you start resistance training with this type of exercise, it is common to feel increased pressure (Valsalva) in the head. If this is the case, just go back to the regular breathing pattern and keep working on that for a while. It takes a while to learn how to keep the pressure in the lower abdomen and not allow it to move to the head.

2.
TIME DISCIPLINE

Time Discipline, in my opinion, is what most people think of when they consider discipline. They want more time. They plan to get up early to have more of it. They make a schedule to organize it more efficiently. Once they have more time, they plan to use it in a wiser way, like training at the gym or working on a new business plan.

Time is a sobering concept. As human beings, we are only given a certain amount of it. And once you use what you have, you do not receive more of it. This is a very important principle, and generally, the earlier we realize it in life, the more potential for achievement we will have.

For me personally, one of the major shifts of thought around time was realizing that it was a unit of my life. Once I had that change in perspective, I started referring to my time as life units in my teaching and coaching.

Life Units

A life unit for me is one hour of my time. Obviously, like everyone else, I have 24 of those hours on any given day. And also, like everyone else, some of those hours are going to have to be spent doing necessary things for survival—sleeping, eating, physical exercise, etc. Generally, when I start to look at organizing the time I have, I will start with these periods that are required.

If we take sleep, for example, yes, we could attempt to have less of it. But when we have less sleep, it will sometimes tremendously affect how we operate each day. If we lower the number of hours that we spend sleeping, it can directly affect our focus and motivation in our waking hours, hours that we are trying to use to achieve our goals on a daily basis.

I'm not suggesting that you can't burn the midnight oil on occasion when it is necessary. I have done this myself on many different occasions out of necessity. But it has been my experience that after doing this for two or three days in a row, I will have to "catch up" on my sleep time up at some point. Not to mention how lack of sleep can affect your immune system as well as the level of stress you carry in your body on a daily basis.

"If you love life, don't waste time, for time is what life is made up of."
- Bruce Lee

With this in consideration I like to take these areas like sleep and look at them to determine a way to achieve their goal in the most efficient and effective way possible. For example, I know I must sleep, but how can I improve sleep to get the most out of the time? How can I learn to sleep better and get more from it? When I proposed this question to myself, it caused me to start a study on the science of sleep and ways that I can improve.

The Art of Sleep

There are several things I discovered that helped me out in using life units that were devoted to sleep in a more efficient and effective manner. One of the first things I discovered with my research was that I needed to eliminate light in my bedroom. The darker it was in the bedroom, the better my sleep seemed to be. How often do you fall asleep with the TV on or sit and stare at your phone or computer before going to sleep?

Exposure to light or less of it stimulates the brain (pineal gland) to release hormones like Melatonin. It will cause a drop in body temperature and other functions, and it will make you feel awake and less likely to fall asleep. Your muscles will begin to relax. Light exposure will affect the release of these hormones that will start your sleep prep cycle.

Before the invention of electricity, we did not need to seek out darkness or ways to create it. It happened naturally with the cycles of day or night, not to mention the changes of technology in the last 30 years that have put lighted screens in front of us on a regular basis. The intensity of the light you are exposed to in the evening will additionally have an affect on your sleep prep cycle.

If you have the ability to control the light in your environment, it is good to gradually use dimmer light as you approach sleep time. One way to do this is buying low-level light bulbs for lamps that you can use in the evening. If you do have to use a computer in the evening, generally, most of them will have settings that you can adjust that will dim the light on a schedule.

One of the things I did was to obtain window coverings that had the ability to completely block out daylight. Once I got that system set up, I noticed a change within two or three days in my quality of sleep. I seem to be able to go to sleep quicker, and it also allowed me to sleep in a little more in the morning if I had time available.

Additionally, one of the other things I did to eliminate light in the room was to remove all electronics from the room. I had to create a new habit of leaving the cell phone in the bathroom. Also, other smaller electronics got removed from the room as well.

I also made it a habit to start turning off or putting down electronics a half-hour prior to going to sleep. This worked out well because I had a routine of preparation for sleep that I would start to do every night. So I just parked the cell phone at the beginning of this routine as part of the winding down process in preparation for sleep.

Your Circadian Rhythm/Cycle

The second change I made was setting a regular sleep schedule. For me, I tried to be in bed before 10 PM every night. And I would set up a time that would give me a few hours of sleep. Due to my personality, I have always woken up early. And when I started setting the schedule, nothing really changed.

I would still wake up way before the alarm would go off. So, in the beginning, I would have to force myself to stay in bed regardless of setting the schedule. But after a couple of weeks, my body started to adjust to the regular schedule, and I ended up not only sleeping better but a tad bit longer in the mornings, which is something I have not done in years.

This is your circadian rhythm. The circadian rhythm is a 24-hour internal body clock that is running in the background of your brain and cycles between sleepiness and alertness at regular intervals. It is sometimes referred to as your sleep-wake cycle. This cycle works best when you set up regular sleeping habits. You should try to set a specific time to go to sleep and a specific time to wake up in the morning and try to stick to it until your body adjusts.

Just these two things had a huge impact on my sleep. I noticed that my sleep quality has improved after about a month, to the point where it almost seemed like I required less than eight hours. At that time, I still tried to maintain the eight-hour schedule, but eventually, I did lower it because the better quality of sleep I got, the less I seemed to need on a daily basis.

Binaural Sound Waves

The third area of change for me was sound. I started out with a brown noisemaker. It had different settings on it, and I played with the different sounds and noticed that some of them had a better effect on me than others. After noticing this, I started doing more research into sound and how it affects sleep. In my research, I discovered binaural sound and how its different brainwave frequencies would determine our levels of alertness.

The different frequencies I learned were;

Gamma (40-100 Hz) - High arousal
Beta (13 – 40 Hz) – Active, alert and focused
Alpha (8 -12 Hz) – Relaxed, calm, and creative
Theta (4 – 8 Hz) – drowsy, light sleep
Delta (less than 4 Hz) – Deep sleep

The Delta frequency was the one I used. Delta waves were first described in the 1930s by W. Grey Walter after producing his own version of Hans Berger's EKG machine. Delta waves are slow, low-frequency brainwaves, between 1.5-4 hertz, that are the dominant brainwave patterns of deep sleep. After learning about these frequencies and subsequently adding them into my nightly routine, this

Trinity of changes made a huge difference in the quality of my sleep time.

As part of designing a proper sleeping environment, I bought the speaker system that I started using to play the Delta frequency at night. The higher quality speakers made a huge difference and just added another element to the positive effect of everything else I was plugging into the environment.

As you see in the list above, all humans will display five different types of electrical patterns or brain waves. These waves can be measured with an EKG or an electroencephalograph. The EKG allows researchers to measure these brainwave patterns. Generally, when measured, all five of these waves are present at any given time of the day. But one could be more active or higher than the other ones depending on what state you are in at any given time. Delta waves are the slowest brain waves and are generally associated with the deepest levels of sleep or relaxation.

Timing Stimulant Intake

It is a good measure to start eliminating stimulants after the late afternoon. Coffee is probably the most commonly used drug in the world. I know that I personally abuse it on a daily basis in my office. A lot of people will increase their intake of caffeine in order to remain alert in the afternoon and sometimes into the evening. The drawback to this is, caffeine will produce adrenaline and dopamine in the body. It takes 4 to 6 hours for your body to eliminate 1/2 of the caffeine it has taken in at any given time.

It also blocks the effects of the brain chemical melatonin that makes us sleepy. Coffee also causes the adrenal glands to release more cortisol, a stress hormone, which taxes the adrenal system. With this in mind, you can easily see how this would carry over into your sleeping hours. So not only can intake of stimulants affect your ability to go to sleep on time, but it can also have an effect on your sleep quality itself. In addition to the timing of intake, it would be good to consider the amount of the different stimulants you are consuming each day.

Although I am a huge fan of coffee, and it is something I abuse on a regular basis, there are times that I have to reduce my intake, and I do so with several alternatives. Here are a few that I have used:

Yerba Mate

Green or White Tea

Matcha Tea

Maca

For those times when I am attempting to lower my intake of stimulants, I still usually have my coffee in the morning with breakfast. But I will switch over to the alternatives listed above in the afternoon and will generally start to slow down on those around three or 4 PM.

The Art Of Eating

The next area I took a look at out of the necessary application of life units was the time you spend eating. Like sleep, eating is something you cannot do without for long periods of time. And like sleep, I wanted to take a deep dive into the study of diet and how it affects you. This is a huge topic. I can't tell you how many books and sources of information I have gone through on this topic.

Interestingly, getting involved with the study shows just how many different points of view there are out there. How do you know who is right? For me, how and what I am eating will vary over time, according to what my goals were at that moment. Was our training harder in the academy or maybe in the gym? Was I going through a period of time where I was not as physically active, and I had to make adjustments accordingly to maintain a certain physical state? Was I taking time to cleanse the body and allow it to heal? Each of these would vastly changed my diet so that I could achieve different goals. This is one of the reasons I refer to the consumption of food as the art of eating.

Dense foods and their effect on the body

At one time in my life, I was a vegetarian for over 15 years. I primarily followed this diet from a suggestion that came from a Kung Fu teacher. I was eating this way because it assisted a certain type of training I was doing at that time.

In the early 90s, I was working in a martial arts academy in Chattanooga, Tennessee. This academy taught several forms of Kung Fu, and one of them was T'ai Chi Chuan. Tai Chi is a centuries-old Chinese martial art that descends from Chi Gong, an ancient Chinese discipline that has its roots in traditional Chinese medicine.

At the time, I was interested in the system because of a study of qi (pronounced "chee"), which is loosely defined as the life force of the human body. The intrinsic bioelectric energy in the body. I was fascinated by the system and started the study in order to learn more about this internal force or energy.

I had been studying Tai Chi for about three years when a group of students and I traveled to Knoxville, Tennessee, to attend a seminar with a master that traveled to the U.S. from overseas. We were going to stay in town for three days, with training to be done on each day. On the second day, I was in a room of about 30 people, and we were working on the form.

This one move, I would stand on one leg and bend over to almost touching the floor. As we were doing this, the Master instructor was walking around the room and making corrections to the students. When she came to me, she

162

placed her hand on my lower back to adjust my position. When her hand touched my back, she said, "humm, you eat a lot of meat." She made the adjustment, then went to the next person.

I was floored because I was eating a lot of meat. I was doing a tremendous about of training in the academy and in the gym, so I increased my intake of protein to help with recovery. Regardless, how did she know? I had never even spoken to her, much less talked about my diet. How could she know this with a touch of her hand?

After the session was finished, I went up to her and asked, "How did you know I eat a lot of meat?" She said, "You hold a lot of tension in your body." Usually, this tension will come from consuming meat. She said that that tension would stop the flow of energy in your body. You will be able to learn the form, but with that diet, it will be hard to study the internal part of the art. Just like that, I became a vegetarian. I went with the guys after that training session and had a salad. I caught a tremendous amount of hell from all of my buddies that evening, but I made the change, and it made a difference in achieving my goal.

During this, I obviously had many discussions in regards to the diet, which also caused me to do quite a bit of study on many different dietary options. There are many different ways to look at how or what you should consume, depending on your goals. So, in my opinion, to say one philosophy is better than the next is very difficult to do. Throughout the years, I have found that people are vastly different.

What will work for one person may not necessarily work for another. What is truth for one may not necessarily be truthful to another. So when it comes down to the decision to eat meat or not to, I believe it depends on the individual and their goals.

One of the reasons I stopped following the vegetarian diet was because of my training. I had gotten to the point where I was training 6 to 8 hours a day. This put a tremendous strain on the body, and in my opinion, I was just not able to get enough protein into the body to recover properly. So at that point, I decided to change my diet again. And for me, the change made all the difference between where I was in life and my goals.

I also don't believe that there is a set diet that you will follow for your entire life. I believe you should study different types of diets and what they do for you. Try one of them out and see what kind of reaction you get from your body. Learn how each type of food or each type of dietary change will affect you. Some foods will help if you are training hard. Some foods will help cleanse the body.

Sometimes taking a break and not eating for a certain amount of time will help your body heal itself. What you have to do is study food and consumption as an art. Search and find out what works for you. The thing is, you may be at a certain time in your life where you're able to eat a certain way. But as you travel through life, your needs may change. As you get older, the way you eat will have to change.

I began to study diet and its effects on the body when I was in my teens. I just always had the mindset to try to improve on all levels. I looked at the body as basically being a machine. As I aged, I knew the system would not work as optimally as when it was younger.

In youth, your body has the ability to deal with and process more levels of toxins if it needs to. Knowing this, I planned to remove or greatly limit certain things from my diet, and I would need to add in more living food as I progressed through the years. (If I had not already done so with my diet at that time). Some of these things on the list were.

Pain Killers
Alcohol
Soda
Sugar and high-fructose corn syrup, Aspartame
Simple Carbohydrates (Refined Wheat Bread)
Dairy products
Caffeine
Processed meat (sausage, bacon, ham, smoked meat)
Fried Foods (Foods High in Trans Fats)
Fast Foods

I chose these items because of their negative effects on the body, which I discovered through the study of holistic nutrition.

Knowing this brought me to the conclusion when teaching students in my academy, I may not necessarily direct them to eat a certain type of food and avoid another. The way I approached it was to just have them think about the density of the food. Yes, I know that there are types of food that can carry certain toxins, and those toxins will also affect the body. But again, I have met people who have eaten the same things, and it has not affected them, so as I said earlier, it's an individual choice in those areas.

Regardless, what I have found is that the denser the food is, the longer it takes your body to digest it across the board. And the longer it takes to do this digestion, the more energy it will burn, and the more time it will spend in the body. Obviously, certain meats are going to fit into that category.

As I said earlier, sometimes you have to include more proteins in your diet. This is common for students I have who are training heavily and long hours many days a week. So with this in mind, you might choose to eat your denser proteins or other dense foods at different times during the day.

For me, depending on how much protein I was trying to consume in a day, I would try to eat heavier proteins for lunch and again at my 3 PM meal. As I moved into the evening, I would choose lighter options like a protein shake or nuts. These lighter proteins were easier to digest and pulled less energy from my body for the digestion process. One of the things I noticed from this is I had more energy later in the day. When I would have the heaver proteins in the evening, they always seemed to weigh me down and make me tired.

This is a very broad way to approach this idea. I started teaching this principle to students initially to get them thinking about what they put into their bodies and how it affects them. If they took an interest in the art of eating, I would then guide them into more detailed studies and guide them to do their own research and find what worked for them.

To quote Sijo Bruce Lee,

Research your own experience.
Absorb what is useful.
Reject what is useless.
Add what is specifically your own

It is not my goal with this book to educate you on the details but more to introduce you to the path. Volumes of information are available on the market that will introduce you to this study. Take the time to research and find the detailed information that will work for you.

Harvey and Marilyn Diamond have some books called *Fit for Life* and *Fit for Life II*. These books are great reads and a starting point for food combinations, timing, and how they affect your body. Also, if you can find it, check out *Tao of Balanced Diet: Secrets of a Thin and Healthy Body* by Stephen Thomas Chang. Doctor Chang gives a great perspective between Chinese Tao medicine and diet and the western diet.

Living Food and its effect on the body
In my own journey, I have found that the more you process or cook the food, the more its living properties are destroyed. higher cooking temperatures will also destroy

the enzymes and nutrients that are in a food. Enzymes are important because they assist in the digestion and absorption of the food we eat. I have always tried to have multiple sources of living food or raw food in my diet with this in mind.

Some of the staples I have had in my diet over the years include raw fruits, nuts and seeds, sprouted grains, and leafy greens. All of these things are high in vitamins, fiber, and minerals and can be easily added to any meal.

Raw living foods also help to alkalize the body, which will reduce the acidity of your internal environment. They have less of a chance of fermenting in the gut and causing inflammation.

Juicing Living Food

I got introduced to juicing in the early 1990s. One of the reasons I was drawn to it is that I could get my requirements of greens and other nutrients for my day all combined into one drink. And since the juicer broke it down, I found that my body could quickly absorb this food.

Generally, my heaviest physical activity is in the mornings. Any time I would need a solid meal prior to going into the academy or going into the gym it would always make me feel heavy and way me down. So I would start to substitute my morning meals with live food juice and a protein drink.

I noticed after doing this for a certain amount of time that my energy levels began to increase in the mornings. I believe this was for a couple of reasons: one, I was getting more living energy out of the food that I was taking in; and two, because it was juiced, it was broken down and easier for my body to digest and process.

I have had times in my juicing journey where I would drink juice and nothing *but* juice for several days straight. One of the reasons I did this was to lighten the body and to give it a break. I also discovered from this that when the body is released from the task of continuous digestion, it will start to cleanse itself. The body will start to eliminate toxins that have been stored in it. I'm going to talk about this a little bit next.

Juicing can have a tremendous effect on your health and body. It is a relatively simple and easily digestible way to get more nutrients into the body. Juicing will also help increase the water content of the body and help keep you hydrated. Between taking a multivitamin and juicing the actual food yourself, I believe that you will get more from the juice than a processed pill. Even if it is something that you are only able to do one or two days a week, the benefits are many, and it will be well worth your time to pursue.

"Let food be thy medicine, and medicine be thy food."
— Hippocrates

Cleansing cycles
Three to four times a year, I will do a cleanse just to give the body a rest. Usually, these cleansing cycles that I do are timed around the season change throughout the year.

There are many different methods of cleansing the body by adjusting your intake of food. For me, one of the best ways was to do several days of juicing.

Living juice has a tremendous amount of energy that the body can absorb, but it is already broken down and requires very little energy from the body to digest since it has been juiced.

Because of this, it allows the body a rest, so to speak. After a day or two into the cleanse, the body will naturally direct its additional energy that is not used for digestion into cleansing.

If you have never done a cleanse, you're in for a treat. There are many mixtures of juice that you can use. For me, the foundation is usually a carrot juice, and when I am in a cleansing cycle, I will usually add raw ginger and beets.

Additionally, I will put in cayenne pepper. These juices have a tremendous cleansing effect on the body. The effect of a cleansing cycle will vary per individual. And if you have never done one before, it could be a struggle.

As your body starts to enter the cleansing cycle, you will feel like you're starting to have the symptoms of a cold. In holistic nutrition circles, this is called a cleansing crisis. Sometimes this cleansing crisis can be severe, depending on how many toxins you have in the body. A relatively clean eater or someone who has followed a good diet may not be as toxified as someone who is not a clean eater.

The amount of toxins that we are exposed to on a daily basis has increased over the years. Our food has become more processed, and the addition of hormones increases the size and growth rate of the different animals we consume.

Also added are additives and other chemicals to extend its shelf life, as well as other additives for coloring and taste.

The use of pesticides has increased over the years as well. Another source of chemical input for the body is toothpaste, lotion, soap or body wash, deodorants as well as multiple other healthcare products that are on the market. Different cleaning agents that you use around the house will introduce toxins into your environment. Not to mention vehicle exhaust and overall pollution that is dumped into the air we breathe.

You have six systems in your body that are designed to dispose of toxins. They are the intestinal tract and colon, the lymphatic system, your kidneys, your liver, your skin, and only your lungs. The great thing about the lungs being on this list is if you are doing the breathing exercises that we have spoken about in this book, you've already started to detoxify the body by improving your pulmonary process.

The question is, how can you tell if your body has become overly toxic from exposure to these different things. Well, there are a few signals that you can look for and recognize. Of course, the lack of these symptoms does not necessarily mean you should not be doing *some* sort of cleansing in your routine.

It should be noted that a lot of these symptoms are connected to chronic disease as well, and it is common in today's society to experience these and then go to a physician, who is going to give you more chemicals to cover up the symptoms.

Our culture has become more drug reliant. This is evident when you see commercials and other marketing advertising drugs to fix minor problems. For myself, if I recognize any of these symptoms, I would generally try to correct them with life changes before getting a physician involved. Here is the list:

Loss of mental clarity

Muscle pain

Joint pain

Continually feeling exhaustion & lack of energy

Weight gain & water retention

Increased inflammation in the body

Headaches

Allergies

If we take a look at what you can do to deal with toxicity, the first thing is to avoid it in the first place. A good place to start is intelligently choosing the food you eat and where you get it from. Generally, with a little research, you can find good local sources for food that has been grown without the use of chemicals or excess pesticides.

As the market has started to become aware that there are individuals looking for these types of products, they have actually increased in availability in the last 10 or 15 years. It's easier now to find meats that have not been grown with hormones. It just takes a little extra time to look for them at the market.

Additionally, you can take a look at the cleaning products that you use around your own home. What kind of chemicals are inside them? There has been an increase in less toxic cleaning chemicals, and they have become increasingly easier to acquire. I purchased air cleaners for my home and office because this is where I spend the majority of my time every day. Doing this increases the air quality that I breathe, probably 50% of my day each day.

Beyond avoidance and changes in lifestyle to lessen exposure to toxins, there are cleansing options. As I stated before, I generally will start most students who want to give this a try on a juice fast. Beyond that, I will suggest the Master Cleanse. The Master Cleanse is a step up from a juice fast in the amount of effort and time it will take to do it. Regardless, the results will follow suit.

Due to its popularity, you can find a tremendous amount of information on the internet in regards to this popular cleanse. I will list the ingredients and some basic directions below just to give you an idea of what is involved in to get you started if interested:

The Master Cleanse
Ingredients:

Two tablespoons of freshly squeezed lemon
Two tablespoons of Grade B maple syrup
1/8 teaspoon cayenne pepper (capsicum) – the red type, *Higher Scoville Heat Units*
12 oz of pure drinking water

Directions:

Squeeze the lemon juice and pour it into a container; add the maple syrup, water, cayenne pepper, and stir.

Eating is part of your life. And you are greatly affected by what you put into your body. The study, learn how to do it effectively, and apply it to your life.

Clean Water

At a minimum I personally consume at least a gallon of water on a daily basis. I think a lot of people take water for granted. 70% of the body is water. It is required not only for life but for all of the processes of the body. It is also intricately involved in eliminating toxins and waste from the body. It is responsible for regulating body temperature. For myself, I follow this basic rule; I'll try to drink a glass of water when I first wake up in the morning, a full glass before each of the meals that I take in during the day.

There is a huge difference between water that has been cleaned through a good filter and what is coming out of the tap in your kitchen sink. I have personally noticed that the cleaner my water is, the clearer I am, and the better I feel on a daily basis.

The filter I have now will not only electronically clean the water but it will also ionize it. This will also affect the alkalinity of the water and remove the fluoride in the water. To someone who has not researched fluoride, that might sound like a bad thing. If it does to you, I suggest taking some time to look into the history of sodium fluoride. Chlorine is actually not much better, and I make just as much of an effort to get it removed from my water as possible. This has had a tremendous effect on me personally.

Obtaining and setting up the filters were surprisingly easy to do and quickly became a part of my daily routine. Good water combined with a proper diet of living food has given me more energy to achieve the goals I have set for myself.

Here are just a few of the benefits of drinking clean water:

reduces headaches
helps mental alertness
benefits digestion
helps with constipation
replenishes skin tissue
has anti-aging properties
regulates body temperature
flushes out toxins & waste products
boosts metabolic rate
reduces the risk of dehydration
moisturizes air in the lungs
helps with joint & muscle health

It's also worth discussing what not to put into your body for hydration. Right away, what tops the list is the consumption of soft drinks. Soft drinks offer absolutely no nutritional value whatsoever. On top of that, they are full of harmful chemicals.

Their high sugar content has been shown to be responsible for the development of diabetes, kidney disease, osteoporosis, bone loss, tooth erosion, and heart disease. It has even been linked to cancer. I have had students over the years come to the academy with a soft drink habit. Some of them go to the extent of drinking 5 to 6 cans of soda each day. Most of them didn't even realize what they were putting in their body until I asked them to take a look for themselves.

Planning Your Awesome

The discipline of your time is also deciding what you want to focus your energy on. What is your end goal? What do you want to achieve? This alone is a vast subject.

I was taught goal setting in the martial arts originally and then later realize what I had been given. The goal was to reach the rank of black belt. Setting your sights on that goal alone is daunting, so we would break it down into smaller steps. These baby steps would be represented by the belt ranks that led up to the black belt. Each belt would have a series of information you would need to learn. But it would also have a certain set of skills that would need to be mastered to a certain level. Just memorizing the information or the list of knowledge was not enough. You have to able to do it and do it with a certain level of proficiency.

Once you could demonstrate that proficiency, you were then placed under stress. So the goal may be just to punch someone in the face. But you have to demonstrate your ability to achieve that goal while two other opponents are trying to punch and kick you as they avoid getting punched in the face themselves.

They would actively counter your being successful. They wanted you to fail and do it often. Getting to the point where you were successful would take a tremendous amount of training, done consistently, and stretched out over time. Nothing would come quickly or easily. It sounds a lot like life!

Failure and the ability to deal with failure were just part of the process. After a while, I started to become disconnected from it. If I failed with something, it didn't even faze me. I just got up and kept going forward. I learned that you could not obtain meaningful success without walking on the stones of failure to get there. After a certain amount of time, failure just became my friend because I knew the more times I fell, the quicker route to get to success.

I also learned that it takes great effort and massive action in order to create change in yourself. And part of that action is going to be the gaining of wisdom from your failures. Achieving a skill on this path would also allow you to experience what it is really like to actually achieve something against resistance. Too often in today's society achieving a goal is made to seem way too easy. I have seen people achieve their goals and then question themselves whether or not they deserve it. They wonder if they actually have what was given to them.

What does this have to do with planning and scheduling your day?

If you understand these principles and ideas in advance, you can plant them into the path you are traveling. You know you have to break down the goal into smaller steps, and those steps have to be achievable pieces that intelligently progress you toward what you want to obtain. You know in advance that you are going to experience failure, and instead of dreading that failure you are actually going to hunger for it because you know it will bring you closer to your goal with the wisdom of the journey.

You already know that you are going to struggle. You know that you're going to put forth the effort, and it may not work. You know you were going to fall, and you're going to have to get back up and then double the amount of effort you are putting forth previously.

For myself, understanding this has benefited me tremendously in life. But after going through it on the academy floor, when I had to set an achievement path for another goal in life, I knew in advance what I was going to have to do. But I also knew the questions that I never needed to ask of my teacher, my mentor.

I've also had good teachers, and I've had bad ones. This has taught me how to intelligently choose a good teacher or mentor. The term I use for one of those creative teachers is a "Sun teacher."

We will be discussing this principle quite a bit later in the book. There is a difference between the moon and the sun. The same can apply to a teacher or mentor. A moon teacher will reflect light. In other words, they only repeat what they have been taught by someone else. There's nothing wrong with this, and in my experience, this is the majority of the population. But what we are looking for is the sun teacher.

The sun creates light, as the sun teacher will create knowledge and wisdom. He does not just repeat what he was taught. A sun teacher is an individual that has learned something, processed it, and trained it in ways that were not taught to him originally. He has the ability to have a broader vision of the wisdom he possesses. And he takes that and breaks it down deeper and gets more from what he was previously taught. This mindset or Mind Shift gives him the ability to almost create knowledge in his given subject on the fly.

As I type this, it makes me think of two of my teachers: Master Pedro Sauer and Master Erik Paulson. Master Sauer is one of the top Brazilian Jiu-Jitsu practitioners in the world. Master Paulson is also one of the top Brazilian Jiu-Jitsu practitioners, as well as an advanced guru in Submission Wrestling. Both of them, in my opinion, are Sun Teachers. Of course, they both can recall and demonstrate the curriculums that they have created for their students and organizations.

But something makes them unique, and I have seen it multiple times over my years with them. I will watch a student ask a question about a problem they're having. And it will be something that's unique that maybe they have not seen before or maybe it's some certain angle that they have not had to deal with before. Both will ask us to demonstrate it for them again and then sometimes to do the technique on them so they can feel what is happening. And then they will literally solve the problem on the spot. They will create an answer, and it will work. They are creating light, creating knowledge right there in front of you.

Why is this important?

We know when we want to achieve a goal that we are going to have to locate someone who has walked the path before us. Someone who has already achieved that goal or a goal very similar to ours. You may do some research and have a list of 100 people or mentors that you could go-to for the knowledge to pursue your goal. But out of that 100, 1 of them will be a Sun Teacher. That is the one you want to locate. It is not an easy task to find these individuals. I have searched for them my entire career in the martial arts. But they do exist, and if you are able to locate one in the given field that you want to pursue, the payback will be 100 fold.

Generally, these individuals are on the cutting edge of whatever they are involved with. They are the ones that are doing things that have not been done before. They are the ones that will hear the phrase "that's impossible," and they will ask, "Is it?" I have heard it commonly said that if you want to achieve something in a new field, then go find someone who is producing the results you're looking for. That is true, but with this principle in mind, you additionally want to find someone who is not only producing those results, but they are changing the industry. They are producing results that have not been seen before, and they are doing it in ways that may not have been done before. This will be that sun student/mentor.

Know Your Goal

Find a mentor, a sun teacher

Ask the right questions because you know the process

Know simplicity is mastery (don't complicate it)

Set your baby steps & timeframes for achievement

Expect to fail & plan for it (*train to win, prepare to fail*)

Plan to give massive effort and action (Effort Scale)

Know it will take continuous effort over time

The Master Filter

When it comes to sitting down and scheduling your time, it is important to maintain a thousand-mile view. I mean that you should check yourself and make sure you're not so busy working in life that you aren't able to take a step back and *work on* life. I am very driven, and I had hard times in my life when I was focused on something so much that I didn't pay much attention to what was going on around me and in my life outside of that thing I was driving towards.

As my business grew, it seemed I had more and more people asking for more things and more time as I was doing this. During that period of time, I believed I could pretty much do anything, so if someone were to ask me for my help or direction, I would do my best to give them some time for a conversation. After a while, I had so many people asking that it was physically impossible for me to do this. Soon I realized that a lot of this time I was giving to people was having absolutely no effect on my goals.

I knew I needed a process to help me better grasp my time and make sure I was using it properly. That's when I created the master filter. It is a list of the fundamental areas of life that were important to me at that time. Anytime someone requested time, a phone call, a private lesson. Anything that would consume a life unit or one hour of my time. Any of these requests would go through the master filter to determine if I was going to spend that time in a fashion that would get me closer to my goals or improve my life in some way.

Here are the fundamental sections of my master filter.

Family

Freedom

Finance

Health

Again these are just the basic examples. Anytime I coach someone on this, this is where we start. Once I find out what is important to the individual I'm working with, we may add a section. Additional sections could be something like; faith or a side hustle. It just depends on the person's goals. When we add on additional sections, we're looking for the thousand-mile view areas of life. In other words, it keeps you seeing a broad vision of your overall journey. So, anything that comes along that I had to make a decision on would go through this filter.

For instance, someone would call the academy and want to speak to me. A common example would be someone wanting me to explain to them how to set up a business. Normally, I might give someone a minute or two of time, but as I said earlier, as the requests grew more frequent, there was no possible way to fit them all in. So at this point, I had to decide what was one hour of my life worth. What would I need in exchange for one of my life units? At that time, I was teaching private training lessons for $200 for 45 minutes. So I told my office manager that I would be more than happy to speak to anyone if they were willing to reserve time and pay for it. I had also instructed her that, if they were willing to pay for the time, to go ahead and request a written explanation of what they wanted to discuss, as well as what my involvement in the project or idea would be.

Let me tell you something, this cut the requests *way* back. It also cut the physical visits to the school way back. But another thing it did was only open the door for the individuals that were absolutely serious about doing something. And later, I came to find these are the individuals that I wanted to speak to anyway, so if we take this back to the master filter.

Let's say Bob calls the office and requests time. He is willing to pay, and he also writes out what he wants to talk about. For this example, let's say he wants to start a tactical training business, and he wants me to help them design it, as well as design the programs he's going to offer. He wants to discuss a percentage partnership for this business.

So I will immediately run this opportunity through the master filter. I'll ask myself how does this affect each of the major areas in the filter. First on my list is family. How is this going to affect them? It will obviously take some time, in the beginning, to design the business and get everything going. But is this going to be a continuous consumer of my time? Or is it going to be set up in a way that after I design everything, I get a percentage, but I'm not physically involved? I have to decide if I have enough available time to commit to this.

I would also need to weigh the financial benefit of the opportunity. Sometimes the financial benefit is so great that it is worth investing my life in. The next section on the filter is freedom. Obviously, this opportunity is going to affect my freedom. But, is it going to continuously consume my time, or is it something that I will spend a considerable amount of time in the beginning, and then freedom will come afterward.

Generally, these are the type of business opportunities that make it through the filter. The older I get, the more important freedom holds. As you move through life, this section becomes gold.

Next is the finance section. Obviously, we would get into the details of the business on this section with Bob. How much time does the business take, how much travel will I have to look into. If this is a percentage-based opportunity, how much of a cut are we looking at? When I do have to physically engage with the business, is it possible to do it electronically, or is it something I will physically have to be there for?

The finance section breaks down into five different types of income that any one person is capable of. For myself, I am only interested in the last two. We'll discuss those sections in a moment.

The last section on the filter is health. I will ask myself, "How is this going to affect my personal health?" I devote a lot of time and energy into maintaining myself on multiple levels. This takes a certain amount of time commitment every day. How will this opportunity cut into my time, or is it going to force me to change my self-maintenance, work, and fitness schedule around it?

Additionally, what kind of people am I going to be interacting with? What are their personalities? If I am seriously considering this business with Bob, I may ask him to meet and spend some time, and I may also want to meet all the other personalities that are involved with the endeavor.

One toxic personality can destroy the whole deal for me. One bad apple in the barrel will make the whole barrel go bad, in my opinion. I have lived this several times in my life, and it is very important to choose the people you're going to be involved with, especially in business. Business can be a harsh environment sometimes, it has been my experience that if I am involved with someone who does not have the personal power, intestinal fortitude, and ethics needed to make it through the hard times, then it's just not worth it. That one bad apple will create more damage than just the failure of the business. One of these potentially catastrophic incidents will be paid for with more than just money.

All of this I will take into consideration before even giving Bob an hour of my time to discuss the opportunity. Using this filter, I have cleaned up the use of my time on a daily basis tremendously. I have also found that I am achieving much more with less time. And overall, it keeps me going in the proper direction of life.

The Finance Filter

This is not a finance book, but I wanted to go through some basic information on the finance filter since we did not do it previously. Again, this is a simplistic look at it. Keep it simple on the front end so that I have the ability to run through the filter fairly quickly to make the decisions necessary on the spot going through each day.

Sometimes these decisions will happen fairly quickly, and opportunities will come up in conversations or business meetings and will be presented as a potential option. If the option makes it through this, you can always do a deep dive into everything afterward to work out the finer details.

Here are the different options in the filter;

Income by the hour
Income by the event
Income by percentage
Income by network

I was introduced to this small list in my 30s by one of the men that I talked into mentoring me in money and business. This list consists of four ways you can create revenue streams. The first one is pretty much where everyone starts. You get paid by the hour. So you exchange one hour of your life for a certain amount of money. This seems like a positive exchange if you are to the point in your life or you have lots of life to give away. One of the ways my mentor introduced me to this concept was by asking me what I was making per hour. I told him I was making $20 per hour. He smiled and asked me if I was sure that's what I was making. That seemed odd to me because I remember negotiating the price with my boss, and I was pretty sure that's what I was making every week.

He explained to me that I only made that money in consideration for the hours I gave away. The reality is if I work an eight-hour day, and I make $160. That $160 should be divided into the entire 24 hours of the day. He explained to me this is actually what I was making per hour for that day. So the hard reality after doing the math was I was making $6.60 an hour.

Then he challenged me again, and he said, "Do you work on the weekends too?" My answer was no. He told me to add up what I made each week. And then divide it into 168 hours of life I had available each week. I did the math again and then laughed as I told him I made $4.76 per hour. He told me we could go deeper into this by calculating the entire month or even the entire year.

Additionally, he said, "And you know we haven't even had a discussion about paying taxes or retirement." The more times I did the math, the worse it got. He told me that the only way to increase this amount would be to create additional revenue coming in through other means. But at the time, the only options were to get another job that would consume more hours each day. I soon realized that if I sold my life per hour, there's no way I would ever be able to get the hourly rate up. This was when he introduced the second level of potential income.

Next on the list as income by the event. An example of this for me would be teaching a Brazilian Jiu-Jitsu seminar. Usually, those seminars will be somewhere between three and four hours long and will pay up to around $3000.

Another example of this would be doing a tile job on a bathroom. It is a one-time event that will pay you a sum of money. You might have to invest a few more hours, but this job may also pay you more money. Obviously, the more money per hour, and the more times I could do this, would influence what I was bringing in over the course of the month or the year. But the trick is I still have to have it coming in at a consistent pace. An additional drawback is that this is something I have to do physically, so travel is involved, and since most of the seminars are taught on weekends, it would consume my free time if I had such a thing.

One additional thing that I had to consider was if I'm doing a pay-by-the-job concept, how would I multiply myself as I moved into the future? Would I be able to train someone with the skills needed to take my place. Let's take into consideration the Brazilian Jiu-Jitsu seminar idea. This will take a tremendous amount of time and effort to get an individual to the point where they could produce a quality product.

So the idea of multiplying myself inside of this business concept would be very difficult. This is something that is very important to keep as part of the decision-making process in the financial area of the master filter. Does the concept you're looking at have the ability to be easily reproduced? Or is it based on your individual personality and not the product, just making it even harder to multiply outside of yourself?

These ideas can look very appealing in the beginning. I have seen many entrepreneurs get stuck in these types of business models, never realizing the difficulty of expanding until after they had already created the business.

The next section was a percentage-based income. There are many different ways to arrange or set up a percentage-based income. Investments and building businesses are just a few. He taught me that what I was looking for in the "percentage by" section was revenue streams that did not require much if any, time investment (life units).

Some businesses you can create, and you get a revenue percentage, but you are spending a tremendous amount of time (freedom) in that business, so it consumes much of your life as well. Now, the percentage may be worth the exchange, and that is something you have to take into consideration. But my mentor told me that if you have many opportunities and can weigh them out, you want to go toward the ones that give you a high percentage of income with a low physical time involvement.

He explained that the more life units you have available in a day or in any given week, the more opportunity to create additional revenue streams you will have. Your time and focus are what allow you the ability and the opportunity to create new revenue streams. You don't want to give away the remaining time. You have to focus your creative energy on creating or investing. He told me that more of these opportunities will move into investments that create a return and not consume freedom as I got older.

Next is income by a network. I have seen the biggest examples of this in my tactical training business. Teaching for law enforcement agencies and military groups is difficult to get involved with. It is a closed system, and if they don't know you, they generally do not do business with you. I saw this immediately in this business.

The more people I knew, and the deeper the relationship with those individuals, the more opportunities and more money I made. It's not that the product was not good, but generally, that was not what closed the deal on the work I did. This is a very powerful principle. Building a network around your business is a huge influence on the success of that business.

The ABCDE Method

Often, when I put a potential group of tasks through the master filter, the ones that survive the filter will generally go through a prioritization method to create a do-list for the day. The one I have grown to use over the years is the ABCDE Method.

I have used many different systems but what made this one float to the top was its simplicity. I did not need a fancy planner or any type of specialized organizer to use it. I can sit down with my notepad and a pen in the morning and get my day organized in under ten minutes. Afterward, I will have a list of the things that I absolutely have to finish for the day. I will have an additional list of things that I should do if the time is available, as well as the third list of things that would just be nice to do but not absolutely necessary. Here is a basic explanation of the parts of the system;

A - Must do
B - Should do
C - Nice to do
D - Delegate
E - Eliminate

An **A Item** is a task that I absolutely must get done that day. Generally, it is a major step to achieve a goal. If there is more than one A Item that is going to be on the list, I generally call it an A2 or A3. For myself, I generally will never have more than three in a day. Not to say I haven't had days with a larger list, but on average, I will achieve about three of these on any given day. And items sometimes require overtime. In other words, if I don't get them done in my normal working hours, it is common that I will stay over and keep driving until I finish them.

A **B Item** is something that will not have a drastic effect if I do not get it done today, but it would be nice to get it off the list. This might be something that will turn into an A item later in the week, but it is not immediately pressing on the current day.

A **C Item** is just an item that would be nice to get done today. There are no consequences if I do not accomplish it. Most of the time my C Items end up on the next list, which is the delegation list.

A **D Item** something that I can delegate. Sometimes I come across many things that are on my list that I can have someone in my office do for me. It might even be something I could hire somebody to do, just afraid of my own time for things that only I can achieve.

Sometimes there are things on my list that I don't even realize I can delegate somewhere else. I have put things on my daily routines and have done them for years, never stopping to consider that it may be something I could pass along to someone else. Then one day, I finally wake up and realize, "Do you know Steve could do this for me? I'm gonna have a talk with him and have him add it to his schedule."

Delegation & Elimination Review

After having the above wake-up call on delegation, I started making it a point to set a section of time aside once a month to look back at the items that were on the list that I created. What I was looking for were the items that could be delegated. Sometimes while you were busy with your head down, working on something, you don't take time to look at your approach with a 1000 mile view.

So I would take this delegation review time once a month and take a hard look at everything to determine what I could pass off to create more freedom. This created such a huge difference in my schedule that I started to also set aside an entire day every six months just to focus on this. It has been one of the most productive things I have ever done with my schedule.

An **E Item** is something that you can completely eliminate from your list. It may be something you're still doing out of habit, but once you sit down and take a look at it, you realize that it has no bearing on achieving your goals. Sometimes these items can be difficult to let go of just because they have become such a habit.

Elimination is something I also added to my monthly and annual review. I had sat down before, and looked back at the items on my do-list, and surprised myself at the things I had been doing for the last month that were absolutely unnecessary.

At the time, I may have thought they were essential, but having the opportunity to sit down and look at it from the perspective of the thousand-mile view or the big picture, I realized otherwise. I just had to take the time to stop and look at what I was doing.

Once you have your list, it is important to remember that you should absolutely finish the high-priority task first. Don't go onto a B item if you still have an A item unfinished. Learn to shut out distractions and gain the ability to focus your intent and energy on completing your most important task. Distractions are the biggest time vampires that will creep into your day.

With electronics set up the way they are, it has become increasingly difficult to remove these time-sucking creatures out of your life. Examples of these enemies of progress are notifications on your phone or computer like email, messenger comments, Facebook notifications, text, and notifications from meaningless apps. You have to take the time and learn how to turn all of these things off, especially during your designated time of creation every day.

The Power Of A Designed Routine

What is routine?

Routine can loosely be defined as a regular course of procedure, a habitual or mechanical performance of an established procedure.

I have used the power of routine to great benefit in my life. Most of my routine started out as my attempt to create a daily habit that was designed around one of my overall goals. As I started to consistently do this, it became gradually easier. At this time, I started to connect other daily training or tasks to the already established daily routine.

One of the businesses I have designed and run over the years was Iron Dog Association Design. It is a business that will design, build and operate international organizations for high-level martial artists.

Like any business you start, in the beginning, you are the janitor all the way up to the CEO. You end up doing everything. One of the tasks I had to do on a weekly basis was the social media marketing for each of these associations. I would usually do this routine on Monday morning. I had to educate myself on how to do some of the areas in social media marketing.

Once I had learned something new, I would add it to my routine. In the beginning, that Monday morning routine took me about four or five hours to accomplish. It never really changed much. It was pretty much the same thing every Monday. It's just one of those things that someone has to do. After about six months, I noticed that what was taking me four hours in the beginning had now condensed down to one hour. I was accomplishing the same amount of work in 1/4 of the time.

This was great because, as a business owner, there's always more you can do. But instead of adding other tasks, I decided to learn new social media marketing skills and then add those new skills and tasks to my Monday morning advertising routine. When I added them to the routine, it filled the time back up to a four-hour time slot. Personally, I thought this was great because I was getting much more done with the same amount of time. This, in turn, produced great results for my customers.

"Success is neither magical nor mysterious. Success is the natural consequence of consistently applying basic fundamentals."
— E. James Rohn

As I continued forward, the same thing happened again. What once took four hours now took about two hours. This was about a year into the building of this particular routine. I decided to do the same thing. I sought more information on marketing, learn the related skills and then add them to my Monday morning routine. And I was back up to four hours. In this cycle, it took even less time.

Within four months, I was back down to a three-hour routine. Over the course of time, I had condensed nine hours of work into three. This was amazing to me, I've always been a hustler, so the fact that I could increase my efficiency like this was incredible. I had initially designed a routine around a goal.

Over time, and by regular repetition, I learned how to condense that routine down to a shorter time while maintaining the same level of performance. And then continued on to add additional items to that routine cycle.

"The secret of your future is hidden in your daily routines."
— Mike Murdock

I have gone back and changed a few things inside that routine many times. Through study and research, I found better ways to do certain tasks in the routine. This would save more time and more effort.

I have continually polished that Monday morning marketing routine to the point of maximum results. In the process of doing it, it has become an ingrained habit. This is the power of routine. Especially a designed, polished routine.

Power of Consistency

Consistency - steadfast adherence to the same principles, course or form. When looking at this definition, the first word that stands out to me is *steadfast*. In other words, regular, steadfast consistency.

Repeatedly doing something consistently over time. It is human nature to want to create great change in a short amount of time. We may set a grandiose goal for ourselves, tell ourselves we're going to start the next day, and then within a week, we start looking for a change in whatever area we are working in. It's not that this could not happen, it is entirely possible, but the majority of the time, it is not common.

Most of us have lives, a family, a job. Some of us are building and designing businesses, so we have a limited amount of time. But the truth is that even with a small amount of time available daily, or even every other day, we can still create great change. And like I mentioned above, even with that short amount of time, with a polished routine, eventually, we're going to get more and more done.

Doing this, daily, weekly, is powerful. The struggle with this is just knowing that it's not all going to happen at once. It's going to be small changes that may happen over months or years. But it is important to know. It will happen.

I have experienced this over the years on the academy floor. Sometimes my weekly routines get so crazy that I'm only able to get in an hour or two a week of training. I would generally break up my training into different areas, and I will plan out what I'm going to do on Monday.

So I will say I'm going to get some grappling in for two hours on Tuesday and then again on Thursday. Additionally, I'm going to do an hour of kickboxing on Mondays and Wednesdays. And on Fridays, I'm going to do about an hour of Filipino Kali, which is various types of weapon training.

"Success isn't always about greatness. It's about consistency. Consistent hard work leads to success. Greatness will come." - Dwayne Johnson

There have been times when I have fallen into this routine for years. It just becomes something I do, and there have been times when I did not ever see or notice the benefit until I would get a visitor that would come in and want to train. So, in other words, someone who was outside my routine, usually a good friend or a peer, would come into town and visit, wanting to spend some time training.

We would set a time and then get together and get started. Usually, I would get a comment from my partner in regards to my growth in a certain area. They would ask me what I have been doing in order to improve or change my game. I would think to myself, you know I really haven't been doing that much. Only average about 2 to 4 hours a week. I know I've got guys in the academy in their 20s who will come in and spend six-hour days doing the same thing all week long. So I really didn't look at those 2 to 4 hours as very impressive. I realized that I have been doing that for almost six years. And after my friend had pointed it out, I began to notice the difference myself.

Things that normally took more effort to achieve seem to come easy. I never really looked at what I did as a great effort. I actually considered it to be very little. But what I didn't realize was that I had done it consistently over all of those years. And I realized that it did seem easy to me. This was very cool because it did not seem to burn me or my weekly routine to get it done. I realized that I didn't have to have a tremendous amount of time devoted to something in order to improve. I could just set aside a small amount of time on a daily or weekly basis.

Make it a routine, and then do it consistently. The change will come and grow like a tree. You can plant a seed and water it. It may be a year or two before anything even comes out of the ground. But by the time the tree pokes up through the dirt, it has already grown an extensive root system. Once it is exposed to the light, it begins to grow even faster. Boom, now the tree is an overnight success!

Routine Task Stacking

We actually spoke about the power of task stacking previously when we were discussing marketing. Some of the things that you have to accomplish on a daily basis will be similar, and you will have the opportunity to put them together in a routine series. I have always referred to this as routine task stacking.

As we have seen, if you put a routine together and you do it consistently over time, you're going to improve with your proficiency in that routine. The better you get at it, the less time it's going to take to go through the routine for the series of tasks. It is easier if all of the tasks are generally similar or in the same area. Very much like the marketing routine, we talked about earlier.

If you are not used to building routine into your daily schedule, you can start with something really simple. Combine two simple chores that are similar and start to do them routinely for a while. With repetition, this will eventually start to turn into an autopilot habit. Once it reaches this point, you can start to add on additional tasks to the routine. Don't be in too big of a hurry to build a too demanding routine in the beginning. Take your time and put them together a piece at a time.

If you've never put together a routine, I would generally suggest doing so by going through your master filter. Pick one of the areas from the master filter, and then design a routine that will help you move along your path to your objective. For instance, say you pick out health as the first category to build a routine. There are several possibilities of building a healthy routine, like going to the gym or improving your diet. Determine what area you want to make an improvement in, decide the actions you want to take in your routine, and then get started.

Remember, keep it simple to get started, and just do it consistently until it starts to become a natural part of your day. You can always add on additional changes once it starts to get ingrained in your nervous system.

Routine Cues

For myself, I have always relied on visual cues that I place around my common areas to signal me and help me remember when to do different routines. It can be a simple post-it note on your computer screen or mirror at home. I have just a list that I kept in my office. I have even purchased certain photographs that remind me to do certain things and place those in various places around my frequented areas.

Daily Themes

Some of your chores that are similar can be connected in a series to save time. I have used this to study multiple martial arts as well as build and run multiple companies. In the martial arts culture, I would assign different areas of training on different days. Something similar to this:

Monday: Grappling
Tuesday: Striking into pummeling
Wednesday: Pummeling to Takedowns to Grappling
Thursday: Striking
Friday: Weapons

In my business, it might look something like this:

Monday: Marketing & Management
Tuesday:
Wednesday: Marketing / Advertising Development
Thursday: Product development and business growth
Friday: Customer Communications

Choosing daily themes has helped me track and achieve greater amounts of work during my normal week. It also gives an opportunity to change up the area that I'm working in from day to day, which helps keep things fresh. I will place the above blocks of time throughout the week in a different part of the day. It is important to remember that you want to set aside time that is free in order to handle those little things that will come on a day-to-day basis.

I will also set aside time for self-education and study. I will usually pick topics throughout the year that are aligned with the goals I'm working on currently. Always understanding the principle of you don't know what you don't, I will use these times to dig deeper and seek greater information on these topics in areas.

In addition to these weekly themes, I'll also set up floating theme days throughout the year. For example, I may schedule a range day every three weeks throughout the entire year. Usually, on this day, I will go through all of the additional training that is connected to this topic. The range is just part of the total theme for the day. Additionally,

I will have certain days that will happen every quarter of each year. Usually, when I start setting my year up, I will put these days in around scheduled training or business events that are already on the calendar.

Electronic Distractions

Over the years, technology has developed to an incredible level. Someone on the other side of the planet can type a few words into the phone, and instantly it is sent to you on your device or your computer. You can be immediately accessible at any time.

This is not always a good thing. For myself, when I set aside time to study or write, I generally try to create an environment where I am electronically unreachable. I turn off the electronic leash. I don't get text, emails, and phone calls nothing. It seems to have become part of the culture to allow these little interruptions. You might not even realize that your attention and focus are being pulled away from what you're doing at the moment and redirected onto little things that may not be as important as what you're doing.

I have had this happen many times. Fortunately, I was able to recognize it and start making little changes to avoid it. Your time is one of the most valuable things you possess. And the thing about time is it will pass quickly. How often have you recognize that the years have passed and they have done so a little quicker than you realize.

How often have you heard the words 'where has the time gone?' It is important to recognize this and to gain control of your time or units of life. And after gaining this control, having the ability to focus where it needs to go in on the things that you need to focus on. Just a small adjustment to your daily schedule will have a huge effect on what you're able to accomplish on a day-to-day basis.

"Work is hard. Distractions are plentiful. And time is short." - Adam Hochschild

One of the best changes I've made in my daily schedule was only addressing email twice a day. I have a specific time set aside where I will answer email. This kept me from constantly picking up the phone and looking every few minutes because of a notification that would pop up.

When I set up this daily change, one of the first things I did was turn off notifications for emails as well as text. I will tell people close to me and in my inner circle that if they need my immediate attention to call me.

Generally, I choose who is around me on a daily basis. The people who are in your inner circle will have a tremendous influence on you and your life. So I choose them wisely. So imagine that I am having a conversation with someone in this group, and the phone pings me for a text. Many times I've seen this happen in different conversations, and the person will pull the phone out of the pocket and break his focus on who he is talking to and be redirected to the electronic device.

This breaks the interaction between you and the person you were having a discussion with. The text may be meaningless, and it just interrupted your conversation with the individual that is standing right in front of you. This is another good reason to turn off those notifications and set a time to address them later on.

3.
ENVIRONMENTAL DISCIPLINE

My first introduction to environmental discipline was from my mom. She would say, "Show me your friends, and I can show you your future." I did not quite understand the wisdom in this phrase at the time, but I did see its truth later in life.

Environmental discipline is basically you taking control of your daily surroundings. It is taking the time to take a look at how and where you live every day and then make changes to it in order to align with your desired goals and future.

Everything around you can have an influence on you, whether you realize it or not. It can affect your

206

opportunities and the decisions you make. It can affect your attitude and your ability, and your energy levels. It can affect your stress levels and your ability to relax. It will affect your habits and your ability to maintain the good ones and get rid of the bad ones. Your physical fitness and your diet. Everything can have a bearing on your journey in life.

In my experience, your environment is one of the things you can immediately adjust, and it will begin to make a difference on where you are going in life. Sometimes changing your environment is easier than changing yourself. Even small adjustments here and there will get things moving in the right direction.

You are a product of your environment. So choose the environment that will best develop you toward your objective. Analyze your life in terms of its environment. Are the things around you helping you toward success - or are they holding you back? - W. Clement Stone

Blessing in pandemic disguise

In 2020 the world experienced the COVID-19 virus. I had never experienced anything like this in my life. It seemed to affect everything and everyone. The virus was spreading worldwide, and in an effort to slow the speed, the government implemented a shelter in place order everywhere. Businesses shut down. People were told not to come to work and attempt to work from home.

Grocery store shelves were emptied out within days. It seemed like the world shut down along with the economy. People were told that you could not go any closer to another person than 6 feet if you did go out. We were told to wear masks in fear of catching the virus. The streets were empty on the few occasions I would go out for supplies. Within 30 days, this virus affected everything and everyone.

In my business, due to the nature of the industry (martial arts), we were told to close our doors until further notice. When this happened, all of my peers started making online video platforms for their students as well as having live classes.

Video training became the only option for them to deliver their services to their students. They all seemed to be in a mad scramble to get this done. Many of them told me that they were working harder and longer than when the doors were open. Not to mention they were more stressed out from the entire event. It was unclear to everyone when the academies, as well as other businesses, would be allowed to re-open to the public, so no one really knew what kind of financial hardship this was going to create.

When the academy closed, I decided to drive up to the VA mountains and spend some time with friends and clear my mind. From what we were being told by the government, we were going to be completely shut down for at least a month to a month and a half.

The place I ended up in was in a small town surrounded by the Shenandoah mountains.

The house where I was staying was on a small mountain where the sun would come up over a distant mountain right outside the front door in the morning, and at night I would watch it go down behind another distant mountain from a sunroom on the other side of the house. This sunroom had many windows all the way around and always seemed to be full of light and energy.

The family that lived at the house was a blessing of high energy and positive attitudes. It was a practice in this house to sit as a family at the dinner table every day for lunch and dinner. Additionally, they were very health conscious. They would make raw juice in the morning, and every meal was prepared clean with health in mind.

Since everything was shut down, there was nothing I could do with the academy. At the same time, all of the martial arts seminars and speaking events were canceled for the next few months because of the impending virus. Even worse for me was the local gyms were closed.

Now, if you knew me, you would know I have not missed a day of training in many, many years. Everything was shut off, and due to this, I was completely free. My schedule suddenly was full of nothing. Now I did think about doing the videos for the students like many of my peers were doing. But I saw an opportunity. I had the ability to completely change everything in my environment and routines for the next few months. So I took a different route.

The first few weeks, I just relaxed and focused on clearing the mind and decompress. I kept my contact with the outside world very limited, so I did not have a lot of noise coming in. I started to put more time into my morning routine, adding a few more motivational points of input and some business-related audiobooks. I started to increase my focus and time that I committed to my morning breath and mind work. I had an app on my phone that played binaural tones. I picked the one for creativity and would listen to it when I would do my morning routine. I completely reprogrammed the first half of my days.

I had been contemplating a few new business ideas for the last year and did not really seem to make any progress on what I wanted to do, so I thought I would just try to pick a direction with my time. I would end up sitting in the sunroom and focusing on this for a week or so.

The environment and everything about it seemed to relax and calm me and my mind. After a few days of contemplation, I decided where I was going to go with my business choices, and I started writing this book. I had spent 40 continuous years searching, studying, and training in multiple martial arts, defensive tactics, eastern meditation, and medicine. The experience had wired me for a lifetime of personal growth and achievement. I had been able to share this with a small group of my students at the academy and through the associations, I help run, but I wanted to reach more people. I wanted to help more people.

Now I was never much for writing. I had made multiple curriculums for the arts and took thousands of pages of notes. But when it came to just put an article together for a magazine, I would struggle with it. My daily schedules were always very tedious and busy, so having time to sit down and focus on writing never really seemed to work out.

But after being immersed in this new environment, my mind seemed to loosen up, and the information started to flow. The words just started coming out and onto the page. I did not even realize what had happened until after a few weeks of writing, I looked up, and it hit me. My new environment had created the conditions for creativity and change. Mentally, all of those little daily worries and distractions that normally came from the businesses I ran were put on hold.

Due to the pandemic shut down, I knew everything was just put on hold for the next month or so, so all those distractions were silenced in the consciousness. Even my daily fitness routine was put on hold because all of the gyms, parks, hiking trails, everything was closed. My time and energy were completely freed up.

I had made a massive change in the environment, and that adjustment created more positive change and growth. The light bulb did not only come on. It got smashed on my forehead. After thinking about what had happened, I realized that I had had this kind of thing happen several times in my life up to this point. At the time, I was just so busy living and reacting to life that I did not understand what had happened. But even those times made sense to me now.

Usually, this type of environmental change is triggered by an unwanted life challenge. Imagine if we could actively choose to make this type of change in our life now. We may not be presented with an opportunity where the whole world shuts down, but we can take an intelligent look at our day-to-day environment and decide how to construct small changes over time, eventually creating the surroundings and conditions we choose.

Now, how can we take this knowledge and make a powerful change in your life? First, let's take a look at the areas you can make changes in.

PEOPLE

Right back to the words of Mom; "Show me your friends, and i can show you your future." It's an easy thing to say but an entirely different thing to do sometimes. Regardless, it is one of the most powerful things you can adjust to in your daily environment.

At one period of my life, most people that happened in my life did so on a whim or coincidence. The only exception was in the world of martial arts. And that, like other lessons, was where I learned the power of choosing the people in your life. I knew I wanted to be a teacher of the arts from a young age. I also knew I wanted to be one of the best.

Most of my teachers, however, never really pushed me to go out and research other arts or other teachers. Sometimes it was even looked down upon. Then in the early 90s, I met Sifu Francis Fong in Atlanta, Georgia. Sifu Fong is a teacher of Wing Chun Kung Fu. But Sifu was unique in that he had an expression of his system that was like nothing I had ever seen in Wing Chun. He was not hesitant to explore other systems and add that information into his training. There were times he would flow from system to system when he was teaching.

I asked him about this one day, and he told me that I should be studying other systems and searching for new knowledge. He introduced me to Guro Dan Inosanto (Filipino martial arts master), Ajarn Chai Surachai Sirisute (Muay Thai master), Sensei Erik Paulson (creator of Combat Submission Wrestling), Professor Jean Jacques Machado (Brazilian Jiu-Jitsu master), Ajarn Greg Nelson (Muay Thai master), and Master Bob Byrd (Judo master).

I was able to get to know these people personally over the years and was immersed in the cultures of their given arts. I decided to move to Atlanta to be closer to Sifu Fong and all he had to offer. It was here I met Sifu Steve Grantham at the academy, and through him, I met Master Pedro Sauer and Master Rickson Gracie. Sifu Grantham also spoke for me to enter the Inosanto Instructor Association, which was a huge step for me. From there, I went on to meet Coach Justo Dieguez, Tuhon Tim Waid, Professor Nicolas Saignac, Professor James Cravens, and Grandmaster Dana Miller.

'You are the average of the five people you spend the most time with.' - Jim Rohn

These men are considered some of the best in the world at what they do. I still think it is incredible to be able to train with all of them. From my involvement with this group of people, I have trained and grown to levels in the arts that I would never have comprehended 40 years ago. I have been given the opportunity from these relationships to operate my school in Atlanta and start a business that designs and runs some of the international organizations for some of the men mentioned above. I could go on for a few more pages listing the incredible opportunities that have been placed in front of me because of these people. Now along with that way, yes, there were individuals that created more drama and havoc than good. They were the ones that seemed to always be surrounded by disarray.

They always seem to be needing something or taking something, never really putting positive energy in, only taking it out. Of equal importance to the above list of people is the fact that I removed those draining personalities out of my network. Just one of the these bad eggs can cause tremendous damage to your journey. If left unchecked, even ignored, they still seem to be a drain on you. I'm sure you have experienced these types of personalities yourself.

Once I see the possibility of this, I applied it to the rest of my life. I have learned that it is tremendously important to choose who is in your inner circle and to guard it vigorously once you do. Placing the wrong person close to you can have a tremendously negative effect if their true colors and character come out eventually. This makes me think of a quote from Jim Rohn: "You are the average of the five people you spend the most time with." The people around you can greatly influence how you think, your attitude. They can affect how you act and ultimately how successful you are in life.

So, if we come back and consider your goal, generally, once you have it in mind, you can take a look and see who the people that are currently doing the same thing or are aligned with that same goal are. I usually start with my current network of people that I know.

Eventually, I may get introductions to additional people who are working in the same direction, either currently or they are in a position that is aligned with my goal. Sometimes it may be as simple as developing a relationship. Other times, much like when I moved to Atlanta in order to train with Francis Fong, you may have to completely change your environment.

It is a drastic change, but sometimes that is what it takes, so it depends on your level of commitment to obtaining what you desire. This makes me think of a quote from Tony Robbins: "It takes massive action to create change." It may come down to whether or not you were willing to take the leap. Take the chance. So, how can we survey our current personal community and make some changes?

So here is an exercise for you:

Consider one of your days, a 24-hour segment of your life. Just as Jim has suggested, who is in that inner circle of five people? Grab a notebook and take note of the top five people you spend the most time with during that 24-hour period. Right away, I'm guessing it's going to be your spouse, coworkers from work, and some of your best friends. Put them down on your notepad.

Once you have your list, you can sit down and take a look at it and ask yourself, who are they? What are they currently doing with their lives? How successful are they? How driven are they? What is their level of ambition? What kind of energy do they give off on a daily basis? Are they generally happy? Did they give you positive energy?

When you discuss new ideas with them, maybe a business idea that you were thinking about...do they support you or did they tell you "that will never work, man," "you will never be able to pull that off." I have heard this myself many times in my life, up until the point the deed was done. Then everyone would whistle, "I knew you could do it all along." It was a good lesson. I realized just how much the naysayers' opinions are really worth. Also, it was very surprising that a lot of these voices would come from members of my family, some of who were very close to me. Learning this took all of the power out of those voices moving forward.

I also learned to turn off the non-action-taking naysayers and only listen to the action takers. Michael Hyatt said, "Never take advice from people who aren't getting the results you want to experience." In other words, the people that are taking action and are getting results. One other very important point I learned in regards to this philosophy is this: Don't be fooled by someone's position or status. Don't be impressed by status, be impressed by results!

Once you have your list, take the time to sit down and look at what you have. You may make a choice to continue spending time with some and not others. It doesn't mean you have to cut them off entirely, but you may consider how much time you spend or invest with each one each day.

You may cut your list down to two people, and that is okay. As difficult as it may sound, don't be afraid to lose some of your personal community or friends. Especially if those losses mean you end up surrounding yourself with the right people, the right achievers who are aligned with where you're going and your goals in life.

I believe it took me longer than normal to realize this concept. At least to realize it outside of the Martial Arts. As I mentioned above, I took the time to choose who I spent time with inside my career. I went to great lengths to place myself in the same environments as some of the best in the industry.

I chose to spend more time with individuals who had achieved and achieved the results I was looking for. But outside of that, in my personal life, I did not invest as much time and energy and choosing wisely. This is something that I have spent a lot of time correctly lately. Even the small investment I have put into it in the last few years has made a considerable difference.

SOUNDS / AUDIO / VISUAL

When it comes to sound, for me, there are two things to take into consideration when you are starting to take a deeper look at your environment and how you're going to condition it. One is what you eliminate, and the other one is what you're going to add to your daily routine. I usually will start with removing the negatives because the more you are able to remove negative audio inputs, when you do get around to adding the positives, they will have a greater effect.

Just as Sifu told me to do earlier in this book, one of the first things I suggest when I'm coaching someone in this area is to take a look at what their daily input is. What do their television habits look like? For me personally, I can't think of too many things on TV that are very constructive or beneficial. The news has become an opinion- and drama-based fear machine.

They present information as absolute reality when in fact, it is only small pieces of what is going on in the world, most of which has become based on personal or political opinions. And everything else I have seen, though it may be entertaining, it's pretty much just meaningless empty noise going into the mind.

I have watched television become a conditioned, sedentary habit for some. They get off work, go home and park their butt on the couch, tune out everything and turn into a thoughtless couch potato. They are bombarded with someone else's content as they sit there for hours and let it go into their minds.

When it gets down to actually making a positive change in my life, none of it has anything to do with moving me in that direction.

What do your radio habits look like? Do you have it on in the car when you get into it and then just ignore what is on the radio as you go about your business, or is it something you have chosen to influence positively? Since turning it off in the early 2000s, I probably have not turned on the radio in years. I met somebody who was very political-minded, and they turned me onto talk radio. I happen to agree with some of her beliefs, so when she suggested the radio station, I gave it a try. So I did agree with a lot of the information that was being discussed. What I didn't realize was that I was being drawn into the discussion.

Many times I would listen to this radio station when I was driving, and if you're familiar with Atlanta traffic, you can spend a lot of time driving. Without even realizing it, I started to get drawn into this conversation and get emotionally involved with it. There might be a topic that was discussed, and I will be connected to it, and by the end of the car ride, I would get out of the car and noticed that even though I had left that environment, I had brought the irritation with me.

This time I probably had listened to the station for about two years. Even when I realized what was happening, even after I got out of the car and had turned off that station, the information as well as some of the emotional involvement would stay with me for the rest of the day. And the interesting thing is most of the topics and the points that were made really had no effect on my life whatsoever. It was time to exercise the off button one more time.

What I found as I ended up going through the same mental cleansing process that I did when I was a teenager. Years ago when Sifu told me to shut off all of this information. Even after I had turned it off, it took a while to get the reaction to it out of my body. I would still have the urge to turn on the noise when I jumped into the car every day. It had turned into a trained physical habit to reach for the switch right when I jumped into the car.

It's strange when you intellectually know it is something you do not want to do, but then your body has an urge to move in that direction. It makes you realize just how quickly something like that can get ingrained into your system as a whole and the effects it can have on you.

So we discussed television and radio. Other things to take into consideration would be gossip. This can be directly connected to what we spoke about earlier, the type of people that you have in your inner circle. Our academy has a small office, and we have three individuals who are generally in the office throughout the day.

We have a set rule at the academy that there is absolutely no gossip spoken unless we are at lunch. It's funny because all three people in the office are hustlers and high-energy personalities. One of our lunch breaks can last about ten minutes. So even if gossip is brought up, it is generally brought up as a joke. Factual information is one thing, but gossip is something entirely different. The sad thing is some people don't know the difference between the two. In my experience, most gossip is just wasted time on nonessential information. Focusing on what other people are doing at a gossip level is a waste of time. Most gossip is created out of jealousy and is spread by the same motivation, all of which can create emotional garbage that does nothing more than consuming your available mental capacity.

These are just a few of the most influential areas to take into consideration when you are removing what can be called negative sound out of your environment.

One area that definitely cannot be left off this list is social media. Social media has a way of mentally pulling you into it. I am involved in social media, advertising for various organizations.

There have been many times that I will get on social media, either on the computer or my phone, in order to do my daily routine of advertising. And after a minute or two, I will find myself caught up in someone's endless timeline or some post that someone threw up that might've caught my eye. I will catch myself in the act, and then I will attempt to go on my way and do my work.

Low and behold, twenty minutes later, there I am doing it again. I almost have to laugh at myself sometimes. I have seen students come in the school that are so caught up in social media apps that you can walk up to them and say hello, and they won't even know you're there. Definitely a source of noise that is fed into your brain.

Since I do use Facebook for some advertising, one of the things I did was unfollow a lot of pages, groups, and people. I cleansed what I see when I open the app. I picked out a few pages that deliver content that was valuable and maybe motivational to me, as well as a few individuals that I wanted to keep in touch with. But I pretty much just narrowed down all of it to a few sources of information.

Even if I do entertain the timeline on Facebook, within four or five swipes with my thumb, I have pretty much seen everything from each one of the sources I had mentioned. And I'm finished. Each individual has their own habits when it comes to social media. It is important to slow down and take a look at what yours are and consider whether or not they are aligned with your goals and where you're going.

Video games

Video games are another form of input into your mental landscape, your consciousness. I have seen positive studies about gaming as well as negative studies. This was always a touchy discussion with a lot of my students due to the fact that it is a hugely popular pastime. I have read that more than 150 million people in the United States will play video games on a regular basis. The average time spent is a little over seven hours per week in the United States.

Regardless of the good or bad, it is another form of electronic input into the mind and in the consciousness. No doubt the effect will vary per individual, everyone is different, but in my experience, coaching high performers is definitely a mental distraction. The individuals I have coached came to me to learn meditation and improve the ability to focus.

Even though they eliminated a lot of the other distractions that we have discussed, a couple of them hung on to gaming out of what seems to be an addiction. They got to the point where unbeknownst to them, this additional input was creating a difficult internal landscape to manage.

Due to this, several of them made the decision to eliminate the habit in pursuit of higher levels of concentration and focus.

I personally have had two experiences with gaming. I've had friends that invited me over in order to play games in the gaming room. They had built out a room in the basement, and it was entirely devoted to gaming. They had a huge screen mounted on the wall as well as chairs that were specifically designed to allow you to feel motion. I would wear a set of headphones as well to improve the experience.

The one thing I remember was we started playing at about 5 PM in the afternoon. It felt like we played for about an hour, and then when I looked up, it was about four in the morning. I was amazed, it was an incredible experience, no doubt, but I had echoes of that game in my head for about three days afterward. Just from my experience alone, it was obvious that it wasn't going to be something I was going to add to my daily routine. I was already gifted or cursed, depending on how you look at it with a very active mind, so for me, this was just a no-go.

Once you have taken out the mental trash, you can start looking at various positive influences in your daily routine. Earlier in the book, we discussed binaural sound and how its different brainwave frequencies would determine our levels of alertness. Binaural sound can be used to improve sleep, improve your concentration, or relaxation. It can even affect your alertness and ability to focus. In addition, we also spoke about the universal frequency that Tibetan monks tune their singing bowls to and Mozart based his music on.

Sound and certain music can have a tremendous effect on your mood, clarity, and multiple other areas. You just want to choose what you're putting in wisely. Certain music can trigger pleasure centers in the brain that release dopamine, a neurotransmitter that makes you feel joyful and happy. Eighteenth-century classical music has been shown to do this as well as increase neuron function and affect your memory and your ability to focus.

I have taught this to the students at the academy for many years. Now the same information did not work for all of them over the years. But I will say each student did find what worked for them. So it is an area that is important to take into consideration when you're trying to discipline your environment.

I will use the binaural sounds in the morning during my morning routine. I'll turn them on when I am doing the breathing and focusing exercises that we have talked about earlier in the book. For me, it has a tremendous effect on these exercises because it helps control the audio input for your internal landscape during them.

Additionally, it is not uncommon for me to walk around with my phone headphones while preparing breakfast and getting ready to move on with the day. I usually keep it on the low-level input, so it just plays in the background. I will usually spend some time studying or writing in the morning, depending on the schedule. During this period, I will also use binaural sounds in the background of music to increase alertness or creativity.

To add this in yourself, there are many different devices on the market that you can purchase. One of the simplest ways I have found are phone apps. Simplicity is mastery.

Generally, in the beginning, if it's not simple, you are not going to do it. Having it on your phone is very convenient, and for most people, you will have it with you the majority of the day.

The one exception is using the Delta tones (less than 4 Hz) during sleep. I purchased stereo speakers and placed them on the other side of the bed so that I can play at a low level during the night. Earphones are not always comfortable while sleeping, and this allows me to mix the tones with some low-level brown noise as well.

Just as a reminder, the different frequencies were;

Beta (13 – 40 Hz) – Active, alert and focused
Related to the conscious mind

Alpha (8 -12 Hz) – Relaxed, calm, and creative
Theta (4 – 8 Hz) – drowsy, light sleep
Related to the subconscious mind

Delta (less than 4 Hz) – Deep sleep
Related to the unconscious mind

Sight & Light
Just as with sound, your visual intake can also have an effect on your internal landscape daily. Generally, there are

a lot of visual cues that you will experience throughout the day that are connected to various habits you may have as well. Your habits will turn into your future, good or bad.

It is important to design and build your habits because it is the little things you do on a daily basis that accumulate over time and integrate change. Just slowing down enough to recognize some of your habits is difficult at times. Sometimes you will have something ingrained in your body that you've done for years, and you may not even realize it until you slow down long enough to take a look.

I discuss this under sight because for myself visual cues initiate a lot of the positive habits I set for myself throughout the day. After a certain amount of time, you may not need those visual cues, but they work nonetheless. If you've ever invested time trying to develop a positive habit, you will know that it can be rather difficult to do. There are many times that I would see that visual cue and still not do what I'm supposed to do. All of this comes right back to the discussion of discipline.

Just on the topic of habits, I highly suggest the book *Atomic Habits* by James Clear. He presents a very clear and definite path for creating new and positive habits.

Visually, one of the things that has a tremendous effect on me is sunlight. I mentioned earlier in the book about the sunroom that I spent about five weeks in during the pandemic in 2020. I always think of this sunroom when I discuss the influences of sunlight. In addition, the office in my school has a huge glass window in front of my desk.

Fortunately for me, it is aimed in the best direction in order to experience the sunset at the end of every day. Sunlight and darkness can trigger the release of hormones in your brain. Your exposure to daily sunlight is thought to increase the brain's release of a hormone called serotonin. Serotonin is associated with boosting mood.

It is also thought to help you feel calm and focused. Darker lighting can trigger the brain to make another hormone called melatonin. Melatonin is commonly known to help you with improving sleep. A continual lack of exposure to sunlight over time can lower the levels of serotonin, which can lead to major depression. Exposure to sunlight causes your body to produce vitamin D.

It has been shown that vitamin D plays a huge role in bone health and development. Low levels of it have led to diseases like osteoporosis and rickets. One of the other areas that Sifu discussed was just the general clutter that I would have around me on a daily basis.

PLACES

Your surroundings have a huge effect on you every day. We have already talked about making adjustments to your sleeping environment. Now let's consider your waking hours.

Though it can be very subtle, the space you spend time in on a daily basis will have an influence on your psyche. Take your home, for instance. Have you ever noticed that some rooms just have a more inviting and positive feel? This may be influenced by the color of the paint or the amount of sunlight that is allowed into the room. It could be changed by the scent of the air.

For me, the amount of clutter that is in my living spaces has a direct effect on me. We discussed earlier the idea of reducing the amount of noise that is put into your conscious.

The points we addressed were inputs like the TV, radio, and social media. A chaotic or cluttered environment had the same effect on me. I never really paid attention to it previously before going through the training. And when I did start making those minor adjustments, the more changes I made, the more of an effect it had. It is not uncommon for the mind to become cluttered with thoughts, emotions, and other things.

This can be *amplified* by the amount of clutter you have around you. This is a major point that is studied in the art of Feng Shui. For myself, I have found that the more simple, uncluttered, and clean the environment, the more calming and relaxing it is. I just eliminated that which did not bring value to my life.

Obviously, this can vary per individual, but it is important to pay attention to how these things influence you. Most of the time, we don't slow down enough to even pay attention. As you gain more control of your consciousness, you will tend to notice these things more often. The good thing about it is you generally can make adjustments to these things to improve your environment. I have found that the small, subtle changes that I make in my personal environment have had a huge effect.

Quality Over Quantity

Have you ever noticed that they just don't make items like they used to? It seems like everything has become a cheap disposable thing. It has become hard to find high-quality anything on the market. As I began to eliminate many unused things in my space, I started to get down to some of the simple basics.

I started to look for high-quality, well-built materials and items to place into my space. Not only do these things last much longer, but they have more character and energy in them. For me, this has created a positive and quieter environment in my most commonly used spaces.

4.
YOUR PERSONPL EDUCATIONAL PROCESS

Part of a warrior's mindset and continuous growth is their self-education process. The teacher or mentor will merely show you the path to pursue the knowledge you seek. You can't solely depend on them to put it in your head. Of course, they're going to present you with information and make suggestions from their experience, but it's up to you to take that knowledge and process it in order to absorb *your* wisdom and experience from that journey. You have to discover *your* truth.

A proper self-education process will help you look past your current source of information, your teacher, their body of knowledge, or the institution they are connected to. It will remind you that there is always additional information, and there are always greater depths of that knowledge under the surface if you dig for it. It will help you create the proper mindset, attitude, and environment that is favorable to obtaining knowledge.

It will create learning environments where you can attempt to apply that knowledge in a safe way that is accepting to failure because we know failure is a powerful teacher. A solid self-education process will take you past the accepted standard of knowledge in any given area. That is why it is important to establish your own personal self-education process; a process that will help you look at any topic in greater depth and detail to get more knowledge and wisdom.

Knowledge and wisdom.

What is the difference between knowledge and wisdom? Both are connected but not synonymous. For me, knowledge is information or facts that people are aware of. Knowledge can be written in a book or be found online, in a classroom, it can be recorded. Someone can know a lot of information about a subject, and they will be considered knowledgeable of that subject.

A person can possess understanding or awareness about a subject, a thing, or a person. Knowledge can be obtained by studying, learning, and researching. A person can easily obtain more knowledge, but the pursuit of this knowledge does not guarantee wisdom. Knowledge can exist without wisdom, but the reverse generally is not true.

Wisdom, on the other hand, is the ability to make proper decisions. Wisdom is a quality that is gained through observing, experiencing, reasoning and living. Wisdom commonly comes from mistakes and the experience you gain from those mistakes. They do not necessarily have to be *your* mistakes. You can observe someone else making a mistake and gain wisdom from that observation.

I can still hear the words of one of my instructors, "Where do you think wisdom comes from son? It comes from fucking up!" What we want to do is learn how to make mistakes in an environment that does not produce elevated amounts of damage from doing so. This is the training academy for the warrior. The training hall is a laboratory, and you can create a laboratory around any subject or topic, allowing you an environment to actively pursue mistakes.

I am a huge proponent of maintaining continuous self-education throughout your life. A higher level of learning and education is associated with better mental functioning. Experts believe that continually learning may keep the memory strong and mentally active. This can become a habit if it is done continuously throughout life. Just as you challenge your body with physical exercise, it is important to challenge your brain with mental exercise or learning.

I will tell the students that I teach in the academy. It's important to be a perpetual student. Your daily life can sometimes become a series of routines. It's not uncommon to repeat these routines over and over today. These routines, after a certain amount of time, start to require less of your conscious mind, and they begin to be run more by the subconscious.

These are the little things you do every day that will sometimes feel like they take very little thought process.

They almost have become automatic, a habit. This is actually a good thing because when a routine is run by the subconscious, it will require less conscious energy. In other words, it needs less brain energy to get that thing done.

The drawback is it does not stimulate the brain as much as when you may have first learned to do those things. So just as we mentioned before, if you do not put the body under stress, if you don't have some sort of physical activity, your body starts to become soft and weaker.

The same concept applies to your mind. So building an educational process for yourself and then using it throughout your life to keep you sharp as well as help you avoid future mental decline as you age is a good thing. This will additionally improve your memory. It will enhance your ability to concentrate and to focus. It'll improve your capacity for critical thinking and your creativity.

"Self-education will make you a fortune."
— Jim Rohn

The study of a new topic is just one part of exercising your brain. It may introduce new thought patterns. It may force you to rethink your opinion on some things.

I have found that a study of one area will automatically connect me to studies of other areas in search of additional information and knowledge. But, we must apply the newly learned information. It will challenge the brain when you learn to move your body in ways that are not normal for you or think in patterns that are new. Ways that will be outside of your normal routine physically and mentally. This, as mentioned above, will force you to use your conscious mind. This is an exercise for the mind. It is important to try to engage as many of your available senses and view them outside of your normal habitual routines.

I was fortunate to have my involvement in the martial arts because they create this opportunity almost naturally, and they do it over and over again throughout your career. Of course, you're going to have things that you have learned and thus become fixed routines, they have become an ingrained habit, and this is good because we need those things to be ingrained in the nervous system when we are placed under stress in a combat situation. But the academy has a lifetime of mental and physical stimulation that will continually push you outside of your comfort zone.

One of the best systems I have seen for this is the art of Filipino Kali. Kali is probably most commonly known as a weapons-based system. In reality, it's one of the most vast and complete systems that exist in the martial arts world. Part of the training is learning new and various-sized weapons and then additionally learning to use them in different patterns of movement.

For instance, you may end up making a pattern with your right hand with a weapon of one size and then make an entirely different pattern with a smaller weapon in the other hand (such as knife-and-stick combo). All of this was stepping on a series of predetermined footwork. To say the least, it's a little bit of a challenge, but this is what is good about it.

Of course, not all of your new topics of study are going to lead you into moving around in training with weapon routines. But you can use the concept in anything you're doing. If you pick an area of study, try to also involve the different senses of the body in the study in some form.

Some of the examples of things I have done in the past would be obviously trying things I had never done before. You may pick up a habit, take a class that is completely out of character for you. It might be something as simple as switching the hand you brush your teeth with. But if you make that switch after a while, it will start to become routine and comfortable for the mind and the body. Realize that at this point, it is no longer beneficial in the way we are discussing, and it is time to try something new.

For those who know me, the idea of me taking a hip-hop class would be extremely out of character. That is one of the reasons I did it for a year. I have done the footwork for various martial arts for most of my life. So adding a new pattern of footwork was not very challenging for me. But going into an environment that was entirely different was a tremendous challenge. I had always moved my feet with the goal of getting something combative achieved.

I never really took into consideration how it looked to someone else, but the hip-hop class was entirely focused on appearance. Some of the patterns would have you move in one direction while you appeared to go in another. It was an incredible experience for me, which actually had a positive effect on the footwork that I applied in the arts.

My experience learning martial arts is different than most other people I've encountered. When beginning to study a new topic or seek information, the common process is to find a teacher or a mentor to study under. You follow in their footsteps and blindly consume the information they have to offer through articles, books, personal communication, classes, and workshops. People can learn a wealth of information through this process, but, in my opinion, it produces carbon copies of the teacher/mentor, therefore, limiting the capability of the individual to engage with and apply the information.

"Poor is the pupil who does not surpass his master."
- Leonardo da Vinci

I wanted to find another way to learn, a way to engage and interact with the information I was receiving. I decided to put together a provocation process.

This process would allow me to take information and consume it based on certain rules and principles that I would follow as I did so. When I would take in a piece of information, I would look at it initially, just as I learned it from my teacher. Then when I applied the series of principles I designed, I would have the opportunity to look at the information from different angles that I may not otherwise see.

Over time, my list of principles and study methods grew until I had a set of them, which I followed when I dove into a new source of information or tried to study a new skill set.

This educational process for me has many times forced me to learn more information at a higher level than what was presented to me initially. Sometimes it would force me to ask questions that I would not normally ask if I were just blindly following someone else's curriculum or guidance.

One of the first things on my list was the principle that simplicity is mastery.

Simplicity is Mastery

One of the best ways to teach someone nothing at all is to teach them too much. I have seen this many times over the years on the academy floor. We will have an overly anxious instructor who wants to give everything he has to the student in a given moment. He will go down a list of things and attempt to teach that student everything. After that instructor is finished with his attempt to instruct, many times, the student ends up just standing there with a blank stare. Completely and totally overwhelmed with so much information, they don't really know what the technique is, much less what to practice at that moment. They are frozen in information paralysis.

When you are self-educating, it is possible to actually do this to yourself. To attempt to seek out so many different angles and aspects of a topic that you end up not absorbing anything useful at all. In the martial arts, as a beginning student, I wanted to learn absolutely everything. I knew from a very young age that I was going to be an instructor, and I wanted to gain as much knowledge as possible.

And sometimes, after going through the big list of techniques that were required for any given art, I would find that I knew the list, but I did not really develop any true depth of understanding, wisdom, or application.

After continuing to train different systems for many years, I have found that almost all of them will boil down to a set of basic fundamental techniques and principles. This basic set of information may only equate to around 10% of the total system.

The thing is, when I look at high-level practitioners, I will see this same filtering down and the application of usable information

I see practitioners who are highly skilled at this small percent of a system, and they are very proficient with it to the point where they will go out on the academy floor, and they will outperform everyone with the basic knowledge they know. They have taken simple high percentage things and mastered them to the point where they are highly proficient with the method or art they do.

Since they took the time to boil down to the bare essentials or the fundamental basics, and they took those fundamentals and trained them consistently over time to a higher level. Sometimes even creating new drills and training methods around those basic fundamentals. In essence, they have simplified what they needed to train and obtain. Instead of creating a bigger list, they actually made it smaller. And making a list smaller, it has become more obtainable.

Since there was less, they had more time to create additional drills and spend more time focusing on intelligent training in creating good habits based on those fundamental ideas and techniques. In essence, they achieved more with less.

Once you have experienced this, as well as the benefits that come along with this simplification process, anytime you start the study of a new area or idea, we can remind ourselves of this learning and boiling down the process in advance. Before I ever begin with new information, I know that from the principle "simplicity is mastery," I will need to actively seek out those fundamental basics or fundamental principles that are in whatever art, system, or method I am looking to study.

Approaching it this way may even make me ask different questions of my teacher that I would not normally ask if I were not approaching it from this perspective. Many times I will seek out additional mentors and teachers that are available in the same area, and I will ask them all the same questions in an attempt to find out what those fundamental basics are. Most often, what you are looking for is your instructor's wisdom at this point. Information that he has found from years of experience and living the topic he is teaching.

If I can decipher this information in advance or at the beginning of the study and then focus my time more intelligently on developing them, I will be able to achieve greater things in less time. I will be able to train smarter and not just harder.

I have heard it explained that in a lot of areas of life, you would find there is a solid 20% that will produce 80% of the results. Using simplicity as mastery, it is our goal to seek out 20% initially. To recognize it early in our search or study of a new topic.

"Life is really simple, but we insist on making it complicated." - Confucius

One of the first things I learned when I started studying in the arts was a jab and a cross. Stances will vary in fighting, but generally, the body is turned sideways. In this position, one arm is more to the front than the other. Generally, a jab is a punch using the lead arm, and a cross is a punch using the rear arm. These two strikes can be considered some of the absolute basics you learn in striking.

When I was first taught the jab, I thought it was great. I wanted to learn many more striking methods. I knew there were many different ways to strike and many different combinations, so I was eager to get on with the list of what I thought was the advanced material. Instead, Sifu had me study this single strike for six months.

When he told me this is what I was going to do, I remember thinking to myself, *I already know this move, what am I going to spend six months on?* That six months turned into a lifetime. To this day, I still study this one move. What I discovered in that six months was this: there is a universe of knowledge that is hidden under the surface of those fundamental basics. We study details on that basic punching method that I had no clue even existed. The amount of depth that we covered in that short amount of time, now that I look back on it, was incredible. But, I had learned more than just the jab. My instructor taught me a learning process that was much more valuable. Always stop and take the time to search for the depth of knowledge under the surface.

Search For The Vast Depth in Simplicity

Now that we understand that we do want to keep it simple, and in the process, we know we have to focus on the fundamental basics of the area of study, we want to enter into that study knowing that there will be a vast depth of information underneath each one of those simple basics.

Keeping this rule in mind, it reminds us to search for this information. All too often, I see people who are concerned with learning "the list." Regardless of how long it is, they don't believe they are educated until they know everything on the teacher's list. They come away from it, having a lot of things in their head but nothing in their skill set.

This is what we want to avoid by finding those basics and looking for the depth of knowledge underneath them. We didn't take that knowledge and work it continuously over time to ingrain skill and gain the wisdom that comes from taking action.

Growing up, I had a good friend and training partner. Eric was a very driven and passionate person for his age. Due to the culture he and I grew up in, it was not uncommon to spend a lot of time sparring and fighting every week.

From this accumulation of action, we both would see that success comes down to a few basics that were performed well and at the proper time. During the 80s, it wasn't uncommon for members of other schools to visit your school and request to fight. It started becoming more *uncommon* in the late 90s, but during the 80s, it was something that was considered normal.

I remember one such instance when we had a visitor at the school who wanted to go rounds (fight) with everybody that was in the class that night. He began stepping up his intensity and taking advantage of some of the other guys who had less experience and time in. I remember sitting against the wall with Eric and watching this happen. We both agreed that the guy was pretty good. He had obviously spent a lot of time developing his game. Knowing that Eric was probably going to be up next, I asked him what his plan was.

He turned his head and smiled, and said I think I'll use a jab. I found this funny at that time because I knew that in the last week alone, we had thrown thousands of jabs. We had done different training drills on multiple pieces of equipment, working just this one punch. The behind-the-scenes years of work that create overnight successes.

And then it was time. Eric was the next one up. He goes out and lines up with the guy. They begin the match. Eric played it safe for the first minute or so of the fight, letting his opponent attempt different attacks, feeling him out for his timing and pace. And then at what I considered the perfect time to throw it.

He dropped that jab square in the middle of the opponent's face, and he immediately hit the floor and the fight was over. He had caught his opponent mid movement. In other words, he was halfway between moves. At this moment, he was off balance and more susceptible to the strike. The punch was delivered with no telegraph from the body and proper power. One basic technique, delivered at the right moment with trained proficiency.

With this in mind, we know we want to pursue our study seeking the fundamental basics. Once we have those basics, we know we want to focus on the depth of knowledge that is beneath the surface. In other words, we don't want to get caught up in all the fluff, all the additional noise that can be added to a thing. Have the ability to focus on what is important.

Sometimes this information is not always readily available. You will have to spend some time seeking the right instructor. In my experience, the individuals who possess this knowledge gain it out of doing. In other words, they have spent countless hours working consistently.

This process always produces a tremendous amount of wisdom from the trial and error process. Unfortunately, some of the individuals who possess it are not interested in sharing it. It may not be where they are on their journey, and that's okay.

It is our job to recognize that and seek out individuals that are willing to pass on what they have gained. It's one of the reasons why searching for a good teacher or mentor is so important.

"Simple things done right, and at the right time, wins fights...and most everything else." - Greg Nelson

No way as the way

Sijo Bruce Lee followed several philosophies in his training and his development of his system Jeet Kune Do(JKD). Many of these philosophies not only pertain to the development of his art and skill but also to other things outside of the arts.

One of the many that influenced me, especially in not only training but the development as a personal education process, regardless of what I was looking into, was Sijo's "Using no way as way, having no limitation as limitation."

Interpretations of this have been argued many times over the years ever since these words were uttered by Sijo. For me, this philosophy is extremely powerful, but I do believe the student has to begin firmly rooted in a good educational process. What I mean by that is if you are starting into a new topic, sometimes you do have to immerse yourself into the status quo. You're going to have to follow the preset learning path for any given thing.

The example I always used is learning to write. We all remember the three horizontal lines from school, the horizontal lines we had to write in between when learning to draw our letters. The middle line will be a dotted line, with the two outside lines being solid. After I draw this for my students, I ask them what they think it is. The most common response is, "this is a road."

I will proceed to draw the letter "A" on top of the lines. But when I do this, I will make the top and the bottom of the "A," then I'll go outside the lines both above and below. I will also usually make the letter excessively skinny. And I will top it off by not crossing the "A" where I am supposed to (middle and on top of the dotted line), but instead, I will do it down at the bottom of the "A." I am probably making everyone's obsessive-compulsive alarm go crazy right now.

As soon as I finish this, I will turn to the class to see a bunch of smiles, and they will get what the image originally was. At this point, I will ask the students how does my letter look? Do I pass the test? And I am usually hit with an onslaught of corrections from the entire class.

With their guidance, I will go on to eventually draw the letter correctly. Once I am finished, I will say, "Okay, if I were to have everyone in this class come up and draw this letter in the way that they do currently, in your own handwriting style, would they all look this way?" And the answer is, of course, "No." Everyone has moved on from this beginning point and learned to express themselves freely in their writing.

I use this example in order to show the importance of beginning your journey of education in any given subject with an organized structure. I believe Sijo Bruce Lee did the same thing himself. When he began the journey in the arts, he started by studying the different structured systems that were available to him. And he spent many years in pursuit of knowledge in these different systems.

But what made him so unique was that at a certain point, he decided not to be confined or bound by these systems. He instead freed himself and his mind in order to search for what worked best for him individually. He began to believe "all fixed and set patterns are incapable of adaptability or pliability." The truth is outside of all fixed patterns. The Living Creature, the Creating Individual, is

Always More Important Than Any Established System or Style.

Where he ended up was equally as important as where he began. We need to look at the entire process that brought him to where he was. In the beginning, he did seek out the established systems of education in the area he wanted to pursue.

He spent time in his education, developing himself, following the usual process as he grew his knowledge. He allowed his curiosity to guide him in testing the things that he had learned. He did not just blindly follow the knowledge. He got together with like-minded people and tried it out to see if it worked for him. He created his own laboratory to see what fit.

Out of this lab came truth and wisdom, and he listened to it and started making changes. He simplified processes by saying, "Adapt what is useful, reject what is useless, and add what is specifically your own." He sought a daily decrease, and he did not add just for the sake of adding something new.

He then took the brave step of stepping outside of the establishment and went on to do it his own way as he saw fit. Passed that, he eventually created his own individual expression, and this creation went on to change not only the industry it was born in but multiple other industries and in areas not related to the arts.

I believe the process he followed is part of the true path of growth and eventually self-expression. If we can take a snapshot of this path, learn from it, we can then apply it to how we pursue knowledge ourselves. It does not matter what area we are seeking growth in, Philosophy can apply anywhere.

The most difficult part of this process is not the beginning. Generally, the status quo has large crowded line of people waiting to get into the process. The system itself generally will have lots of company. The difficult part is when you start to break away and seek to find out what works for you. This takes a lot of bravery to do this because, in general, most people feel safe in the arms of conformity, and they seem to be threatened by individuality.

The trick is, don't listen to them. Listen to yourself, and if you're lucky, you'll find a few like-minded individuals along the way, just like Sijo Bruce did.

"The height of cultivation is really nothing special. It is merely simplicity; the ability to express the utmost with the minimum."- Sijo Bruce Lee

Let's take a look at what their journey might look like.

Set your goal

Immerse yourself in the environment (status quo)

Commit time to learn the fundamentals (seek to understand first)

Test the knowledge you are given and find what works for you. (Your Application Laboratory)

Research (continue to seek for additional knowledge) it may be something you were not taught.

Simplify, but don't clone, *"Adapt what is useful, reject what is useless, and add what is specifically your own."*

Believe in yourself and listen to what you have discovered.

Obtain or create your goal, your individual expression by using his "way" as "your way."

Think the thought the Thinker thought...

Through years of training, I have developed my own educational process I follow when starting a new area of study. I will usually plan out my year in advance, and I will pick several subjects I want to dive into or learn and arrange them on my calendar for the year. Usually, what that looks like it is me picking a subject that I will dive into each quarter of the year.

The framework to the process is a series of principles that guide me through my research and development. These principles keep me honest with myself, keep me open-minded, and force me to do the work that sometimes human nature will nudge you to let slide.

Human nature tends to fall in the direction of complacency. One of the primary principles in this process is the "Think the Thinker's Thought" principle.

As I was training and coming up in the martial arts, one of my teachers would tell me to "Think the thought the thinkers thought when they thought the thought." I would ask what this meant, and he explained I should not just accept information blindly from teachers. Instead, seek to understand what the original creator thought when they thought the thought in the first place.

What spurred the Thinker to think what he was thinking when he invented a specific technique?

Seek to understand their environment, culture, and what problems they were trying to solve when they put together the information. I was taught to identify the systems these creators utilized, then to study and train those systems. Think about what were the creator's physical attributes; big, small, strong, or weak? Did they have any physical disadvantages they sought to overcome? Seek to better understand them in order to better comprehend the wisdom and knowledge they have passed down.

This principle of the "Thinker's thought" is not new. Many great instructors study more than just the history and do the physical practice in a system. Sifu/Guro Dan Inosanto has always told us to study the culture around the art, and it will better help you to understand the art. This statement has turned on lightbulbs for me over and over again throughout my years of study. Following Guro's advice has led me to find and learn deeper levels of understanding in every area where I applied his educational process. Not just in the martial arts but in multiple subjects I have studied over the years.

Sijo Bruce Lee designed a new thought pattern in the creation of Jeet Kune Do. I believe the principle of "Think the Thinker's thought" is vital to have a deeper knowledge of that system because of the way Sijo Lee created it. This principle is one factor in how I developed my journey in Jeet Kune Do.

I wanted to understand the systems that the ideas, principles, and techniques were taken from or studied in order to design the new thought pattern, i.e., Jeet Kune Do. I identified Wing Chun Kung Fu, Chinese Boxing, Shaolin Kung-Fu, Boxing, and others as the systems that influenced Sijo Lee, the Thinker.

I then sought out and studied with who I considered the best instructors and/or sources of knowledge of these systems. I have a different definition of study than most people. To thoroughly study something requires more effort than just practicing moves or reading a couple of books. It requires the student to challenge the information given, to seek out the "why," learn about the origins of concepts, and to grow through the systems.

Devote time and discipline to the art to achieve advanced levels of rank. In all martial arts, this journey will change you on multiple levels. This process will check your ego and make you grow in ways you cannot experience by just doing a study of the art or system.

Be a perpetual white belt. This means to always look for opportunities to learn. Keep your mind open, be accepting of new information and ideas. I believe this is one of a warrior's most valuable skills. With the open mind of a child, we should strive to learn in every aspect of the journey. Because children have an open mind, they can learn and retain new information quickly, much more so than an adult. This is because as we get older, we develop preconceived notions, judgments, and points of view.

Our mind's inner landscape fills up with junk that blocks our ability or willingness to receive information at that speed and depth. Many times, we will reject new information because it does not fit into our ideas of what is valuable, or we don't value the source of information.

We also must realize we can learn something from every person and every experience. As we age, we tend to slow down, and it becomes harder to learn. I have always told other instructors in the academy, as a warrior educator, it is your job to fight that pattern to continue to always grow and learn.

At the time Sijo Lee developed JKD, the culture on martial arts considered it a bad thing to study multiple martial arts. Yet Sijo Lee did not follow the norm or opinions of the collective. He was able to have an open mindset of learning to study multiple martial arts, then to utilize his knowledge and experiences to create JKD. To have a deep understanding of JKD, and to "Think the

Thinkers thought," you must be able to achieve this level of openness in your studies and practice.

This is all the more reason to strive for the mindset of learning. I believe all of the knowledge gained will help you understand the "Thinker's thoughts" better and hopefully understand the skill you are studying.

Being open to learning and challenging what I learn has shaped my journey in martial arts. While growing in these arts over the years, I started to notice that some systems were better in some areas of the combat blueprint than others were.

The Combat Blueprint is a framework I learned from Chinese Boxing. It was originally called "the encounter." This blueprint lays out a basic structure of an encounter with an opponent. It begins with pre-contact footwork while you are outside critical distance.

Next is the entry where you advance on your opponent until contact is made. Then you deal with the contact that was made by clearing it or going around it. Lastly is the finish, where you decisively end the fight. I have studied and experimented with this framework of the blueprint to develop my own version that goes into further detail in the study of range, using weapons, multiple opponents, and the ability to apply techniques under stress.

As I began to develop my version of the Combat Blueprint, I saw the need to supplement areas of training that might be overlooked in one system but would be the focus of another. In addition to this, I started to see the need for the development of training methods to bridge the gap between the major areas of the Combat Blueprint. At times

I would say to myself, "Someone should find a way to smoothly transition between each range or concept."

Then I would have to pause and realize, someone has done that. They did it at a time when the study of multiple systems was considered a bad thing. Now we have the freedom to do this, and we have access to abundant knowledge and information. All of this helped me understand better what Sijo might have been thinking when he started to piece together his principles and ideas into his own unique system.

It's one thing to learn and repeat knowledge and another thing entirely to understand knowledge at a deeper level. I believe it is the warrior instructor's responsibility to strive for greater depths of knowledge and understanding. If we do not carry the torch, who will? Like Sijo Lee, strive for improvement with an iron discipline, seek greater depths of knowledge, and do so through multiple sources and methods. It is people who do this, that push past the normal idea of "effort," these individuals will influence the world and change it.

This educational process can be used to study any area that we choose. Anytime I get into a new subject, this is one of the first study filters that I will put that subject through. Just as mentioned above, this will force me to approach the subject from many different angles that I may not have normally considered. It will make you ask questions that you would normally not ask.

The Study of Gap Art

"Gap art" is the study of what happens between actions or events. I was first introduced to the principal by Grandmaster Dana Miller, and the example he used was the time of musical notes. Everyone learns the same musical scale, but not everyone sounds the same or feels the same when they play the same music. Some will have a different timing or placement between the notes.

Another example of this is the jab. The jab is one of the first basic punching techniques you learn in many different systems. In general, it is taught to everyone who starts to take a look at standing striking methods. Generally, if you're not using the punching hand, you rest it on your cheek or forehead.

When the time comes to apply it, you will place it lovingly on someone's face. So it goes from point A to point B. The hard part is figuring out how to make that happen. And the study of the gap between point A and point B (in other words, what does it do between the gap on the way to its meeting the face?) is what we're talking about here. So if we are using the analogy of the jab, what is the setup that allows us to break through our opponent's defense and make contact.

Another example would be a business meeting in order to close a deal. Arranging the meeting, and getting everyone together with the Point A, successfully signing a business agreement would be point B. In the gap study, the magic that happens between those two moments of time is extremely valuable information.

We spoke earlier about the principle of simplicity being mastery. We covered the importance of not necessarily obtaining more things intellectually but studying a greater depth of the functional basics you already have. The Gap Art principle teaches us that if we learn a series of techniques or ideas, we must also take a look at what happens between those moments. Is it a shift of weight, a tilt of the body that allows the punch to land? What is it that makes it work?

Is it proper body language and an expression that helps close the deal in the business meeting? Knowing this principle can remind us to seek out those intricate details. It reminds us to ask the questions of our mentors that we may not normally ask. It's just one more tool to keep us honest and reminds us to dig a little deeper into whatever subject we are placing in front of ourselves.

Studying the "gap" is one of the ways to seek that greater depth of knowledge that we spoke about earlier, being below the surface of the basics in any topic. You may choose two or three fundamental basics that you apply in any given situation. But the routes into those techniques, the path you take to achieve them, can be a wealth of different variations. This will broaden your knowledge of your basics while still maintaining simplicity. And as we know, simple basics have a greater possibility of surviving under stressful conditions.

The Art of Failure

Failure is one of the biggest things people struggle with. I have lived through the struggle myself, and I have watched it for many years on the academy floor from students striving to obtain their goals. After 40 years in the arts, I have had the opportunity to watch the effect of failure on many different personality types.

Their reaction to it would vary from person to person. Some individuals would seem to have the ability to shrug off failure. It didn't even seem to faze them. Some individuals would be completely shut down by failure. It's seem to bruise their ego so terribly that they would rather give up and walk out the door of the academy instead of facing and dealing with it. Many of them I would have the opportunity to speak to, and counsel and one of the things I heard the most if they fell short because of expectations they had built in their minds. In their minds or they had built a vision of themselves obtaining the goal and doing it at a certain level of proficiency.

When they fell short of the skill or did not seem to measure it to the proficiency in the vision, their reaction to it was so heavy it was shutting them down. I remember seeing this so much that it got to the point when in a discussion with a student, if they spoke about expectations that may be a little bit larger than reality, I immediately saw it as a red flag.

Not only for them but at the same time, I noted this for myself. I had many goals that I wanted to achieve in my career. And I have done the same thing many times. I would see the visual expectation of the performance. After seeing this in my students, I started making it a habit to avoid these mental expectations based on performance. Instead, I would set visual goals around a specific achievement.

I knew I was still going to work hard and consistently. I knew I still had to achieve those performance milestones, and I had to do them at a high-level. But I just excepted the fact mentally that I would achieve them in my way, Alan's way. And since I had not been in that position before, I did not know what that would really look like yet. And in my experience, after getting to the achievements personally, I ended up performing better than I would have thought.

This is the same discussion I would have with those students that were on the verge of quitting. I would tell them I know it is very difficult to do but try not to set expectations in your mind. Just try to do the work as best you can put in consistent time, and then achieve the goals you have set your own way.

"Far better is it to dare mighty things, to win glorious triumphs, even though checkered by failure... than to rank with those poor spirits who neither enjoy nor suffer much, because they live in a gray twilight that knows not victory nor defeat." - Theodore Roosevelt

The second type of feedback I would get back was they would compare themselves to their classmates. In other words, if they were achieving the same goal or attempting to demonstrate a technique next to their classmate, in their mind, if the classmates seem to do better or present the technique at a higher level, witnessing this would shut them down as well.

I'm sure at some point; everyone out there has had to deal with this. Expectations and comparing yourself to the people around you will be a black cloud in your mind. It's easy to just tell someone, look, you should just not do those things, and you should not think that way.

Regardless it is not an easy task to harness the mind and control it. You can't always be mentally present to keep those dark clouds out of your mind. Sometimes they will slip back in there, and you will have to deal with it. Like everything else that we learn to do in the arts, most people think of demonstrating physical techniques. You have to practice those techniques and those physical moves over and over again until they are ingrained into the nervous system, and they become part of you.

Cleaning up and controlling your mental landscape is no different. You have to approach it, in the same manner you would when you're learning those physical techniques on the mat. Just like going to class, I will have to plan to take time out of my schedule to sit down once or twice a week and focus on working on and in the mind.

This will help you improve, but you will notice that some of the best opportunities to train these things will come along when you least expect it. Life will throw a little curveball at you in that one moment you were not prepared for it.

Those moments are going to be some of the most powerful training opportunities you will find. Life will throw a punch. You will miss the block. The punch will hit you square in the face, and you will have an emotional reaction to it. That moment will be one of the best internal classrooms you will ever get to walk into. Sometimes your mind will run away from you, and sometimes you will recognize it, and you reigned it in. The better you get at this, the better you will be able to prepare and deal with failure.

There is no escaping failure

I'm going to go out on a limb here. I'm willing to bet that no one has ever achieved anything significant without going through multiple moments of failure.

I know for me in my career, there was an abundance beyond measure of failure. And one 30-minute sparring session with one of my teammates would reveal it. You will miss blocking that punch hundreds of times. And that punch will smash you right in the mouth, and there it is, failure. It is inescapable. It is going to happen. And it seems the harder you try to avoid it and the more time you spend doing so, the more it will come around and hit you in the face.

It is important to accept and understand that it is just part of the process and that the process will never change. Failure can contain some pain and embarrassment.

Due to this, it is human nature to naturally fall into a pattern of avoiding failure. I've always thought that those seeking to walk the path of a warrior know how to develop the habit of going into failure instead of away from it. Especially when you are in the process of learning a new skill or technique. In my opinion, it's much easier to learn all of those mistakes on the journey instead of arriving at the destination and making them when it really matters.

Failure is one of the most potent teachers

259

It is my experience both in life and on the academy floor that some of the most powerful failures are some of the biggest teachers.

What do I mean when I say a *powerful failure*? Well, failure in life will affect you differently at different times. Some things you are more invested in, and maybe you have more emotional energy connected to an event or thing. Sometimes you will fail at something, and you will shrug it off within a week. Other times you will have a failure that will haunt you for years. Some failures will create great pain, either emotionally or physically. These failures are the ones that will drive the chisel deepest into the stone of the mind and allow doubts to fall into the cracks they make.

Though it is not pleasant to think about, these moments and those failures in those moments are probably some of the greatest teachers you will ever have in your life. Why do I mention this? It is common to avoid failure. And sometimes, when you're sinking, you may start to do things to lighten the damage of the failure. But the reality is, those failures that hit hardest will teach us the most. We gain the most wisdom and knowledge out of those events, and they will stay with us the longest.

When we are in the middle of those types of life events, we just want to get out as quickly as possible. We just want to get it over with. But if we know in advance that it is a teaching moment, it is an opportunity to gain wisdom. We can slow down and allow that wisdom to sink in a little deeper. Maybe even take the time to look for all of the little lessons we are supposed to be learning at that moment. Sometimes we will just see the big one, the big lesson.

The times there are a series of smaller ones that are connected to them that we need to learn too. Maybe if we could have the ability to pick those up at that moment, we would not have to return to them again later on in order to learn them.

In my life, I have learned to do my best to be in the moment at these times of opportunity. In the first part of the experience, I may feel like I'm drowning and trying to fight my way to the surface. But once you have struggled your way to the surface of the water.

Once you have taken in that deep breath and you are able to start to calm yourself in your body, you will see these teachable moments for what they are. Once you have found a moment of peace, take advantage of the situation and search for wisdom. Search for the lesson that is being shown to you.

"Failure is woven into the fabric of achievement."

A warrior plans to win but prepares for failure

Earlier I was discussing a sparring session with a teammate. And that teammate was having a really good day. I seemed to taste the leather of his glove over and over again during that year-long 30-minute session.

And just as I mentioned above, failure in sparring is going to be like breathing in life. It's going to happen, and it's going to happen a lot. Well, until you start to gain experience, wisdom, and knowledge. But that takes time, and it takes a lot of failures.

In my own experience, it seems to happen so much that I just got used to it. It almost got to the point where I just ignored it, and I would just shrug it off. I can actually remember having training sessions, getting punched in the face, and laughing about it. Failure is woven into the fabric of achievement. We know this, and we accept it.

Additionally, it's important that you take the warrior's mentality on failure, and you start to prepare for failure. A warrior will have a failure process. A method that they will use to study failure and attempt to get the most knowledge and information out of it as possible. They want to know where the weak points in their armor or their weaponry is located so that they can then spend time working to develop and strengthen it. You have to be honest with yourself in moments of failure.

Sit down and take a good look at what has happened and what you did to get yourself there, or what you failed to do. This is a huge step in effective self-improvement.

The art of failure

So what is the formula that I use to keep myself in check and be open to educational failure?

1. Keep your ego in check

Your ego is who you think you are or your mind's perceived identity. This identity is usually constructed of your personal experiences, history, memories, abilities, opinions, beliefs, together with your identification of your body. All cultures develop a self-image as a normal part of growing into society. The problem is when it doesn't necessarily match up with the reality that we exist in. Also, if that self-image is negative or overly positive (to the point of being delusional), it can create problems.

Keeping your ego in check is easier said than done. And it's not something you can do once, and then you've got it. Keeping your ego in check is something that you have to stay on all the time. To me, it's like wrestling a bull to the ground. That bull definitely does not want to go down, and if you get him there, he is not going to stay. It is a continuous effort.

It takes a certain level of self-awareness just to know that you are in the ring with the bull. So you have to keep a persistent eye open for that guy, and you have to start looking well in advance because you know he's going to be there.

I have seen the struggle take place many times on the mat. I have watched someone's ego completely shut them down after failing at something they were achieving. I have even seen individuals give up martial arts entirely from this bruised image of themselves.

We all have experienced this. The trick is to recognize when your ego pops up and starts to interfere with your learning process. This can kill your ability to gain new information, knowledge, and ideas, which can in turn influence your future growth.

One of the best pieces of advice I can give, and have done multiple times in the academy, is to try not to connect your sense of worth and your happiness to your achievements. Do not measure yourself by what you have achieved, your job, or your possessions. Obviously, this is a common thing, and it can be very difficult to change thinking patterns around it.

For me, this is one of the virtues of a warrior and one of the reasons to follow the warrior mindset. Their ability to connect their worth to who they are and what type of person they are becoming, what they say, and what they do.

Ego can supply an individual with a lot of drive and passion for achieving more. This is not necessarily a bad thing, but in the incident above, it could be a very damaging thing if it brings you to the choice of giving up to protect your ego. Swallowing that big pill and continuing on the path of growth and advancement can be a difficult chore sometimes, but it is absolutely necessary to climb the ladder of success in any arena.

Additional advice I almost always give to students in the situation is to practice the gratitude drill. It is easy to get so focused on the win or loss that when the loss comes around, it's difficult to accept. If you recognize this moment, it is an excellent time to practice the gratitude drill.

Consider the things that you possess in order to get you to the point where you are. You are healthy, your body is operating well, and it is allowing you to come into the academy and get on the mat and train multiple times a week.

There are many people in the world who cannot claim that. You have nourishment, and you get enough of it to operate that amazing machine you are trapped in, in order to come into the academy and get on the mat and not have to worry about being hungry while you train. There are many in the world that cannot claim that.

Do you have a powerful support system? More than likely, you have a family at home, but I *do* know you have family in the academy. The environment at the school is filled with individuals who will go out of their way to help you just as much as they go out of their way to catch you in a submission when you're training.

The truth is, once that training is over, they would get up and follow you home and help you move your whole house if it were required. Not many people can claim a support system that powerful in the world. These are just a few examples of the gratitude drill. It has a way of putting the ego in perspective and getting you back into action.

2. Get up there

This is a quote from my teacher, Master Erik Paulson. Coach Erik was the first American to win the World Light-Heavy Weight Shooto Title in Japan. I would hear him use this quote when talking to guys that were getting ready to fight. I would hear it come up as we would walk on the mat to train. To me, "get up there" means exactly how it sounds. Get out there and give it everything you've got. Don't hold back. Live in the moment and experience what you're doing. That experience will educate you. I have seen guys hold back many times on the mat because they are worried about how they will look to others.

Or they are worried that if they try something new and they fail at it it will put a scar on their reputation. That is one thing I have always admired about Coach Erik. He will get out there with anybody and train and learn. He is constantly looking for new information, new ways of doing things, and he will attempt to learn that information from absolutely anyone.

With this in mind, anytime you are getting into a new subject or topic. Don't be afraid to go all in. Check your ego at the door and make the mistakes. Don't let them faze you in the least, and keep going with no worries about what other people think. Get in there and take action.

3. Your opponent as a partner

I have heard Master Pedro Sauer tell his story of how he began training in Gracie Jiu-Jitsu many times. He was good friends with Master Rickson Gracie when he was a young man. Rickson took Pedro to meet his father, Grandmaster Helio Gracie at his school in Brazil. This was an eye-opening experience for him.

He was pretty much walking into a room of killers. He would talk about how in the first year, he was submitted multiple times every night he was in class. He never seemed to be able to get anywhere with any of the guys he was training with. Instead of quitting, what he started doing was every time someone would catch him in a submission, he would immediately get up and ask his opponent what he did to him. He would ask him if he would teach him what he just did. Again and again, this would happen. After some time passed, he noticed that he was getting caught less and less.

He said that after a while, he knew what everyone's favorite move was in class. And he learned how they would set up each move, so he would literally see them coming before they did it. Pretty soon, he was avoiding all of the submissions he was familiar with. And he was learning to get out of different positions that he normally was getting stuck in previously. As time would pass, he would start to catch the same techniques on his classmates.

This is a tremendous thing. I have seen many times on the academy floor students will get caught in a submission. They will get so irritated with what just happened that they completely shut down. Their ego completely closes them off to even learning the least little thing from the experience.

If I can, I will usually have a talk with these guys and tell them Master Pedro's story. The ones that can understand what he is trying to teach will start to do the same thing. When they get caught, they will check the ego, get up and ask their opponent what they just did. They will ask them to teach them and help them.

The guys that get this are the ones that start to progress much faster in their studies. They are also the ones that end up gaining the most wisdom and knowledge later on in their career. They end up learning from everyone!

I have owned and operated a tactical training business for about fourteen years now. We work with military groups, law-enforcement groups, as well as security and protection groups. In this business, it is common to acquire a contract between you and the person you're going to work with. In this process, you have to place a bid on a job.

Usually, you're not the only person that is bidding on the job. So you have to compete with other people to get to work. Obviously, you will win some, and you will lose some.

So one of the times I lost the bid for a contract, I actually found out who the business was that obtained it. I happened to have a mutual friend who knew the owner, and I asked him for an introduction. When I finally got to meet and talk to the owner, I told him congratulations and immediately asked him how did you do it. I knew it was not a price thing because we had bid very similar amounts on the contract. What got the contract for him was how he was going to present the material. And he was gracious and open enough to tell me what he did. I learned a tremendous amount that day, and I have applied that wisdom moving forward. I am also still good friends with that man to this day.

So in your educational process, for whatever method or skill you're learning, if you have an opponent, don't be afraid to reach out and learn from him. Sometimes they will not be open to this, and that is okay, but in my experience, way more often than not, they are open to it.

I have found that most of them will jump at the opportunity to meet other high achievers that are in the same industry. You may even find out that the relationships you develop outside of the business will be way more valuable than anything else you will gain from it. That is exactly what I discovered.

White Belt Mindset

I have been fortunate enough to be the defensive tactics instructor for the Executive Protection Institute (EPI) for almost thirteen years now. Dr. Richard Kobetz created EPI and was one of the leaders in growing the executive protection industry in the United States, if not the world.

Dr. Kobetz would commonly say in class that "You don't know what you don't know." I also think of Grandmaster Dana Miller, who I vividly remember saying, "The problem is, you think you know, but you don't know."

Both of them could not have been more correct. When learning from Dr. Kobetz, I did not know what I did not know. I did not even have the vision to understand the knowledge that was out there in relation to the subject. I would learn something about an area and think I had a decent grasp on it, but I had not yet seen the ten other areas that were connected to it just over the horizon.

There is always more wisdom, and there is always a deeper level of knowledge to be gained. In my experience, this has applied to absolutely everything. I will think I know a subject because I have studied it for a certain amount of time, and maybe I have had this thought pattern for a considerable amount of time. I have stayed in the state of "thinking I knew" for years until the day I raised an eyebrow and wondered if there was something else to this thing I was doing or teaching. Because of that curiosity, I would start to look for information and knowledge. Sometimes it was because of necessity.

I have trained in the gym weightlifting for the majority of my life. I was fortunate enough to get introduced to it when I was fourteen years old. I remember learning a technique like the basic fundamental move of bench press. And, of course, I thought I knew what I was doing. So I would go to the gym and do that bench press the same way for years. And then, one day, I realized I was getting a little older, and my body was responding differently to the work I was doing in the gym.

It was out of this necessity that I sought out a professional in order to learn more about the science of weightlifting. I was introduced to a vast ocean of knowledge that I had no clue even existed. I have learned things that have allowed me to do things physically in the gym that is very uncommon for fifty-year-old. It seems like the more knowledge I take in, the more of the science I understand, the more I can see myself doing this until the end of my life. It has helped me learn to work smarter, not necessarily harder, and achieve the same if not greater results.

Now for the quote from Grandmaster Dana Miller. He stated correctly that I thought I knew something. And it was because of that thinking that I knew that I was blocked from actually learning what I did not know.

This is worse than what was mentioned before. Your ego can get in the way, and it will whisper in your ear that "You know this, and there's nothing else left to see." And because of that, he said you will absolutely never see it. Thinking you know can be devastating to your future growth and advancement in anything you do.

In my experience, thinking that you know is a safe place to be for most people. I have had the opportunity in what I do to meet many people that thought they knew. And they would defend that belief till the bitter end. I think that they have this defense mechanism because the truth is, if you let down the defense of ego and actually look at what is out there, you will find that there is such a vast universe of knowledge that you will never have the time or the ability to obtain.

I am not a big believer in the term "master." It insinuates an end, and after looking in that universe of knowledge, I believe there is never an end to learning. I also believe that if you think you have arrived at the moment when you have something mastered, that you have shut yourself off mentally to any type of future growth. You're pretty much dead as far as growth is concerned.

I personally don't ever want to be in this position. I want to be that perpetual student that is constantly seeking knowledge and growth. So with this in mind, I have to continuously remind myself that I really know nothing. I am a perpetual white belt that is stepping on the mat for the first time.

I want the set of eyes of an infant, a child that is taking in life and its experiences for the first time, hungry for information and knowledge. This mindset is a mental skill you want to develop in your educational process. The skill of keeping the ego in check and the mind open.

Small Consistency - Big Change

"A white belt is just a black belt that did not quit." This is a quote that I was introduced to by Master Pedro Sauer. I have watched him many times over the years give away multiple levels of rank to people who are on different points of their journey in Gracie Jiu-Jitsu (GJJ).

He will usually tie the belt around their waist, shake their hand, and then he will say the words, *"Great job my friend, don't stop training, keep going."* This seems like a small thing, but it is a mountain of truth once you stop and think about it. Jiu-Jitsu is not a skill that is obtained quickly.

If you're not familiar with GJJ, it takes anywhere from 10 to 13 years of your life to get to the rank of black belt in Gracie Jiu-Jitsu, which is what Master Pedro teaches. Along the way, you will work for and gain all of the levels of rank leading up to that point.

Obtaining each of the lower levels of rank takes a considerable amount of time and effort as well. They literally require hundreds of hours of training on the mat. If you were to look at this whole journey and see just the end, it can be very daunting. I cannot tell you how many students I have had that made it to the rank of blue belt (blue belt is the first rank achieved after white belt in Brazilian Jiu-Jitsu) and then just stop because the journey between that rank and the next one seemed almost impossible.

You see, the amount of time required will double after the blue belt, so it is easily twice the amount of time and energy required to make the next rank.

You have to break those big goals down into small bite-size goals. They have to be small enough that you can look at them and believe that they are obtainable. Once you have set that micro goal, you then have to design your consistent daily habits in alignment with achieving it.

In the academy, the example of this is setting aside two or three days a week at the least to make it into class to study and obtain new material. Even with this, it just might not be enough. You might have to come in a couple of extra days, or maybe early to class.

With that early time, you will meet up with a partner and spend additional time doing drills. This may be above and beyond what is normal for the operations for most students of the academy. A large portion of the population will only show up for class, and then they are done for the night. And that's fine.

But then you will have those select few that will come in an hour early every class and get on the mat ahead of everyone else in order to get additional training time. They make it a habit to show up to class early and because of that habit, they are able to do it consistently over an extended amount of time.

One may look at it and say, "That is just an additional hour before class." But if we do it consistently over a year, those short hours add up to a tremendous amount of time and a huge amount of change.

This is a small principle that could have a huge effect on life. Knowing this, regardless of the goal we want to achieve, we know we need to create habits that will equate to those extra efforts being put in on a consistent basis. An extra hour here and there consistently over time. Small efforts done consistently over time can create great change.

We also understand that there really is no rush because there are no shortcuts. It is better to know it is going to take time and then decide to use that time as intelligently as possible. In other words, train or work smarter, not just harder. Take the extra time to look at what you're doing. Find the 20% of work that is going to produce the 80% effect and then repeat it like a running machine over the required amount of time to make a massive change.

Wisdom comes from an active "Sun Teacher" Mentor

I was first introduced to this idea in the early 90s, and the first time I was introduced to it it was in relation to being a sun student. It was explained to me that there are two types of students, one will be a sun student and the other will be a moon student. The moon student is someone who theoretically reflects light. In other words, they will learn from their teacher and then they will turn around and repeat exactly what they were taught. They will reflect the light they were given.

The sun student is looked at as a creator of light. This kind of student has learned the information and then spent time with their own experimentation to gain their own knowledge and additionally go deeper into a subject matter. They don't take it at face value. They use the principle of "you don't know what you don't know." They always know that there is a deeper level of knowledge, and they take the time to seek out that knowledge. They always know that there is wisdom that will come from consistent hard work overtime in the area that you study.

Sun personalities are generally very passionate and driven about what they do and, most of the time, looked at as high-percentage achievers. Individuals like this go on to be very influential creators and influencers in their given industries. One example of this is Bruce Lee. Due to the way he processed knowledge and his unyielding search for more knowledge, he advanced the Martial Arts industry as well as industries, and he pushed them well past what they were before his involvement.

I mentioned this earlier in the book when I was talking about Master Pedro Sauer having the ability to create new Jiu-Jitsu moves on the fly. So I learned this as a student. I focused on either searching for mentors in the martial arts or other fields that I wanted to get involved with.

I begin to refer to this type of person as a *sun teacher/ student* or mentor. We spoke about conditioning your environment in your network. In other words, choosing the people that you spent time with on a daily basis to help you attain your goal.

I believe that one of the top sources of wisdom and knowledge is from a living mentor. So when I start looking around at the different options of individuals that potentially could be a teacher, this is one of the major things I'm taking into consideration. I will ask myself, "Is that a possible mentor a creator, is he an inventor, is he someone that has influenced and change the industry he is in?"

Of course, he has to be someone who is willing to be in a position of a mentor or a teacher as well. These individuals are hard to come by. I think I've only known four of them in my 40 years of Martial Arts experience. But what I have gained from those four individuals has been monumental in comparison to the other teachings that I have come across. So it is well worth taking the extra time to search for those individuals and place yourself under their tutelage.

Some of the characteristics of an innovative sun teacher will be: they are a divergent thinker, they are not afraid to move away from what the norm is, away from the standard. They will have an insatiable sense of curiosity, they are not afraid to ask questions, and they have the ability to think outside the box, putting things together that are not normally put together. They are constantly asking, "What if I were to do this?" They will have a tremendous passion for what they do.

The four individuals that I have personally been around almost seem to give off energy. People are drawn to them because of this. Sun-type individuals are not afraid to share their knowledge. They are constantly trying to teach and give away information to help the people around them because they know teaching is an advanced level of learning.

The Learning Triangle

Sifu/Guro Dan Inosanto first introduced me to this concept in the late 1990s. At the time, I didn't realize that it would end up on this list of my educational process.

When I finally realized it, I was sitting on the mat at the academy with a student that I was teaching. We were going back over a technique that I had just shown in class, and he had asked me for additional details. I went through the details with him, and he made a comment that he had been doing it wrong the whole time. And I asked him if what he had been doing was working for him. He told me that he was successful with it almost all of the time.

I was intrigued and asked him to show me what he was doing. So he immediately grabs a partner and shows me the move. Watching it, I said to myself, "That is really cool,

I've never seen it done that way before, but that is a damn good idea." So the next time I was training with my partner, I gave his version of the move a try, and it actually was easier than what I was already doing. The thing he found by mistake actually became a common move that I use even to this day. That beginning student had taught me something extremely valuable, and it was way more than a technique.

After thinking about what happened, I realized that this was the exact principle that Guro Inosanto had taught me many years ago. When he taught the learning triangle, he had a photo of a triangle that was sitting on its side.

So the top of the triangle was pointing to the left side of the page, and the bottom was pointing to the right side of the page. In this illustration, you are on the point of the triangle. The teacher will be on the baseline of the triangle at the top right corner. The student is usually placed at the bottom corner of the right side of the triangle. And for this illustration, your peers are placed in the middle of the baseline. So they are straight across from you horizontally.

Guro used this illustration to show that you can learn from each of these points. Obviously, you can learn from your instructor. But you can also learn from your peers, and you can learn from your students. This illustration is important because it keeps you in check, and you can keep your mind open so that knowledge can come from any of the above directions.

Even if you are in a teaching situation, keep an open mind as to what you can be taught. In my experience, you will start to find there is a lot of things that will come from the teacher-student exchange. Train your mind to stay open, and don't miss that valuable wisdom.

Teaching Teaches You - Give Back

This is probably one of the most powerful educational tools that I've come across in my career. I did not start teaching professionally until the early 90s. Up untill that point, I had done a tremendous amount of training. And at the time, I thought that I understood the material that I was immersed in at a great level.

Once I started getting into the classroom setting and started to teach other individuals, I realized I might not know as much as I thought. I had not been teaching for a month or two before I started saying to myself, "I don't know anything about any of this." I would almost have to laugh at myself at times for ending up in situations that I completely had no answer for a student.

If there's one thing I hate, it's not having an answer for a student. Anytime I would end up in that situation, I would gracefully say, "No, I do not know, and I don't have an answer, but I will go and find one for you."

This was a very important part of the process. I never tried to make up an answer or teach something that I didn't know. I would simply admit that I didn't know it, and then I would take a note so that I could seek out a source of information later that would educate me on the topic.

This happened many, many times. I took notes, and then I would spend many days digging for answers and additional knowledge. This process has taught me more in my career than I can possibly express. Teaching has forced me to dig into multiple subjects at a much greater depth than I had originally been introduced to them.

With this in mind, as part of your educational process, go teach. Go find some outlet that you can pass on your information to someone. It doesn't have to be in a classroom setting. It could be a volunteer situation. It could be a mentor situation. I have spoken many times about the process of finding a good mentor. Sometimes they are hard to find, but I will say this.

Good ones will teach because they know teaching will make them better at what they do. It will make them grow.

Creating A Learning Environment

We discussed environmental discipline earlier. This is an extension of that idea. Self-educating has always been a huge part of my life. Because of this, I have found setting up a designated environment for studying makes a tremendous difference in your ability to focus and absorb what you are pursuing.

When I focus on a topic, I will dig out every source of information I have on that topic, including all of my handwritten notes. Usually, the study will look like a bomb went off with all of the open books and notepads around the room.

I'll do this in order to go back and review all of the sources of information I may have had previously on whatever topic I'm focusing on. Any new sources of information that I will get will go through the same process. Because of this, I will have different tables in the study, both permanent and portable tables that will only go up when I'm diving deep on a topic.

I will do a lot of thinking on whiteboards and easel boards, so I will have several hanging on the wall that I would use to process different information.

I like using the whiteboards because after accumulation, I will usually go through the process of elimination. In other words, taking all the information, I have been absorbing and boiling it down to the functional basics that I'm looking for. The whiteboards make this easier because of the ability to erase the information or rearrange it if needed. Additionally, I will usually try to pick a room with the most available sunlight. This has always had a positive effect on my ability to study and focus.

The point is, if you can create your own environment that is conducive to your self-education process, it will increase your effectiveness. Have a place that is comfortable where you have access to seek additional information, review the information you have currently, and then a place to process that information and boil it down to your functional knowledge.

Additionally, when you enter into this environment, it will help you mentally shift into a learning state. It will become an environmental trigger for learning. Very much like going to the gym, as soon as I walk into the door, my body starts to get ready for the impending beating it's going to get in the weight room.

Exercise Educational Consciousness

We discussed consciousness and awareness earlier in the book. I wanted to bring it up again now as an area where this skill can be applied.

I recently spent the day at the gun range with my good friend, mentor, and instructor, Coach Dennis Rousseau. During the day of training, we had several discussions in regards to some of the other classes he was teaching for his regular employment.

He mentioned that he had people in the class who were not entirely present for what was going on in the class. Some of them even spent time looking at their cell phone while he was teaching.

He said that several of his students struggled with the ability to focus for an extended amount of time. During this discussion, I mentioned that I refer to the lack of the ability to collect your focus as a lack of educational consciousness.

As part of his educational process that we are discussing here, I believe a warrior should develop the ability to enter into a state where he has an elevated level of focus and a higher level of available consciousness.

Of course, this is someone who has spent the time to develop and grow their level of awareness and focus. This, as we have mentioned earlier in the book, is a challenge in itself that can take someone years of training to obtain.

Once you start to gain the ability to do so, one of the most important areas that you can apply this skill is in a classroom or learning environment. This is especially true if you are working with someone who is taking the time to be a mentor to you.

"The key to growth is the introduction of higher dimensions of consciousness into our awareness."
- Lao Tzu, Chinese philosopher, 6th century BC

A mentor is someone who takes extra effort in teaching you. They go the extra mile to help you understand the topic at a deeper level. They take the time to go into extended explanations or use multiple explanations until they can see that you understand the concept or technique at the required depth.

They understand that true growth of knowledge and wisdom is more than just putting information into someone's head. Sometimes it involves changing their perspective. You literally have to change the way they think about a thing. This is a huge undertaking in itself.

Mentorship is more challenging than just teaching. It takes more energy and dedication. Because of this, it is something that once you recognize, you as the student should take the additional steps to be more attentive, more focused, and have more of your available consciousness actively available when knowledge is being passed.

I refer to this as exercising your educational consciousness. Have you ever felt like you had to see something or learn something multiple times before you finally got it? I believe that a lot of that repetition can be due to a student not being fully in the moment or fully available mentally.

Our culture has started to turn into a culture of distraction, sometimes requiring continuous stimulation. As I have said, I believe it is part of the warrior's code to continuously seek growth and upward movement. It is also important for them to invest time to develop their ability to educate themselves or to accept instruction from others.

Like anything, this can be developed with consistent effort over time, and a small part of that is your ability to gather together your awareness and your ability to focus on absorbing information. I believe the beginning of developing this state is first controlling the breath and then eventually exercising the focus trail discussed at the beginning of this book.

You Never Arrive

In my industry, I have seen instructors train for years, and they will reach a certain rank in their system. In their minds, they look at this achievement as an arrival at a level or in the attainment of mastery.

Due to the stop pattern, they relax in their pursuit of additional growth. In their minds, they have become what they have always sought to become, so when they finally "arrive" they relax they slow down on their pursuit.

I have seen a stop pattern in more than just one industry. An individual will go to school, put in a certain amount of time, and they will receive a piece of paper that says they are a thing and they have arrived.

They hang the paper on the wall and go to work. They don't continue to seek knowledge or growth. It is my belief that as a warrior, you never arrive. It's one of the reasons that I'm not a big believer in the title "master" (even though it is a title often given as a show of respect in the martial arts world, but I give that a pass as it is something I say to *my* teachers).

This title, if you take it too seriously, insinuates that you have reached a point of attainment or growth. And I believe this mentality is the beginning of the end. With this in mind, I believe it is an important principle in the educational process to realize there is no arrival. There is no ending moment where you're going to relax.

True wisdom evolves over time. It does not sit still; if it does, then you will not continue to grow. You can learn information about a topic, and then five years later, there will be new information. This new information may even contradict the stuff you learned five years ago.

It is continually changing and evolving, and due to this, you have to continually pursue knowledge. I believe life is the same way. There is no arrival.

Life is a struggle. I commonly referred to it when talking to my students as a fight. You have to fight time, deterioration of your body, and deterioration of your health.

As you move along to your journey, you are in a battle. If you let up on your forward pursuit, if you let up on your drive to continually improve, this is when you start to deteriorate. Personally, I believe there is no resting point. You're either on the upward angle of growth in all areas, or you are falling backwards.

5.
DISCIPLINE OF STATE

Websters loosely defines a state as a mode or condition of being; a state of readiness, a condition of mind or temperament; a condition of abnormal tension or excitement.

In the wrong state, you will eat badly or consume sugary foods. You will skip your morning run or the gym.

In a lower state, you will lack passion, drive, motivation, and energy to act. The state you are in will determine how you interpret everything around you. Think about the last time you were in a bad mood. In this state, everything around you can be disturbing and irritating. The amount of effort you put into something in the state is minor. There seems to be an internal abundance of negative self-talk in this lower state.

In an empowering state, you will show up early, put in extra energy and work, go the extra mile. There are more drive and passion in higher levels of state.

Changing the state you are in can change your decisions and actions. You will speak to yourself differently when you are in an elevated state. In neurolinguistic programming or NLP, it is said that the concept of states refers to the mental and physical processes we experience at any moment.

Most of the time, our state will depend on how well our bodies are functioning at the moment or our internal process. It could be based on our emotions in the moment or our interaction with our external environment.

Most of the time, we are unaware of our state changes. But we can change state any given day at any given time. Our body chemistry will change due to what we eat or how much water we drink during the day. Our state can be influenced by how much oxygen we breathe into our bloodstream. It can be influenced by your internal dialogue or self-talk.

Most of the time, we don't even notice these changes as we go through our day. But if you pay attention, you will notice changes in your breathing rate, heart rate, or posture, and how you hold yourself physically when you experience a state change. Fortunately for us, we have the ability to choose what state we are in.

Fire and Water

I started studying methods of state change in my mid-teens. At the time, I had no idea what I was learning. My teacher told me that as I go through my normal daily routine, I would pass through different phases of being that were affected by my physiological state, my mental state, and my surroundings. He would explain at certain times in life that if you are in a higher state, you will be elevated to heightened levels. Sometimes it would be higher levels of focus, other times, higher levels of energy and personal power. He explained that with the proper mental cues, breath control, and adjustments to my physiology, I would have the ability to recall those moments or states and tap into the benefits they would have to offer.

We started out by just recalling experiences in life where, due to your surroundings and experiences, you were placed into an elevated state. He would ask me what I would remember about the state, breath rate, posture, how I felt, the things I thought, etc.

Through visualization, he would get me to try to re-create elements of that moment. I experienced a certain level of success with this, but I had even greater success with what he had me do next. He told me that there would be more of these moments in life. Moments where you will feel exceptionally energized, clear or focused. Moments when you will feel physically strong.

He told me the next time you recognize that you are in one of the states, I should take the time to sit down, breathe and focus on all of the elements that I was experiencing. He wanted me to make a mental and physical recording of the state I was experiencing. I was supposed to take note on my posture and physical expression of the body.

The clarity of the mind in that moment, the level of focus, was absolutely incredible, and he wanted me to recognize what my heart rate and breathing rate was in the moment.

Additionally, I was supposed to take detailed notes on the emotions that I was experiencing and the effects they were having on my mind and body. He told me to take the time to take note of everything. And as he said, as time passed, these moments came. Some of them came just because they were part of life's journey. Others came because they were opportunities that were created by my teacher. After taking note of these powerful moments of state, I began to practice recalling the traits of those moments when I needed them. This was an amazing thing to me, so when I started to experience the ability to do it, I dove into it and started to devote a lot of time to developing it.

I started to categorize different states that I had experienced and was developing the ability to recall. I gave them very simple names at the time. One was "clarity and focus," another was "strength and power," and the third one was "calming relaxation / release." Sifu noticed the progression and one day sat down and told me about some additional triggers that I could add to the practice.

"The breath is the bridge" - Breathing Trigger

The first change he taught me was in relation to my breathing. Up until that point, I had only done a full cycle breath as he taught me in my morning focus exercise.

He introduced me to the idea that speeding up the breathing cycle or slowing it down would have different effects on my mental and physical state. He told me certain breathing patterns would relate to certain states that I was attempting to recall in my training. And if I learned how to put the two together, it would amplify what I was trying to do. I found that a faster breathing rate with a focus on sharp movements of the abdomen wall greatly enhanced the "strength and power" stare. I could feel the body react to the increase of oxygen in the system. The temperature of the body would increase in preparation for action.

The above mixed with controlled breath holds, in relation to moments when the body needed to express maximum strength, greatly improved performance. An example of this is when you pressurize your abdomen when you are trying to push a car. Very similar to the power breath we talked about earlier in the book. All this, mixed with the mental cues, amplified everything I had been working on previously.

What my Sifu taught me was that the first physical trigger for entering into a state was the breath. At the time, I did not realize the intelligence of what he was doing. I have seen other systems of thought that will connect state change to something like clapping their hands. But breathing is

289

something you do on a regular basis. It is primarily programmed into the body.

Breathing is something you're going to do even under a great amount of stress. This actually makes it a perfect trigger. All you have to do is set the breath rate and pattern around the state you are relating it to. Of course, physical and emotional changes will be related to it as well, but the breath (pattern) was always the original creator of change.

Emotional Triggers

Earlier in the book, we talked about where the emotional center is in the body. Generally, it is in the chest close to the heart. We mentioned in previous chapters that we wanted to lower our breathing cycle in the torso in order to avoid amplifying whatever emotional state we were experiencing.

So, for example, if I were angry at someone for something they have done and I recognize that my breathing is high in the chest, I may want to get myself in check. In order to do that, I would attempt to lower my breathing to the abdomen and away from the heart center or the emotional center of the body. I would want to "sink" the emotions down to root myself.

As we were discussing amplifying the states, Sifu brought up this concept. He explained to me that sinking the emotions is used in the beginning to manage emotion in the body, so it doesn't control you. But it can also be used to amplify emotions when it is needed.

He pointed out that some of the states I was working on created certain emotions that were connected to euphoric,

290

positive states. If I were to connect a chest breathing pattern to these elevated states and emotional experiences, they could be amplified and used in a positive manner as part of the state change.

The example he gave me was an actor. An actor will use thoughts that are connected to emotional moments in their life in order to re-create a state of anger or sadness for the scene they are about to portray. In essence, they are creating a state change in order to add more emotional energy to the performance.

This is very similar to what we were trying to achieve, only instead of acting, we were applying it to the physical performance while under pressure. I found that this had a powerful effect on my spirit and willpower at the moment I needed it most.

I remember in the following months after that lesson. I put many hours into training the different state exercises. I was learning to use them in many different situations in life. It was an amazing discovery to me. This was not always about fighting, though that is how I originally learned it.

An example that I have used for most of my life is the state when I'm with family or loved ones. It is my goal to create a positive, high-energy state around my family or my inner circle in order to be a positive influence. I have met many people in life who you could easily call a "Debby Downer."

Whenever you are around them, they seem to be so low on energy that they literally suck it out of you. You end up feeling drained after being in their presence. I never wanted to express this to people that I cared for, especially the ones that are close to me.

So, anytime that I know that I'm going to be in that situation, I will take a second or two to reframe myself mentally and physically and gather myself consciously in preparation to be fully in the moment. I have used this in preparation for speaking engagements, critical business meetings, and first impressions. This practice has never failed me as far as the return I would receive from existing at my highest state.

The Human Antenna - Posture Trigger

I have used the term "The Human Antenna" to reference a student's physiology for many years. One of the reasons for this is I believe that how you hold yourself and where you place your posture has a direct effect on everything else in your body. I also use the word "antenna" because I believe the body is energetically connected to everything around it. You possess a bioelectric field, a field of energy that shares and exchanges with all things around it. And like an antenna, if it is bent and crooked, it directly affects its ability to connect to those signals or energies.

Additionally, it will affect the bioelectric energy that is in your body. This is something that will be discussed in the latter half of the book. For now, we want to introduce it because it has a direct effect on the state that you are in. You also have complete control of where you place yourself physically. In my experience, your posture and your breathing patterns are two of the first triggers that you can use to adjust or completely change the state you are in.

You can try this now, stand up and adjust your posture. Straighten your back and hold your head up. Shoulders back, chest out and put on a big SMILE. Open up the body, now start your full-cycle breath, inhale deeply and let the body expand. After a few breaths, do you recognize a slight change in your state?

Most individuals will experience a positive change in how they feel both mentally and physically. And the wonderful thing about this is that you are in charge of these things. Of course, if you are not paying attention, you may have your mind on something else, and your body position goes to where it has a habit to go.

So you have to be mindful, and in the moment, you have to recognize what position your antenna is in. Sometimes you have to make this correction several times throughout the day. But the more you make these adjustments, and the more you correct them, the closer you come to make it an ingrained habit. Straighten your antenna and change your state.

I was taught the different postures could have different effects on what you were trying to create. Earlier I told you to straighten your back, pull your shoulders back and smile. This could have a positive, uplifting influence. Another option would be more of a primal physical state. You may round your back, your stance, and your gaze may come out of the top of your eyes.

Posture can create a physical trigger for a state of action. Most of the time if you are forced into a situation where you have to react to something physically, you will make most of the changes automatically. This, very much like the breath, is because these types of posturing are also a primal reaction.

They are generally already hardwired into your nervous system. How much of the program is hardwired in will vary per individual, but in my experience, everybody has had a certain amount of this programming. All we have to do was recognize that it is there and then work on improving its effectiveness and application.

If you become aware of them and start practicing intention with your physical placement, breathing, and emotional energy, you will improve these state changes, and you will be able to elevate them to the point where you will get more out of them when it is needed.

So far, we have looked at the three primary trigger methods that I teach. These three options are very simple methods of connecting your physiology to your state change. Here are the three that we have gone through:

Breath Triggers - The timing of the breath cycle or hold

Posture Triggers - The appropriate physical placement

Emotional Triggers - Connection to empowering emotions

Animal - Stress Training

After our introduction to the methodology of state change, Sifu started to introduce us to what he called "the animal state." This state's purpose was only for combat. What made its study unique is we practiced it while we were placed under tremendous stress.

This type of training was not everyone's cup of tea. Quite honestly, there was only a handful of men at the academy that were even interested in it. At that time, I thought all Martial Arts were trained in this way. I had no clue that it would be any different anywhere else. I thought it was just part of the journey.

Sifu would formulate these stressful training environments in different ways, but most times it was fighting with the other participants in the class. The fighting was hard. You would get hurt. You would experience great disappointment. You would get angry. Every emotion you can imagine that would be connected to that type of situation we experienced, and we did it on a regular basis. We got to the point where it was just normal operating under those levels of stress and violence. At that point, Sifu began to develop a specific state he called the animal state.

I remember him taking us to a photograph that he had hanging on the wall of the academy. The photograph was of a tiger. This tiger, when you took a look at it, was ferocious. It was staring straight into the camera bearing its teeth. You could see drool coming out of its mouth as it crouched low, ready to attack whatever was in front of it.

When Sifu brought us to the photo, he would say to us, "Take a look at that tiger. What do you think he's thinking?" My answer was he looks like he is very upset, very angry.

Sifu looked at me and said, no, he is just being a tiger. He's not angry, he is not upset, he's just a tiger, just an animal. He explained to us, this is the mindset, the state you want when you fight.

We went on to study this concept in-depth for many years. We looked at how the posture changed and molded into a combative nature when it was placed in a violent situation.

We studied the breathing rate that was connected to this posture and state and how it affected our physiology, how it would increase our strength, endurance, and stamina. We learned how this state would affect our ability to endure pain and push past what we thought our physical limitations were.

We learned how parts of the brain would start to shut down when placed under tremendous amounts of stress and pain. As stress elevates and your body responds with the fight or flight response, it will start to limit your ability to access the prefrontal cortex. The brain can switch from its higher cognitive functions into the primitive part of the mind, the hypothalamus.

We would always refer to this area as the midbrain. Think about an instance when you had to speak in front of a crowd. Have you ever had that moment before you go up on stage where you seem to go blank and just forget everything? That is an example of this switch into the midbrain when you are placed under stress.

He also taught us the areas that would stay present in the fight. We learned that there is a huge difference between what we train in the normal class environment and what we trained in the animal state. Habits, reflexes, techniques that were trained in this state seem to be rooted deeper into the body and the midbrain.

Once you learn to do something under this amount of stress in this state, it is ingrained in the body at a deep level. He taught us that this was a state we can tap into or switch on when the situation requires it. Obviously, not all situations will call for something like this, but if the moment arrives that you need it and you do not possess it, that is not a good day.

The thing about the pearl-sized midbrain (hypothalamus) is that you can only put in a certain amount of information that you're going to be able to access under a tremendous amount of stress. You are only going to be able to teach the caveman a certain number of simple tricks.

That poor guy is going to be dealing with the impact of the response, tunnel vision, difficulty speaking clearly, short-term memory loss, diminished hearing, and loss of coordination because all of those are symptoms from this. *All of that* will happen if you have not trained your "animal mindset" to switch on when you need it. So with this in mind, you have to keep it very simple. I also believe that the exercises you choose to practice have to be as close as possible to the primal reactions that you already have programmed in your system, and they should be built as major motor skills.

So with this in mind, you have to take the time to study the information that is available and boil it down to the simple fundamental basics that meet these requirements. It doesn't matter if you are training the midbrain in preparation for a business meeting or getting in front of a large group of people, or preparing for a fight. The same requirements will need to be met.

It's not that you cannot program in minor motor skills to the midbrain. But in my experience, you were only going to be able to choose a few because of the amount of continuous repetition under stress that is required to ingrain it.

I will usually start off the foundational skills with major motor movements and then add in the smaller ones as we move forward in training. The student becomes more accustomed to the harsh environment and the chemical dump in the bloodstream that is related to it.

"It is better to be a warrior in a garden than a gardener in a war."
- Unknown

Now, are the more intense levels of this something you need to experience to benefit from? Absolutely not, but what you *can* do is learn from my experience. One of the main things I learned from training this mindset is how deeply ingrained into the mind information will become when it is practiced or trained under a stressor.

Stressful training environments can be created in many different ways. I have heard stories from my students who are in the military of going through experiences like this in their training. Additionally, they had told me of experiences they had had when they were placed into live combat and how the training affected them and helped them get through the situation.

How can you create an environment to train yourself?

It is believed that the body and midbrain cannot differentiate between the stress experienced during an emergency incident and the stress experienced during a high-intensity workout. So these types of workouts can be used to create the conditions to start to play with these ideas.

Obviously, they may not be the motor skills that you require in your particular occupation, but they can be used as an introduction to the training in order to become familiar with the responses of the body when under stress and help you to be able to deal with them.

Also, it will only be a physical stimulant because the drill is just a physical drill, so it does not introduce methods of dealing with the internal dialogue that you will have to deal with certain situations, but as I said, it is a beginning.

Another option is to just place yourself in the environment that you are preparing for. For instance, if you are dealing with anxiety from public speaking, look around and find a group that is getting together with the intention of working on this.

In other words, find a classroom with like-minded people that are willing to help create an environment for everyone involved. Your team will know what you're there for, and this will give them the ability to help you deal with the stress response as well as improve the given skill you're working on. It just takes action, get out there and locate your classroom and start making change.

Anchoring Peak States

Anchoring is an internal state that is triggered by external stimulation. Anchoring is actually something you will do all the time naturally. I can just say the word "spider" to Jennifer, and I can literally see her change state. Her eyes will widen, and sometimes her shoulders will rise from the tension.

Another example is, say you smell a fresh apple pie, and it takes you back 40 years to when your grandmother used to cook the pie, just the scent of a pie may mentally put you in her home with her. Some phobias that we possess are based on anchors that are connected to life events that we may not care to remember.

The spider phobia that I mentioned above may be connected to an event where Jennifer had a bad experience with a spider. Now due to that, every time she hears the word, it changes her state and affects her physically. These anchors that are connected to phobias are not the ones that we really want in our lives. But we can use anchoring to connect our external and internal states to the present and improve our current state.

You can use anchoring to recall those maximum performance states that you may have experienced in the past and bring them into the *now*, where you can use them. It could be as simple as feeling happy, and that happy feeling and connected internal state could be triggered with some type of physical action like snapping your fingers.

Imagine something like you're getting ready to perform in front of a group of people, or you're getting ready for a public speaking event, and you need that extra something. You can activate your anchor and change your state.

To create the anchor, I like to wait until I am experiencing a peak, powerful and emotional state. Yes, you do have the option of using one from out of the past. This is common. You can go back and immerse yourself into that moment using all five senses and recall that peak state. But in my experience, I have had more luck creating powerful states but waiting until I was in one and then recording that state and connecting it to the anchor that I wish.

When you are in the moment, you want to get fully associated with its peak, so you can pull the trigger on your anchor. Remember to take notes on this powerful state, write every detail down that you can remember about your emotional, mental, and physical state. Reference all five of your senses.

This is important because you're going to use this to recall the state again and again later on in order to ingrain it into your system. Once you have the state and your chosen trigger, remember that practice makes perfect. The more you can practice returning to this peak state, the better you will become at it, and the more accessible the state will be at any given time that you need it.

Here are some examples of anchors I have chosen over my training career. You will notice that I connect several of them to different breathing patterns. *The breath is the bridge!*

Animal = Clenched fist & inhale to growling exhalation & forming the C Spine/ a primal curved spine.

The Gratitude state = Trigger for in the moment mindfulness. (A mental trigger)

Strength and power = Strong, forceful inhalation & widening of the eyes.

Clarity and focus = The one-minute inhalation followed by a quick exhalation.

Elation Happiness Love = Three taps of the index finger.

Calming Relaxation / release = Long slow exhalation while dropping shoulders.

Rooting & Grounding

My Chinese boxing instructor Professor James Cravens defines rooting as "a skill of keeping a heavy and relaxed energy in the lower half of the body." One who is rooted is bottom-heavy and connected to the earth. Utterly rooted.

In addition to this, I learned that levels of tension and control of intent in the body could also greatly affect your ability to be grounded. When you are startled, you can feel energy and intent rise up in the body. Sometimes the shoulders will rise.

When you have this moment of physical tension or a rise in intent, you are less connected to the ground and less centered. Other things can affect this in the body. As you become angrier, the level of tension in the body will increase, and the intent of the body will start to rise.

Obviously, this would have a negative effect if you were in a combat situation with another person. But it will also affect everyday interactions with people. When you lose control of your emotions, the body is soon to follow. As you become less centered, less rooted, it is a downward spiral.

We spoke earlier about syncing the breath lower in the torso. In addition to that, we want to have the ability to keep our tension levels in the body under control and keep the intent in the body or the energy in the body low as well or, simply put, we want to keep rooted. Staying rooted keeps you calm, centered, and under control. You generally are less reactive to external stimuli. This will come across to the people around you as relaxed confidence.

Here is an exercise to help you feel what rooting is like. You will need a partner for this to help you out. Stand up with your feet apart. You want them slightly wider than your shoulders. Once you have this low base, we are going to try to contract all of the muscle structures in your upper body. When you do this, raise your shoulders up toward your ears.

After you have done this, have your partner push on your shoulder from the side. You are pushing into the stance. You're not pushing yourself forward or back. Obviously, it would be easy to just knock you over, but it's not the point of the exercise. They are going to give you a good steady push, nothing too hard but have them build up the pressure slowly so that you can have the time to feel what your body is doing.

Eventually, even though they are pushing against the stance, they are going to be able to push you over. Now we're going to do the same exercise again. This time I want you to try to completely relax your body, let your shoulders slumped like a rag doll, let your arms dangle at your sides, and point your index fingers down at the ground like you're pointing out a rock on the ground.

Try to completely go into a physical state of dead heavy energy. One thing that will help you at this point is to have a long, relaxing exhale. Let all of the body's tension run down the legs and into the floor.

Now have your partner do the same type of push. Again, not too drastic, have them start lightly and gradually build up the pressure until they're able to tilt you over. What you should notice on the second attempt is that you will feel heavier to your partner.

It should take more effort for them to move you because you will be more rooted to the ground. The intention of the body is sinking downward. This will give you an idea of what a grounded state feels like. Now we can look at a few methods to get more tension out of the body.

Wu ji Grounding Exercise

In Chi Gong, correct body alignment is called the Wu Ji Posture, where "wu" means none, void or nothingness, and "ji" means extreme. So this loosely translates into a stance or posture that has no extremes.

We did a variation of this earlier in the book, this is going to be similar, but now we will be in a standing position. Stand with your feet about shoulder-width apart. The feet will be parallel to each other, and you want your weight evenly distributed between the two feet. If you have too much weight in the back of your foot, your heels will throw off the alignment of your spine.

Your first goal with this exercise is to attempt to align your skeletal system in a way that it is balanced and aligned. This alignment allows the bone structure to support the weight of the muscles, organs, and flesh. If we can create this alignment so that the bone structure holds the weight, we can then attempt to turn off the residual tension that is held in the body. An example of this would be the knees. If I fully flex the muscles in my leg in order to straighten, this would create tension in the muscle structure of the legs. My goal is to align the femur bone on top of the tibia.

If I can get the alignment correct between these two bones, it would allow the muscles in the legs to relax and just hang in a loose fashion. This articulation of the bone structure can also be done in the hips and lower back. Naturally, the alignment can be found in the upper torso, the neck, and the head. Your chin is tucked, and your spine is straight.

It is commonly explained to students to have the idea of a string or rope that is pulling up from the top of the head, lifting and straightening the body. All of the joints should be slightly bent and relaxed, and your shoulders should be hanging and relaxed.

Since our bodies are all built differently, finding this alignment can take a little bit of effort and time. But that's part of the goal and the exercise. Once you find this alignment, let your arms and hands hang at your side. You want everything balanced in a straight line.

Once you have achieved this, close your eyes and start a full breath. Mentally focus at the top of your head, try to relax the top of the head, and let it release.

Next, move down to the forehead and temples. I usually have students visualize a ring of light that they are passing down the body. When this light reaches a certain part of the body, we will try to release the tension from that area. And then, we will move down another few inches and attempt to let go of the tension in that area as well. We will do this exercise and travel all the way down to the feet, imagining letting go of tension and passing it into the ground.

As you do this exercise, you should start to feel heavier on the earth, more rooted and grounded. You can actually do this mental pass down the body and then up three times.

Once you have reached a point where you feel relaxed, and like the tension is passing out the feet, you are ready for the next step. Next, visualize growing roots deep into the ground underneath your feet. This exercise can be done anywhere between 5 or 10 minutes.

If you find certain body parts are difficult to relax, don't spend too much time focusing on it in the beginning. Go ahead and pass on to the next area of the body. With time you will gradually be able to loosen and relax the entire body. It is also normal to feel tingling or itching in the body when you're doing this.

Sometimes your muscles will contract slightly as they are learning to release tension. If you feel the tension in an area, it may be because you have not properly aligned the skeletal system. For instance, you may be leaning a little bit forward, and it will cause your lower back to tense.

You may feel the tension in the back of the neck because you may have a slight tilt forward in the head. Since you are standing for this exercise, you're going to experience a lot of alignment body tension.

As I have said, this will take some time to recognize, address, and then correct. This is one of the reasons this exercise is considered a more advanced version of what we did earlier in the book. If you do this exercise laying down, you do not have to deal with skeletal alignment, which is most commonly done with muscle.

So take your time, listen to your body and make small adjustments as you practice. It won't be long until you command the drill and start gaining greater benefits of muscular tension control.

Steps for creating your own peak performance states

Okay, now build your own recallable states to help you reach a performing state at any time you need to do so. The following are six steps that I teach to my students for developing a peak state.

Life moment recording

Choosing an anchor / trigger

Amplify the moment mentally

Add a breath amplifier

Add an emotion amplifier

Create and follow a state training routine

The Mind Hit

We have discussed how the mind can be an important tool or weapon. Knowing this, it is also an important target. The principle of the mind hit comes from Chinese boxing. We have discussed drills previously that help you clear the conscious mind and make it more readily available to you.

This is a very important principle for a student of the warrior arts. Just to train properly or to practice anything properly, you need access to your focus, your conscious mind. The more you are able to access this, the more you will be able to increase the effectiveness of your education, training, or anything you focus on.

Anytime you work to create states or to have the ability to recall them, especially the ones that are going to be related to stressful environments, your ability to maintain control of your focus and concentration while under stress is imperative.

"Take your opponents mind out of the fight and there is no fight." - James Cravens - Chinese boxing maxim

This is even more important in a physical exchange for a warrior. Knowing this, if we have the ability to disrupt our opponent's mental focus, it will allow us to take advantage of the lapse of concentration. This same principle can apply to a heated conversation, a business negotiation, or navigation of a business deal. It could be anything that would serve as a mental distraction for your opponent.

This type of distraction could have the same effect on the opponent as what you want to avoid. It could remove them from the mental state they are in. Put them in a reset mode or take them out of the state entirely, just taking them out of the exchange or fight is a rare gift in combat or in a negotiation.

John Boyd was a fighter pilot in the Korean war. John created a way of thinking during a conflict that taught its users how to disrupt the thinking process of their opponents. This tool was called the OODA Loop. OODA stands for Observe, Orient, Decide, Act.

He taught that these four stages in the decision-making process had to be traversed by both you and your opponent. So the individual who made it through the process the quickest and took action generally would win the encounter.

This decision-making process is something your opponent will go through regardless of whether or not they are getting ready to engage in a physical exchange, a business meeting, or a heated conversation. I was introduced to this concept at the Executive Protection Institute, where I have now taught bodyguards and private security professionals for over 14 years. Professor John Musser teaches the OODA Loop as part of his executive protection program at the school.

One of the biggest challenges, Boyd believed, is our inability to properly observe and orientate ourselves in our actual reality.

Obviously, things are going to change, especially if it is an emergency event. When these things change, people will often fail to adjust their perspective to what is actually going on around them. They will continue to think of the world as they feel it should be or how they have seen it in the recent past.

In other words, they cling to pre-existing cerebral models. This can obviously be bad for you if you are in a stressful situation and you have to deal with the fight or flight response of the body. Part of the OODA Loop model is obtaining the ability to observe reality for what it *is* and not get overly connected to old thought patterns. We will hold onto these patterns because we are familiar with them, and they feel comfortable and safe, but that is not always reality.

So the first part of the OODA Loop is to *observe* what is going on around you. This is directly related to what we have spoken about previously in the book in our ability to obtain more control over our conscious mind.

Our ability to focus and be in the here and now and pay attention to our environment and what is actually going on and how it relates to us is crucial. In the self-protection industry, they will have a series of mental conditions or states that they will use to signal where you are on the stress continuum.

This first level of awareness is referred to in that industry as being in condition yellow. Condition white would be completely unaware of your surroundings. In other words, you are just mentally switched off. So when you are in condition yellow, you are in a higher state of conscious interaction with your environment in the here and now.

For the security professional, if you are in a restaurant, you are paying attention to where the exits are as well as where the bathrooms are. You may actively choose the location you're going to place yourself and your client.

This stage of the OODA Loop could easily be framed in running a business. If you are observing, you are aware of your financials in the other areas of the business that will give you realistic feedback of what you have in front of you.

The second "O" in the OODA Loops is *orientation*. Orientation is your ability to take your feedback from your observation and determine where you are in relation to the situation. Often this is done with mental models. In martial arts, a good practitioner will study many different models that can fit into a situation. There could be weaponry involved, it could be a striking contest, it could be a pummeling or standing grappling exchange or you could end up on the ground.

Each area I have just mentioned will have certain models that are taught and trained depending on the art. I personally do not like to choose models based on a system or method. I like to take a look at what the absolute primal actions are both from your opponent and from you. It is best to study many different possibilities. To simplify this, you are going to learn as many different techniques and methods of using them as possible.

This modeling is how you mentally orientate yourself in the OODA Loop. You may be in the middle of an exchange, and you will notice your partner shift into a position that is familiar in relation to something you have trained previously.

At this point, you don't even have to think. All you have to do is act. Although these mental models are good for creating structure in orientation, they can also be a bad thing because you can become overly connected to them and not have the ability to make adjustments on the fly.

You may attempt to orientate yourself in a stressful situation and realize you have no preset mental models that align with what's going on. At this point, you have to have the ability to throw out the models and build your own. To simplify this, you are consistently going through the "what if's" in your environment. You are making plans (mental models) for them just in case that might happen.

"Be polite, be professional, but have a plan to kill everybody you meet." - General James Mattis

The next part of the process is to simply decide what to do. Take a look at your options and quickly pick what action you're going to take. It may just be your best-educated guess, but that's okay. The main part of the process is that you make a decision, and you do not get frozen sitting there going back-and-forth between your options. If you find yourself in the situation, if you want to train yourself to decide, pick one and then take action.

Going back to the mind hit. This is basically what you want to do to your opponent. You want to hit them mentally and scramble their OODA Loop. Interrupt their thinking process and slow down their ability to eventually get to a decision and take action. If you can do this, it will allow you the time to take action yourself, beat them to the punch.

6.
WILLPOWER & DRIVE
DISCIPLINE

Webster's dictionary defines effort as a conscious exertion of power: hard work / a job requiring time and effort.

A person's individual drive and effort ethic is directly connected to their ability to achieve their goals. Over the years, I have seen personalities that have had a natural ingrained drive that seemed to push them to want to achieve more and go farther.

Equally, on the other end of the spectrum, I have seen individuals who seem to lack the ability to tap into their own willpower, their own drive. These individuals sometimes would have methods they have learned in their journey to try and develop this energetic drive, while others came to the academy looking for answers to develop better willpower and discipline.

I commonly see in students and have experienced myself the impulses to let things slide as you go throughout your day. Sometimes they are small things in the beginning, like eating something that may not be on your diet, not making your bed today, letting those dishes sit in the sink because we will "take care of them later."

These smaller things left unchecked will eventually start to affect the more important things you were trying to achieve. Maybe you are trying to start a new habit, and because you may be in a little bit of a hurry today, you decide to go back to an old habit because it feels quicker instead of reinforcing the new habit.

Sometimes we give in to this because of laziness or procrastination. I believe these small moments when we give in and do not do those little things we know we should are the beginning of developing willpower in the overall amount of effort you can put forward. Human nature (that is, the human mind and body) has a natural inclination to find the easiest route or method. It is so easy to take your hands off the wheel and just cruise through this course of low resistance.

The small moments are what we have to fight at the beginning of the process of willpower, effort, and drive development. We must, in those small moments, fight against the easy path of laziness.

Examples of these will be not doing those dishes right now, not picking up that piece of trash, not taking that moment to clean up after yourself, not giving in to that useless habit that you are trying to change or put down. In those little moments, the first step is to overcome your natural inclination to let it slide and take action.

This is the beginning of developing your drive and willpower. Giving in to the small urges will build up. It starts becoming easy to just let it slide. But the opposite is also true. If you start adjusting your willpower ethic on a small scale in the beginning, it will build up to larger opportunities later. In other words, it gets easier to "ramp up" your energy and self-control.

It's just like training in the gym; in order to make a muscle grow, you will gradually increase the weight you will put on the bar. Over time, you gain the ability to handle larger loads of resistance. Students at the academy will a lot of times get introduced to this at incremental level.

You may be placed into an environment where you do not have the willpower to get a task done. If this is a challenge, we will usually back down to a smaller challenge, much like what I mentioned above, and we will have the students gradually work their way up as their willpower ethic increases.

Obviously, this can be done on the mat by just backing off the resistance and building it up slowly. But having the students do it throughout the day as they go through their normal routine always seems to increase their growth exponentially inside the academy.

I would nickname this the "extra mile drill." It was a very simple thing that sometimes was difficult to do.

Willpower and effort I consider a lifestyle. If you are looking to strengthen your willpower, it's not an exercise you're going to do, and suddenly you will possess more of it. It is a life change, and like any major life change, it has to start small and then build up.

It is also a perishable skill. If you take a little time off from your small efforts every day, then eventually, you will be back where you started. Willpower itself is a habit that has to be disciplined into the human-machine.

The Effort Scale

I was fortunate enough to get introduced to weight training when I was 14. I was equally fortunate to have good mentors around me to guide me and teach me what to do. It didn't take long for me to see some physical change, and that sealed the deal.

It has been a highly beneficial habit in many different ways. I always noticed over the many years of the gym culture how as time passed, you would see some individuals at the gym create great physical change, and then you will see others that would look the same year after year.

Quite honestly, the majority of the crowd in the gym never really change much. One day I looked up, and I noticed the guy in the mirror was having the same problem. It was puzzling to me at first, but then I realize that as I had grown older, the effectiveness of what I have been doing the majority of my career in the gym and started to not have the same effects. I was not getting the same results that I was experiencing years ago.

I had heard from many sources over the years to expect this, and it was just part of the process. I'm not good at accepting those types of thought patterns, so I looked back in the mirror and asked that guy, "are you really putting in as much effort as you can?" No, I was putting in what I considered a decent amount of effort. The truth was, I was not pushing it as hard as I had potential for.

This was an eye-opener for me at that time in my life. It was time to take a good look at what I was doing and the outcome from it and be completely honest with myself if I was getting the results I was looking for. In the martial arts, I had learned to push myself to my limits many times. But it is an entirely different environment in the gym than it is in the academy.

So I decided to start stepping up my effort. Within a few days, I could hardly walk, and when I was able to, I looked like a duck waddling. Quickly I realized that my ability to recover like I did when I was younger had diminished.

Since I was dealing with a few physical limitations, I decided to dive deeper into the science of weight training.

This goes right back to what we spoke about earlier in the book. I really did not know what I did not know.

The truth is, over time, I had settled into a comfortable routine and effort. I pretty much was just doing a maintenance program, and that's what I wanted to change. I started to look for a mentor in the industry. I went to my normal process of looking for a teacher or a source of knowledge. I was fortunate, and then I found two individuals that were not only tremendously experienced but they were also sun teachers. They were *creators*.

I started to learn the science behind building programs designed around my goals and how to set up periods of effort. I also started to discover how to measure your recovery depending on your age and design the program according to your potential.

In other words, I started to understand how to train smarter, which would give me the ability to train harder and at higher levels. I learned how and when I could exert a tremendous amount of effort in order to gain the change I was looking for. I immediately dove into the information and started going to work.

Even as I move forward with training, I continue studying this science. Even to this day, I learn more and more as I move forward. The result of this turned into a tremendous amount of physical change in multiple areas. I was actually getting more done with less than I considered possible.

All of this physical change was noticed by several students at the academy. Several of them asked me what I had changed in order to produce the results. I saw this as a great opportunity (as we mentioned earlier in the book, one of the best ways to learn something at a greater level is to start teaching it and start mentoring someone else). So I started sharing the information that I had learned.

I noticed after some time passed that even though I taught the guys everything they needed, they still were not being successful at it. They would come back and ask me what they needed to tweak or what they would need to change to get the same results.

I accompanied a couple of them to the gym just to take a look at what they were doing. They were sticking to the plan and using the science just like they should be. The thing I noticed was the amount of effort. I would tell them you need to push a little harder, "You need to step up your effort." And the response I would get back was, "I'm giving it all I've got." My response was, "But are you really?"

It took them a couple of tries in order to get around their ego. But once they were able to do it, they realized that they were not making the effort required to make the changes they were looking for. The way I explained it to them at that time was by introducing the effort scale.

"It is only through labor and painful effort, by grim energy and resolute courage, that we move on to better things." - Theodore Roosevelt

The effort scale is a super simple concept. Pretty much a scale of 1 to 10, and you determine where you are on the scale. Did you ask yourself the question, "Am I able to step this up a notch?" This should be one of the key things you ask yourself every time you go into the gym or the academy.

I found that most people will put forth the effort, and they will think, "This is the highest level of effort I have." If we sit down and take a look at it, and we are honest with ourselves, we quickly realize that we are nowhere near what our limits are. Not that we want to push it all the way to 10. But generally, there is always room to step it up a notch. For me, once I started to take it up one or two clicks on the scale, I started to see a real physical change in my body.

A good measurement for me comes from answering this question: "Am I truthfully getting the results I was looking for?" If I'm not, then it's time to go back and take a look at my effort scale. Of course, I also took a look at improving my knowledge of what I was doing, and this had a tremendous effect on it as well.

One of the reasons I always say you should be a perpetual student is this: You are always a white belt, and you are always looking for deeper knowledge and information. Even when you think it's not there, trust me, it's *there*. You might have to look a little harder, but it is there. Now at the beginning of this chapter, we had a definition of effort, and one of the key parts of the definition was this: *conscious exertion of power.*

To me, this is a huge piece of the puzzle. You learn to increase your effort in the moment and in the now. And then you keep that consistent over time. The ability to do these two things will create a tremendous amount of change in whatever you're focusing on—diligence, hard work consistently over time.

This not only will help you reach your goals in life but in my opinion, it will strengthen your character. I have seen this many times with my students on the academy floor over the years. So, where are you on the effort scale today?

"Leaders are made, they are not born. They are made by hard effort, which is the price all of us must pay to achieve any goal that is worthwhile." = Vince Lombardi

Passion Source

Passion can be defined as intense, driving, or overmastering feeling or conviction. or a strong liking or desire for or devotion to some activity, object, or concept. There are different things in life that can supply the motivation to you. These things will vary per individual. It just depends on where you are on your journey. For some people, it is their kids. For others, it can be a spouse or family. I have worked with highly motivated individuals by their goals and what they wanted to achieve in the future. They had created a visual image of where they wanted to be in life, and this visual image gave them a lot of motivation and passion.

I have met highly motivated individuals because of a past event, whether that event was good or bad. Some of them had experienced a painful and negative event in life. So they are very motivated to avoid a repeat of those events, and that drives them towards their current goals. There can be many different examples of this. All of these things can be what I call a passion source.

A passion source is a personal event or possibly a thing that gives you drive, energy, or passion. What it is that creates this energy is not as important as what you do with it. I'll teach my students that regardless of the source, you have the ability to mentally connect it to daily activities and routines that will take you closer to where you want to be in life.

Doing this can bring greater amounts of drive and passion into those activities. They can motivate you to achieve them with greater effort and energy.

This doesn't necessarily have to be a positive event either. Some of the most powerful passion sources that I have had in my life were events that made me angry or disappointed. One example of this would be a business failure. I've actually had this happen several times in my life, but I can remember one instance where the business failed due to another individual.

At that time in my life, it was extremely irritating to me. The one good thing that came out of the event is that I redirected my irritation and disappointment into action. It drove me for years in the future to double my effort in the other endeavors that I had moved on to. To this day, the thought of that event can create a passion and a drive for me to move forward and do better. It has actually become a positive thing because of this.

Find a motivator / accountability coach or culture

This is something that I have helped create in the academy many times over the years. Sometimes I end up being the individual that is in the coach position or the motivator. Other times I've seen individuals develop relationships with other students in the academy because that individual supplied them with a certain amount of motivation, or they held him accountable for what they knew their goals were.

The academy is a family environment. Everybody, there is walking on a path, we may all be in different positions on the path, but we all know what it is and where we're headed. I tell my students all the time that it is part of their responsibility being senior students to help motivate and guide their younger brothers and sisters on their journey.

I teach this as part of the culture, we expect it to be that way, and we educate the students to do it. This is not always the reality outside of the academy. Regardless of this, the principle is just as applicable. If you have set a goal for yourself, taking the time to break down the chain of events that are required to get you from point A to point B, then you've clearly defined your path, and you may have even set a timeframe on each of those sub-steps on your way to your end result.

If you have this together, share it with someone you know is going to press you with accountability. You may even have a discussion with him about doing this for you. We spoke about surrounding yourself with the right people. This will come right back to that principle.

Does your inner circle have the philosophy of mutual accountability? If they do not, are they the type of people that would be willing to learn to do this and then apply it with you? Very much like what we do inside the academy, we want to create a culture of accountability and motivation. Inside the academy, they have me, Sifu Alan, creating the environment, we set the rules of what students are supposed to do in order to support each other.

We demonstrate between the senior student's respect, motivation, and accountability. In your circle of friends, you may have to create this environment yourself, but as we said before, if you have the right people around you, it should not be too difficult to do. Remember, it is a two-way street. Right now, you may be asking for assistance from your friend, but if both of you understand the process, it will not be long until you are supplying the same support to the other members of your circle.

I have walked into various cultures unexpectedly and discovered they were similar to this. And generally, I am very self-motivated and highly driven. But when I walked into this one particular culture, it seemed like I was behind. Everyone in the circle of that culture immediately expected me to step up.

I would go so far as to say they did not ask. They *demanded* that you step up to the level of everybody in the group. But at the same time, they gave a tremendous amount of support. Do this, and what you will be able to achieve with these groups will be amazing.

Finding this environment sometimes is hard, and it may be difficult to get accepted into it if you do. Some high-performance groups in the business industry are not open to everyone. So sometimes you may have to create this yourself, and you may be the leader of it in the end.

I have been a part of or have the ability to create this type of environment outside of the academy several times over. It was done in an industry that had nothing to do with the Martial Arts. But the environment was created just like the one I experienced when I grew up in the academy.

The guys in the group really did not even know where the information for the culture that we had built came from. And I don't think any of them really cared. All they knew is they had a group of guys that would give off a tremendous amount of respect, drive, and accountability.

7.
DEALING WITH THE UNKNOWN

Uncertainty and the unknown

The unknown. If there are constants in life, uncertainty is one of them. Feeling a lack of control in your situation and having a shortness of answers about the future. Fear of a bad performance at an upcoming competition or a public speaking event. There are unknowns everywhere you look in life.

Our brains seem to be hardwired to make dealing with uncertainty difficult. When we are forced to make quick decisions without adequate information, the untrained mind will move from thinking with the rational brain into the limbic system and the hippocampus.

This midbrain system does have other roles in the brain. It is believed its primary function would be to control emotions. It is also believed this is the area where emotions such as anxiety and fear are created or generated.

As we covered earlier, this is where the fight or flight response lives. In the time of the caveman, this overwhelming fear or caution was probably very conducive to survival.

When I first learned about this, I was simply told it was the midbrain. Sifu would refer to it as the primitive brain. Although it can vary as far as reaction per individual, uncertainty and other stressors can force us to react with the midbrain. This can trigger emotional reactions, and thought patterns can cause us to make decisions that might not be conducive to success either in the moment or in the future.

Processing the unknown

Uncertainty affects everyone differently, but rest assured, it does affect everyone. One of its effects is obviously anxiety. Everyone will feel it, but not everyone deals with it or processes it in the same way.

I have seen the entire spectrum of reactions to uncertainty on the academy mat over the years. Some students seem to have a greater ability to deal with the anxiety that commonly comes along with uncertainty. They seem to have a higher threshold for it naturally. Then again, other students seem to have a higher anxiety reaction, so it has a greater effect on them, and they seem to struggle to manage their reaction to it.

The students that seem to have less of a resistance to anxiety will spend a lot of time in their head worrying about an upcoming competition or test. Will I remember everything I need to know? Who is going to show up to watch? What will they think of my performance? What if I don't pass? Will I do something wrong or awkward in front of everyone? They almost seem to be lost in their head, trapped by the thoughts of the upcoming endeavor.

Then you have the opposite end of the spectrum, the student who seems to look at the upcoming test and just say, "Who cares, I'm not that worried about it. I will do my best, and we will see what happens."

They almost seem like they're looking forward to it because they're excited about the experience's potential adventure. Both students, having a completely different reaction to the same event. The same moment in time. It's not that the adventure-seeking student never has a reaction of anxiety for any event. It just means that they may need something that is a little more drastic to trigger the response. Neither response is incorrect, and everyone is going to be at a different place on the journey.

I see this generally because it is my job to create those situations for the student. One to see their reaction, and two to introduce the concept of training in order to condition their reaction to a greater amount of stress or uncertainty. And for those who have a higher reaction to an event, maybe they even overreact. What I mean is the reaction to the thought is out of proportion for what it really is. I've seen these individuals benefit the greatest from the training we would do at the academy. I would go so far as to say they are the ones that need it the most.

It is one of the incredible things about the ecosystem of the academy. You can create opportunities to train many different skills both physically and internally on the mat. Situations can be created, and many times they will just come with the environment. These situations will give the students the opportunity to train their reactions, how they deal with different things on the mat.

These skills can carry over into life. In the academy, you are going to learn these things with your team, your family. They generally are in this with you. Even though they may not be in that situation at the moment, and they may be the ones creating it for you. Within a week, they may be the ones receiving it from an elder classmate. The thing is, that's not always the case in real life. That's one of the reasons why learning it in an academy can be an ideal place to practice.

Dealing with the unknown
There are different levels of training for a student or any individual to learn to deal with these things. They can range from just making decisions in a life-based or tough

situation, all the way up to being forced to make a split-second decision under an extreme amount of stress.

What one would have to do is train their brain in moments of stress to move away from the limbic system and into the rational brain. As Sifu would say, don't let the midbrain control you; quieten it and think. As we've said before, thinking with the midbrain generally is connected to a fear-based knee-jerk reaction. This is not conducive to good decision-making.

People who are trained in good decision making will recognize their brain's reaction and movement to the midbrain and put a stop to it before it gets out of control. They will gain a more stable mental level before making a life decision when faced with unknown possibilities. So, what can you learn from the students in the academy? Here are some of the fundamentals I will see applied over the years.

Breath

The breath is like a leash on the primal brain. In moments of great stress and anxiety, stop and take a full cycle breath. Focus on feeling the breath pass through your nose and throat. Fill the body with air, expand your torso, lungs, and rib cage, as it all fills from the bottom to the top.

On top of being responsible for a multitude of positive conditions inside the body, the breath is one of the first physical actions you can focus on that will pull you out of negative thought patterns of the past and future and bring you into the "now state."

The breath is the first step of mindfulness. This is how I usually teach students to focus on the breath internally. This can bring them out of their mind and into the body, and then gradually, they will work their way outside of the body to their surroundings.

Next time you feel yourself feeling a bit out of control, or you start to notice that your mind is wandering in the direction of negativity, with anxiety-creating thoughts, take a moment to breathe and focus on it. The number of inhalations is up to you.

I have learned that it varies per individual. Use what works for you. You'll be surprised how relaxed, calm, and steady you will feel after a moment or two of this exercise.

Practice mindful consciousness

This is something that we discussed earlier in the book when we were going through our morning-focused training and breathing exercises.

We develop the ability to quieten the mind, tame rogue thoughts, and gradually regain more control of our available consciousness in order to be in the here and now, not only in the drill but throughout the day. We want to be in a mindful state of consciousness. Are you aware of where you are at the moment and what is going on in the here and now? If you have not had an opportunity to train that exercise to this level, now is the time. It could be as easy as just being aware of how the chair you're sitting in feels. What is the texture and feel of the desk that you're sitting at?

Sounds that surround you, the light that is in the room. How do you feel physically? Practicing a mindful consciousness will pull you out of the primitive midbrain and into the rational brain. Being in the moment can also keep you in the "yellow alert" state we spoke about when discussing the OODA Loop. It is the orientation stage of OODA. I have found that this heightened level of awareness is an additional buffer when dealing with sudden unanticipated events.

The Gratitude Drill

Gratitude has the power to transform anxiety and change your perspective. The gratitude drill will usually follow the mindful exercise above.

Once a student pulls himself into the here and now and is able to focus and be in the moment, he will be better prepared to face the day. I tell my students to take a moment and do the gratitude drill each day. Ask yourself how you feel, if you feel healthy and strong. And remember to be thankful. Are you around good friends and people you trust? If so, be thankful.

If you take the time and look around, you can find something to be thankful for. Even though sometimes it can be hard, life is an amazing gift. You just have to take the time to recognize it.

I have watched this mental drill change the entire attitude, energy, and posture of a student in a matter of seconds. It has a way of pulling positive energy out of a situation that will charge you physically and mentally if you allow it.

These positive thoughts have a way of silencing fear and activating rational thinking. Obviously, if you are struggling with negative thoughts, this can be a challenge, but it is possible, especially if it is something that you are able to train on a regular basis. Just like exercising a muscle, it is important to exercise your gratitude.

The more you are able to train your gratitude drill, the easier it will be to recall and use it in times of stress and anxiety.

Focus on taking action

Once you have gained control of the mind, you have to work to maintain it because this is not a state that will maintain itself on its own. It takes active willpower on your part to maintain this positive state. You are going to have the same thought patterns that you were struggling with previously come back to you.

It's important to know that this is going to happen and to be prepared for it. It is common when old thought patterns stray back in to give them power by focusing on them and dwelling on them too much. So it is important to see them clearly as they come back into your consciousness.

Recognize them for what they are, and then repeat the process. You may have to do this quite a bit if you have not done this exercise before. But I promise you, the more you do it, the better you will get at it. I have watched students do this over and over again for more than 40 years. All of them that were persistent and accomplished great things with these skillsets.

Now that you are in a now state, one of the best ways to maintain control of the mind is to focus it on action. Sit down, and you can take a look at your situation. Weigh out the pros and cons of what you have to deal with. Take the time to look at the multiple possibilities of outcomes.

Generally, when I am doing this, I will have a talk with some close, trusted friends. I will usually do this in order to gain perspective. Sometimes we only have the ability to see things in our way.

Discuss with others what you're dealing with, ask them what they think your options could be. Open up and listen and take those suggestions into consideration. Going through this process will allow you to come up with Plan B, plan C, and plan D. Sitting down and making a plan can create a sense of control for you. Now it's important to remember that even though you make this plan, life changes, and the situation changes.

You may have to sit down and do this a few more times. You might have to have that discussion with a trusted friend a few more times. If the situation changes and throws a wrench in your plan, don't let it take over your mind. It's important to know that this is probably going to happen.

If I know that it's going to happen in advance, I can look for it in the future. I have even told my friends that I have the discussion with, more than likely, I'm going to talk to you again in a few days when life throws a wrench in this whole mess.

Once I have developed my plan, the next thing I will do is create daily routines and habits in order to take organized action in the direction of the plan. Nothing allows the man to stray back into his old ways of worry and anxiety than having nothing to do. Creating your daily routines can give you a visual plan to take action on.

This allows you to focus your energy on the baby steps needed to take forward action on your plan and not get lost mentally in the past or the future. On those occasions when the mind will stray, pulling it back into an ordered state can mean getting immersed in your daily routines.

Don't let perfection destroy your action. Once you are taking action on your plan, keep going. One of the biggest things that I have seen that will bring a plan to a screeching halt is being overly focused on being perfect in what you do.

Do not worry about perfection. Focus on action. The truth is nothing we do will be perfect. There's always going to be slight flaws and error in our journey. We know this, and we discussed this earlier in regards to failure.

Truthfully failure is just part of the process, and we know that. Since we know it, we expected it. We are looking for it. I have white belt students in the academy be completely physically shut down by this before. This is not what we want.

The Black Belt Test

In the early to mid-90s, I was working with a grandmaster of Chuan Fa. Sijo (grandmaster or founder) would arrange a training camp in the wilderness of Minnesota once a year.

The camp would last a week or a little over. It was on a campsite that was out in the middle of nowhere. The site was very well-made, and it had cabins for all of the students as well as a large building that was a cafeteria.

We had the ability to train out in the large open area between the cabins, or we could move all of the tables and chairs in the cafeteria to train indoors. Most of our days were spent out in the field training and working on multiple forms and drills.

The cool thing about this camp was that Sijo would arrange for multiple other masters and instructors to be present to teach during the week. It was an incredible experience and a great opportunity to get introduced to different systems and training methods.

It was not uncommon for teachers to schedule tests for their students during this time so that they would have the opportunity to do the presentation in front of everyone. Generally, we all knew in advance who was going to be testing, and they would let the student know so that they could spend the months prior to the camp in preparation.

We arrived at the camp on the first day, and I started setting up in our individual cabins. We went through the day as was normal with our training. It wasn't uncommon to start training around 8 or 9 AM and go through until 9 PM.

That first day was no exception. I will always remember how sore I would get after the first day. It was a shock to the body to be out in the sun and be that active for over 12 hours. It was late in the evening, and we were just finishing up with dinner, and we're getting prepared for some of the last classes for the night. This is when Sijo came up to me and informed me that I was going to be taking a test.

This test was going to be in front of all of the masters that were present. I immediately asked him what I needed to prepare for. And his answer was, I'm not going to tell you, you will find out during the test. This is the first time this ever happened to me. Before I always knew what I would be presenting at a test, I always had some time to get ready for it. After he informed me of this, I simply said "yes sir" and finished the evening classes and went to the cabin.

Please understand, dear reader, I have always taken training very seriously. It has always been one of the more important things in my life. So, needless to say, this situation created a huge opportunity for anxiety. That is a kind way of saying I was freaking out.

At that time, I didn't realize that Sijo was creating an opportunity for me to deal with the unknown. In reality, he had seen me do the demonstration, the forms, and the techniques many times in the past. The test really wasn't about those things, but of course, I did not know that.

He was testing my ability to deal with the unknown and all of the things that come along with doing it. Even though at the time I had some training in dealing with this type of thing, the reason I'm giving you this explanation right now is that I remember completely losing it at that moment.

After he told me about the test, probably for the next three or four hours, I sat in the cabin with my mind running wild. It probably wasn't until about 1 or 2 AM in the morning before I gathered myself and realized what I was doing. My thoughts were running away and doing more damage than anything in the actual situation, in the here and now, would ever do.

That's when I remembered my different exercises for reining in mind and gaining control. It took me about 30 minutes before I was able to calm down enough to go to sleep. When I woke up in the morning, I was immediately conscious of what was going on, and as soon as the midbrain started to speak, I would shut it down and bring myself into the present. I continued to do this throughout the day, and the test went off without a hitch.

The reason I remember this example personally was because of that few hours I spent in complete and total control of myself. My emotions had been powering all of the mental thoughts that were running wild in my mind. It has stuck with me for my entire life. After the test a little later in the day, Sijo had a conversation with me in regards to dealing with the unknown and what that meant as a warrior.

A Warrior's perspective

There are different types of warriors in society. There are many different ways to walk the path of the warrior. A warrior is someone who strives to be ready to deal with conflict. They prepare to deal with violence. Conflict is full of unknowns. You are never really sure of the outcome. The outcome could mean different things depending on the situation. It could range from great physical pain and harm all the way to death.

Unless you are a fighter in martial arts, you generally will prepare for it, but you're hoping to avoid it. As a fighter, you are guided by a set of rules, a referee, and a medical tech who is waiting outside the ring.

For some, it is their job to go into situations of conflict. They know there is no way to avoid it, only to do their best to prepare for it. This is an entirely different level of dealing with the things we are discussing.

You imagine what the individuals in those positions have to deal with mentally. And they have to do it not only once, but every time they're on the job. For 14 years now, I have had the incredible opportunity to be the defensive tactics instructor for the Executive Protection Institute as well as the Vehicle Dynamics Institute.

The Executive Protection Institute is one of the top executive protection training schools in the United States. Dr. Richard W. Kobetz founded the Executive Protection Institute in 1978. Doc K. actually created the "Personal Protection Specialist (PPS)" title that is used in the protection industry everywhere today. The Vehicle Dynamics Institute is the top advanced driver training school in the U.S.

During this time, both of these great schools have given me the opportunity to work with men and women in the military, law enforcement, and the executive protection industry. This work has given me the opportunity to meet some of the most amazing people and have the opportunity to learn from them. Teaching them, having them go out in the field and using the information, and then coming back with feedback has been an incredible learning experience. These men and women deal with the unknown and uncertainty at tremendous levels and do it repeatedly as part of the job.

Through the Vehicle Dynamics Institute, I had the opportunity to work with a group of high-level Special Forces operatives. These guys were placed in situations that were tremendously stressful, both physically and mentally. I had the opportunity to be present when they were receiving training in regards to monitoring and controlling their physiology using breathing techniques.

In addition, I got to give input on my own experience in this area. This was an exceptional opportunity for me because the guys would go and use the information and then come back and give me feedback.

This feedback loop allowed me to tweak and improve a lot of the information and skills that I taught for this type of environment. It also had a tremendous effect on the type of training I was doing back at the academy with the guys. It motivated me to dig deeper into the topics discussed, which led to more growth and advancement of the material overall regardless of who I was teaching it to.

After starting on this material, I also had the opportunity to work with several groups in law enforcement and the guys who would come through the Executive Protection Institute.

Interacting with these guys allowed me to find one common ground between our two industries. This common ground was a warrior's perspective on dealing with the unknown. We all expect it, and we train for it so we will be prepared. But the warrior will actively seek out this environment and place himself in it on a regular basis because he sees the benefits of the environment.

No, I'm not saying go out and find yourself a gunfight to get in. What I'm saying is they will all create opportunities that will force them into high-level stress situations, so they have the opportunity to train control of their physiology while dealing with it.

Seeking out the unknown

A warrior seeks out the unknown because he knows it is growth and wisdom. It is not always a comfortable exchange, as we all know.

Life can throw something at you out of left field that you were not expecting. It'll put you in a situation that you don't particularly enjoy or want to be in. But after you get through that event and on the other side. It is common that you look back and learn from the experience.

You come away from it with a greater depth of wisdom and understanding, not only about what may have happened in the life event. You will learn things about yourself that may not have been evident before.

It is human nature to avoid these types of events because of the inconvenience and potential pain it promises. But the warrior sees the process for what it is. He understands it's better to learn and gain this knowledge in advanced preparation than to be thrust into the event when the stakes could be higher.

"Uncertainty is the only certainty there is, and knowing how to live with insecurity is the only security."

- **John Allen Paulos**

This is one of the reasons the warrior seeks the environment. He will look for opportunities to create these learning environments in his training. He wants to pick up those little bits of knowledge and wisdom and collect them. He hopes that the accumulation of all of these golden nuggets will add up to a collective skill level for when that potential future event comes to test his metal. It could be a negotiation or a public speaking event for the businessman or entrepreneur. It could be that self-defense situation where you're protecting your wife and kids on the street for the martial artist. It could be a gunfight for the law enforcement officer or the mission for the Special Forces team. Using the unknown as a tool of preparation is a common thing in the warrior arts.

One example of this in my industry is the test that I spoke about earlier. The thing about that particular test is that it was a test of the unknown. But I did have a general idea of what was going to happen. And though it was mentally stressful, it was still a relatively low level of stress and anxiety to deal with.

Another example of taking a look at would be sparring. Sparring is a form of play fighting. You can do this on different levels of intensity depending on what you're trying to create. The difference between this environment and the test is dependent upon the level of engagement between you and your partner (or partners), the threat of pain, and the threat of embarrassment (bruising your ego).

If you are having a physical exchange with one other person, and that individual is more trained and has more experience, then you have to put all of that aside and step on the field in search of that lesson. You have no idea what's going to happen, and you are forced to make decisions and reactions in a split second.

Additionally, in sparring, you get to pay for your mistakes immediately. You do not only have to attempt to apply a move or technique, but you have to be able to do it while maintaining control of your body, your emotions, and your mind. This is one of the reasons you have to have the ability to vary the level of intensity.

If you have a good partner, he will know how to create just the right amount of pressure to force you to apply what you're doing just a little bit past your limitation—doing this consistently over time forces you to have growth.

How could you apply this to life outside of the academy? One of the first examples that come to mind is public speaking. I may start out just practicing on my own. Eventually, I may invite a friend to give me critiques. Beyond that, I may seek out a local public speaking group and put myself in front of strangers and people I don't know. I may invite verbal debate on the subject I am presenting.

This obviously starts to increase pressure. Then I work my way up to putting myself out in front of the public openly. This may sound like a relatively easy process for some, but for many, the thought of just speaking in front of a few friends will create a tremendous amount of anxiety. A lot of that anxiety comes from the uncertainty of their reaction, what they think.

Regardless, for growth, we know that we have to go into that unknown and put ourselves out there. We have to put our egos in check and be open to suggestions and learn from the mistakes. Sometimes when we do step out, we do it with hesitation. But I tell my guys on the mat, the warrior seeks those mistakes and bites them. He wants them because he knows that is the fire that will make the metal strong.

Knowing without knowing

For our ancestors, it was a point of survival to rely on their gut instinct or intuition. That moment of knowing without understanding where the knowledge comes from. How many times have you been in a situation where your gut told you that what you're getting ready to do might not be a good idea?

Whenever that happened to me, I always thought about the cause of this "gut feeling," and I did not see a logical reason to feel that way, but nonetheless, the feeling was still there. Then after moving forward, I would realize that it was a bad move after all.

You've no doubt had this happen before, too. Afterward, when looking at the situation with hindsight, you remember that gut feeling that was telling you not to move forward with the decision. You just had a hunch, but you couldn't seem to explain why.

Professor Gerard Hodgkinson at Leeds University in Leeds, West Yorkshire, recently published his team's research in the *British Journal of Psychology*. They found that intuition is a psychological process by which our subconscious uses past experiences and certain cues from its present environment to make split-second decisions while under stress.

They believe this process happens so quickly that it's not even noticeable to the conscious mind. "People usually experience true intuition when they are under severe time pressure or in a situation of information overload or acute danger, where conscious analysis of the situation may be difficult or impossible," says Professor Hodgkinson.

Now the question is how can we, as high performers, tap into this unconscious process? In my experience, one of the first steps is quieting the mind. We have actually already discussed this earlier in the book.

When we were taking a look at the exercise to develop focus, one of our goals was to gain control of the noise we are experiencing internally, we discussed how this would give us more access to our conscious mind in order to focus on being in the here and now. For me, after training this for a few years, I started to experience what my teacher called "knowing without knowing."

The quieter my mind became, and the more I was able to pull myself into the moment, the more I seemed to be tuning in to what I called intuition. It seemed I had just gained the ability to listen for it more.

A common example that I have experienced is thinking of someone seconds before the phone rings, and that person is who is calling. The gut feeling that something is just not right with someone you know, maybe a family member, so you reach out to them and find out they actually are going through a life crisis.

Sifu eventually introduced me to drills that trained this idea in order to improve it and eventually went on to implementing the scale in sparring with an opponent. So, in other words, he started to place me in gradually more stressful environments in order to force me to have the opportunities to listen for this internal voice.

This was difficult for me. When I was placed in stressful situations, I would get very focused on what I was doing. In other words, I would gather up all of my consciousness and focus solely on my opponent. I had no room to listen for anything else, any other valuable data. After a while of not accomplishing what Sifu was looking for, he had a talk with me and told me that I had to get to the point where I was not giving my opponent as much of my mental energy.

He told me I would actually get to the point where I would just ignore them. I wouldn't even look at them. First, it was very difficult for me to believe, much less achieve. And I'll be honest. As I was attempting to learn the process, I got smashed in the head quite a bit. After a while, I finally got to the point where I could "let go" and just be quiet. To my surprise, the quieter my mind became, the more I started to hear that intuitive warning that something was coming.

There were times when I would not only receive the intuitive warning, but I would respond without thought. I remember my opponent asking me how I knew to move at a certain time. And the only way I can explain it was that I did not do it, "IT" did it for me. Sifu was right. In the end, the less I was fixated on my opponent, the more this type of thing started happening.

Gut Trust

During this process, one of my major sticking points was being able to just trust my gut. I can remember many times feeling the internal nudge to move. I wouldn't believe it, so I would stay where I was at, and then I would end up getting punched in the face.

So the intuitive signal was there. I just didn't trust her enough to listen. This was probably one of the biggest obstacles for me to get around. Later in my teaching career, I found out that a lot of my students struggled with the same thing.

First, they would get to the point where they can listen for the intuitive signal. Then, they started to hear the signal, but they didn't believe it. Like myself, it took them a little while to get to the point where they trusted enough to not only listen but react on its cue.

Intuitive action

My training partners and I used to play a game, and the way it would work is we were all standing in a circle facing inward. We would stand in a wide stance and have our arms up in front of us. The game would start by passing a ball from person to person.

This ball was filled with about 1-2 pounds of brass shot. The ball was so tightly packed that when it was thrown, it would maintain a round shape. When the ball came to you,

you had to catch it and then immediately pass it off to someone else. You were not to hold onto the ball for any amount of time at all. You want to treat it as if it were 300° and you wanted it out of your hands quickly.

Now, with everyone playing the game treating this ball the same way, it would start to zip around the circle very aggressively and quickly. When we started playing this game, due to the potential for pain when you got hit with the ball, you would zero in on the ball and keep your eye on it everywhere it went.

When the game really got going, it was difficult to see where the ball was going and keep up with it sometimes, and then you would get zapped by the ball.

We played this game for a few years before Sifu told me to try and not focus on the ball. He told me I wanted to try and ignore it, just like I ignored partners in a sparring session. As you can imagine, this was difficult. Every time I could hear the ball leave someone's hand, I could feel my spirit flinch and create tension inside my body.

I told Sifu about this, and he told me, "Part of the exercise is controlling your own energy." He said fear would cause a person's body to tense and their energy to rise. When this happens, you are completely out of control of your body; you're letting fear physically control you.

He told me I had to get to the point where I could completely let go. I needed to be able to sink into the stance and control myself regardless of what was going to happen. He reminded me as well what he had said previously, "As you are doing this, you still need to not focus on the ball." In other words, I needed to get to the point where I was not fixated on it.

This took quite a while, and it took a lot of getting smashed in the face and the body with that tiger ball. And then, one day, something changed. The ball was buzzing around like it normally did, one of the times taking out its victims. I was doing what I was told. I was not fixating on the ball. I just figured it's going to hit me, so I'm just gonna try to do what I'm supposed to do and just ignore it.

At that moment, my hand moved. I could hear that someone had snatched the ball in midair. And I was surprised to look down at my hand in astonishment. It was me! I did not have one single thought of grabbing the ball or moving my hand to catch it. Yet there it was in my hand. I sat there for a second and stared at it as all the guys gave me hell because I was slowing up the game. That was the first time I had experienced intuitive action.

The last part of this was learning not only to hear the intuitive signal but to respond to it without thought. This is when my partner would think about making a move. My intuitive action would pick up the signal, and "It" would immediately respond. This connection between intuition and action was the final goal of the different drills and exercises my teacher had given me.

The 6 - 9 Changeability Principle

I first learned the 6 - 9 and ability principle from Chinese boxing. A boxer using this principle does not need to reload or chamber his moves. He's in a constant state of readiness, and even when he applies his moves, they are done in a fashion that would allow him to change his direction or technique instantly.

He is never overextended in any direction but instead rooted and centered, enabling him to react instantly. He constantly attempts to avoid extreme conditions. He strives to maintain a non-rigid suppleness and relaxation. This principle is based on classic Chinese writing called the *I Ching*. Generally, it is a book used for fortune-telling by chance. This is done on the numbering system. In the system, six and nine came to be known as the numbers of change. And this is where the theory got its name.

When dealing with an unknown situation, especially when we have to make decisions quickly and possibly under stress, the 6 - 9 principle can be applied. The ability to not completely overextend but instead maintain the ability with each move to still be centered and able to change into something else. Move in any direction and adjust to a changing situation. It doesn't have to just be applied to fighting, obviously. The scale will be available in a conversation or a business negotiation. Making a quick decision could possibly overextend you and put you in a position where you're vulnerable.

"You must be shapeless, formless, like water. When you pour water in a cup, it becomes the cup. When you pour water in a bottle, it becomes the bottle. When you pour water in a teapot, it becomes the teapot. Water can drip and it can crash. Become like water my friend." - Bruce Lee

An example of this might look like this. We'll say you are in a business negotiation. And the person you have your meeting with has laid out several alternatives. They are trying to create a situation where a decision needs to be made during the meeting. There is no urgency to the decision. It's just that they want to get it done at this time.

Let's say the individual starts to put pressure on you to make a decision on the spot. You decide to try to mainta

in changeability, so you say, "I will narrow the decision down to these two options, but then I'm going to need to think about it and get back to you." So you may have eliminated a few options for your opponent. He knows that you do not want to do anything outside of what the two you have left on the table.

Additionally, you have asked for time to think about it, which will take you out of a stressful situation so that you can be in a mental state to think and make a proper decision. You have maintained the ability to change.

8.
BIOELECTRIC DISCIPLINE

Bioelectric discipline

The next thing we're going to discuss is the topic of what I call bioelectric energy. This is frequently linked to the study of bioenergetics in the west. This is a field in biochemistry and cell biology that concerns energy flow through living systems.

The goal of bioenergetics is to describe how living organisms acquire and transform energy in order to perform biological work. In the east, it is studied as a practice used to cultivate balance and grow the vital force of the body. This study is referred to as qi gong, chi kung, or chi gung, which translates to "life energy cultivation" or "energy work."

This practice has roots in the Chinese culture dating back more than 4,000 years. The practice of chi gung generally will include coordinated movements of the body in various forms of breathing exercises and is used for exercise & wellbeing, meditation & relaxation, self-cultivation, and of course, the martial aspects. It is practiced worldwide today.

Its practice is based on the belief that the human body has a bio-energy field that both runs through it and encompasses it. If someone can become aware of this energy field, with practice, it is believed that they can influence it and potentially cultivate it to make it stronger.

I was introduced to the concept in my mid-teens. At that time, I was primarily concerned with the combative aspects of the martial arts. So when I was first introduced to the training, I looked at it as just an additional study that was required to progress to areas I actually wanted to pursue. I looked at it as a side study, fortunately for me, I did take anything that was put in front of me as an educator seriously, and I took notes. I did my best to advance in the knowledge.

I have always been a "prove it to me" student. I always carried a healthy amount of skepticism when looking at any new material in the arts. I will admit, at first, I wasn't too sure that I believed what I was being told.

But I had two teachers in front of me that were able to do things that I could neither explain nor reproduce. This amazed me and intrigued me, so I decided to pursue the information in practice. I figured that if I put the time in, someday it would come to me, and I would understand it. The training was broken into five areas of study:

Medical qi gong
Martial qi gong
Spiritual qi gong
Scholar qi gong
Health qi gong

Looking back, I did not realize the monumental amount of information and training that was in front of me. What I thought was going to be a small side study turned into an ocean of information and knowledge.

I am extremely grateful to the young "me" for putting the time and effort into the pursuit of this knowledge. Because at the time, I didn't understand the benefit it would bring me later in life.

My teachers did tell me that the information would become more valuable as I got older, but it was another thing I did not understand at the time. But they were absolutely correct.

I originally got into the arts just to learn how to fight, and along the way, I got introduced to the warrior concept of continuous self-development and growth. As we have discussed in this book, that philosophy pushed me into the deeper understanding and development of the human-machine on multiple levels. What I discovered was that qi gong introduced another area of study that needed attention. And that study was the bioelectric systems of the body.

As I said, I was skeptical, but after several years of training, I started to find that what my teachers were telling me did exist. It took time to slow down and quieten the mind enough to be able to recognize it.

But one day, there it was. They proved it to me after all. Since then, it has become a major part of what I do daily to maintain myself, my health, and my daily energy levels.

Western science has not been able to measure the study of qi gong and thus categorize it as a pseudo-science. I am not attempting to counter that. All I'm doing is sharing with you what it has done with me over the course of the last 40 years.

What can Qi do for you

My experience with this practice has been immense. Over the years, it has never ceased to give me more than I have given to it. It has improved every area of my life. It has allowed me to do things in the martial arts that I did not think was possible.

The scholar aspect has allowed me to pursue self-education that has taken me past anything I could've possibly imagined. The medical aspect has allowed me to help students, friends, family, and multiple other people along the way. And finally, the health aspects have given me longevity and strength far beyond what I had expected.

The health aspect is what I would like to focus on with you. We have looked at disciplining multiple areas of the mind and body. And when I put the list together of areas I wanted to take a look at, this study was a major one.

I honestly hesitated to put this chapter in the book just because of the reputation these training methods have in the west. But I personally have benefited from them so immensely that I decided to discuss it as an area of growth. Though it may take you a little while to become familiar with bioelectric energy if you actively pursue it you will find it. I will not have to tell you. You will see and feel it for yourself. You will also grow to understand the benefits of it.

As far as my personal health goes, the study of this bioelectric energy in the body and the ability to grow it and maintain it has helped me be healthier, stronger, and it has given me longevity in life.

These are the same qualities I would see in my teachers. Now I have instructors who are in their 60s, 70s, and 80s, and they are still vital and active and are able to get out and pursue their goals as they continue to enjoy life even at advanced ages.

You, too, can benefit from this. The study can become a part of what you do either daily or weekly in order to maintain the same longevity and vital energy. Here are just a few examples of what I have experienced and what is available to you as well with practice:

Approved available daily energy
Improved relaxation & sleep
Reduced stress & improved overall wellbeing
Improved recovery from injury or training
Emotional balance and control
Improved focus, concentration & memory
Increased bone density & ligament strength
Improved athletic performance
Improved posture, balance & flexibility
Improved pulmonary function

The How To

Okay, this is the first exercise that was given to me in order to become familiar with this field of study. I started with this one and learned many of these exercises by the time I actually got to the point where I was experiencing this energy fully. It was that epiphany moment, the instant when the lightbulb finally came on. Simplicity, I was right back at the beginning. This exercise was called the chi ball exercise.

The body will have different points where these energy fields will be stronger. The two we are going to use in the drill are called the Lao Gong points and are in the palms of the hands. This point is also one of the major points used in acupuncture as well. If you were to make a fist and pay attention to the spot between the tip of the ring finger and your middle finger, you will find the spot. This is generally the location of the Lao Gong point.

Now, while standing with your arms hanging at your side, turn your palms inward. We want to bring the hands to the front of the body, with the palms facing each other.

We would like to do this with the least amount of tension in the arms, wrists, and hands as possible. Imagine bringing your hands together in a prayer position with the fingers downward. Now separate the hands by about one inch. Keep the fingers separated and open with a very light effort.

We don't want to over tense the hands. Just expand them in order to keep them open. Focus your attention on the palms of the hands and begin to move your hands gently in small circular motions. As you do this, try to maintain about one-inch distance between the palms of the hands.

What you're looking for is a slight magnetic pull or push between the hands. It will almost feel like you're playing with two small magnets that will either repel or pull toward each other. You may additionally notice a tingling sensation or a heaviness in the area as well. Our primary goal is to locate the feel of that positive magnetic field.

It's that simple, but at the same time, it may take some time for this to happen. That is okay, and it is very common. Some people will pick up on this very quickly, and others take time.

Everyone I have ever taught this to eventually gets it, as long as they continue to play with the idea, and it led to greater things later. Once you have experienced this ball of bioelectric energy between the palms, continue to work with it and just become familiar with it. Energy work is just that, taking the time to practice and work with it consistently over time.

Key points to remember:

Keep the body in a loose, relaxed state.

Keep the arms and hands relaxed (no tension)

Keep the shoulders relaxed and down

Keep the palms of the hands facing each other

Use a slow steady breathing pattern

When you have experience in this field, you can start introducing the breathing patterns we spoke about earlier in this book as you do this drill. As you introduce the breathing patterns, you may start to notice that different breaths will affect the energy field in different ways.

Primarily you are looking to notice a change in either the pulling or pushing of the field. It's similar to playing with two magnets. You can situate the magnets in a way where the magnetic fields will push them apart, and if you turn one over, you will feel them pull toward each other. This is the same sensation you will feel between your palms with practice.

Additionally, you may also be able to start feeling this field with the hands farther apart. With practice, I have been able to make this field grow up to two feet between the palms of the hands.

This drill is primarily just to introduce you to the study of bioelectric energy in the body so that you become familiar with it. That is the first step. As it is with anything that you seek knowledge in, it will take time to develop further.

Once you have gotten this far, if it is something you want to pursue and grow in, it is best to find a good instructor. Remember, when you are searching for one, simplicity is mastery. This area of study can be so overly complicated that you can become paralyzed with information and never make any real growth. So, keep that in mind when you're interviewing potential instructors. It should be simple, and it should be effective and applicable, especially if you are someone with a limited amount of time both in life and in your daily schedule.

These applications should be simple so that you are able to apply them in your daily routine and gain benefit from them. As well, I am going to offer more information and instruction on my website sifualanbaker.com if you are unable to locate someone as a teacher.

Conclusion

Jim Rohn said, "Unless you change how you are, you'll always have what you've got." Warriors and high achievers know this and will continually seek to improve themselves daily.

I was taught this principle in the warrior arts and later applied them to entrepreneurial and business pursuits with great success. Along the way, I got immersed in the culture of self-improvement, and I quickly realized that I already knew a tremendous amount of what they were teaching,

I had just traveled a different path to learning them. I also noticed that there were additional areas of information that I had learned that I did not see in that self-development community. This is unfortunate because a lot of this information had an incredible influence on my personal growth and development.

So I started teaching this information as part of what I taught inside the academy and through seminars around the

United States. I would often get the request to write the information down in book form.

After seeing this information help other individuals better their lives through the arts, I finally thought to myself, *It's time to write that book and share this with everyone else*. And that is what initially started the project that became this book. My goal was to introduce to you some additional ways to look at discipline in relation to the body in the human-machine.

Though I tried to get as much knowledge into the book as possible, the reality is it is simply an introduction to these areas. If you have gained knowledge that has assisted you in growth, go out and find additional sources of information to continue learning and growing. If you cannot find that information, get in touch with me, because it is my additional goal to create an outlet that is accessible to the community as a whole in order to share this information as well as additional information on the topics discussed.

About the Author

Sifu Alan Baker is an internationally recognized martial arts & self-defense expert. He has been training continually in the martial arts since 1981 and teaching since 1990. He has 40 years of continuous experience in the arts. He has been recognized for developing the Warriors Path Tribe and is the founder of the Civilian Tactical Training Association, he has appeared in several national magazine articles.

In the course of his career, he has attained the level of black belt or higher in multiple disciplines of martial arts, as well as multiple instructor level certifications in additional systems under some of the industry's most renowned teachers, such as Tuhon Dan Inosanto, Master Pedro Sauer, Sifu Francis Fong, Sensei Erik Paulson, Ajarn

Chai Sirisute, Ajarn Greg Nelson, Tuhon Tim Waid, Grand Tuhon Leo T. Gaje, Jr, Professor James Cravens, Master Bob Byrd, Guro Don Garon, Grandmaster Dana Miller, Sifu Paul Vunak and Coach Justo Dieguez.

In the tactical training field, Sifu Baker has taught countermeasures and defensive tactics, firearms, and edged-weapon programs through his AMAC Tactical Training Group to Fortune 50 corporate security teams and law enforcement / SWAT teams throughout the United States from the Marietta SWAT team here in Georgia to the Cincinnati SWAT team and the California Highway Patrol unit just to name a few. He has been privileged to work with and design training programs for the Department of Defense, CIA, and other specialized government and military groups like the U.S. Department Of Homeland Security.

Sifu Baker is a certified Armed Personal Protection Specialist (PPS) and the Defensive Tactics Instructor for The Executive Protection Institute (EPI) in Clarke County, Virginia, where he created a specialized defensive tactics program for Protection Agents (Bodyguards), named Protection Response Tactics (PRT). Sifu Baker's AMAC Tactical Group also teaches the defensive tactics for Vehicle Dynamics Institute located in New Jersey. VDI & EPI are considered the top schools for teaching Executive Protection (Bodyguards) and tactical / security driving in the World. Mr. Baker is a licensed Private Investigator in the state of Georgia and has worked as a protection agent for several top names in the entertainment industry.

Alan is also the Association Director for the Combat Submission Wrestling Association (CSW), and The Francis

Fong Instructor Association (FFIA). He is on the KFM International Team and acts as a manager for the US in the Keysi Fighting Method Instructors Association. The CSW Association was founded by Sensei Erik Paulson and develops professional martial arts coaches around the world. The FFIA was founded by Sifu Francis Fong and trains professional Wing Chun Kung Fu instructors. Alan has designed and implemented business plans for multiple international associations for some of the top names in the martial arts industry.

Dedicated to the passing of two great teachers and mentors: Scooter Sellers and Mike Jolley. You both will be missed! Also to the driving force in my life: Jennifer

If you enjoyed the book, please leave a review on Amazon. Reviews help new readers discover my books.

Printed in Great Britain
by Amazon

77890616R00210